GODS
★
SPIRITS
★
COSMIC GUARDIANS

Examines the encounter experience in all its forms, from
religious vision to men from Mars, attempting to reach an
understanding of what such experiences have in common and
what is behind them.

GODS

★

SPIRITS

★

COSMIC GUARDIANS

A Comparative Study of the Encounter Experience

by

HILARY EVANS

THE AQUARIAN PRESS
Wellingborough, Northamptonshire

First published 1987

British Library Cataloguing in Publication Data

Evans, Hilary
Gods — spirits — cosmic guardians: a
comparative study of the encounter
experience.
1. Psychical research — Social aspects
I. Title
133   BF1031

ISBN 0-85030-597-7

*The Aquarian Press is part of the
Thorsons Publishing Group*

Printed and bound in Great Britain

2   4   6   8   10   9   7   5   3   1

CONTENTS

And is there care in heaven ? and is there love
in heavenly spirits to these creatures base,
that may compassion of their evils move ?
There is: else much more wretched were the case
of men than beasts. But oh, the exceeding grace
of highest God, that loves his creatures so,
and all his works with mercies doth embrace,
that blessed angels he sends to and fro
to serve to wicked man, to serve his wicked foe.

How oft do they their silver bowers leave,
to come to succour us, that succour want ?
How oft do they with golden pinions cleave
the flitting skies, like flying pursuivant,
against foul fiends to aid us militant ?
They for us fight, they watch and duly ward,
and their bright squadrons round about us plant,
and all for love, and nothing for reward;
Oh why should heavenly God to men have such regard?

EDMUND SPENSER, The Faerie Queene, *canto viii*

In these studies of deeply religious women I have had no thought of
directing a campaign against mysticism itself. They were all courageous,
generous and most mortified servants of God who did immense good and
made a profound impression upon all who came in contact with them. But if
anyone, on the ground of their ardent aspirations and high standard of self-
conquest, regards their alleged communications with the next world as
warranting belief in a divine guidance and supernatural knowledge imparted
to such souls, it seems to me that his conclusion is a rash one.

FATHER HERBERT THURSTON, S. J., Surprising Mystics

I do not know if what the spirits say and teach me is true, nor do I know if
they really are the people they call themselves; but that my spirits exist is
beyond question.

S—W—, a patient of Carl Gustav Jung

For me, they are all one and the same — an extraterrestrial contact, a
spiritist contact or the case of a religious visionary.

SALVADOR FREIXEDO, one-time Jesuit priest, *interview in* Karma 7, 1985

PREFACE
DELPHINE AND OTHERS

Delphine is 18 years old. She works in a chocolate factory in an industrial suburb in central France which is not much frequented by tourists and sightseers. In 1982, though, sightseers came to the town in their thousands, and Delphine was the sight they came to see. For Delphine had been visited, she claimed, by the Virgin Mary, the mother of Jesus of Nazareth.

'I know my apparitions were true. Why would I have invented them?' Five years later, Delphine still does not question that her experiences were what they seemed to be at the time. And true, no doubt, they were — for her. But would they be true for you or me? Would they be true for a behavioural scientist whose job it is to determine what goes on inside our minds? Or for a theologian whose job it is to evaluate events related to the belief-system of which the Virgin Mary is a component part?

This book is a search to find out what sort of truth there may be in encounter experiences like Delphine's. I believe that something important happened to her in 1982. But I am not at all sure that what she thinks happened to her is what *really* happened to her.

Equally, I am not convinced that what the scientists think happened to her is any nearer the truth. I have a great respect for science, because science has shown itself very good at helping us see how happenings which seem to be random and arbitrary are governed by some kind of sense and order. My respect diminishes, however, when science, because it is unable to make sense of something, instead of recognizing its failure, chooses to explain it in terms of something known but manifestly inadequate, or worse, denies that the thing exists at all.

This study starts from the premise that 'something' happens in encounter experiences such as Delphine's. Its aim is to establish the nature of that 'something', and it recognizes that if we are to reach a worthwhile conclusion we must be prepared to question every assumption. We must have respect for the witnesses, but we must be prepared to find that they are mistaken. We must respect what science says about those experiences: but we must be prepared to find that science is mistaken. We must respect those who believe that these experiences occur on levels of reality beyond the reach of science: but we must be prepared to find they are mistaken.

In 1982 Delphine took her place in a long history of alleged visionaries. Her experience was not essentially different from hundreds of others, through the centuries and long before Christianity came on the scene, who had visionary encounters with otherwordly entities, so that not only the theologians of the belief-system to which Delphine subscribes — the Roman Catholic Church — but mythologists and folklorists too have their views about people like her. But so at the same time do the psychologists and the psychiatrists and the psychoanalysts, and with them the sociologists and all who concern themselves with the interaction of the individual with his cultural milieu.

Very likely Delphine had no idea what she was letting herself in for, and we may say that she had no choice in the matter. But she is no exception to the rule that 'no man is an island': in assessing what happened to her, we are bound to relate it to what happened to all those thousands of others who have had similar or comparable experiences. If I have taken Delphine as my starting point, it is simply to give myself a fixed point to refer to. In a previous study[58] I took for my starting point another 18-year-old, Glenda, who at the age of twelve had been visited by a 'spacewoman' in her bedroom. I might equally well have taken a former vet in Wales who told me how he had been harassed by the agents of Satan, or the young woman in Wyoming who explained to me how she is really a denizen of another planet, occupying an earthgirl's body while she accomplishes her mission on Earth. Each of these people claims to have had an experience which is more or less unbelievable to the rest of us; there is not one about whom opinions are not divided as to what 'really' happened.

For a few months in 1982, Delphine was news. A century or so earlier her fellow citizen Bernadette Soubirous made news when she had much the same kind of experience. In Bernadette's case she sparked off a cult with the result that today millions of people every year make a pilgrimage to her home town of Lourdes. Their reasons are varied, but I suppose most of them would say they believed that what happened to Bernadette in 1858 was 'real'. Ten years before, some other young girls in New York State claimed to be in contact with the spirits of the dead, and sparked off a worldwide movement to which millions today adhere. In our own time, cults are forming all over the world around individuals who claim to be in contact with extraterrestrials.

Where, among all these claims, or among the counter-claims that say these people were victims of delusion, is there any truth? Does it lie with Delphine, who insists 'my apparitions were real' or with the doctors who diagnosed her as 'a hystero-epileptic whose banal delirium has been stimulated by a pathogenic milieu'? This study is a detective story with a single purpose: to understand what is happening to Delphine and the others.

The right to question
This book is about very important experiences. Important to those who

enjoy or suffer them at first hand, important to those of us who at second hand try to learn from them something about humankind's relations with the cosmos. Because these things are so important, they are apt to generate strong feelings, particularly among people who have found a way of intepreting them with which they are satisfied — who are convinced, say, that Teresa d'Avila really spoke with God, that others have really been possessed by Satan, that they can really speak with the dead at spiritist seances, and that beings from other parts of the universe are really visiting Earth.

For those of us who have not yet made up our minds, it is impossible not to question some of these beliefs; but I have sought to do so in a way which questions not so much the experience itself as the way we interpret it. Not from politeness or consideration (though I hope I have also been polite and considerate) but because I recognize that *whatever they are* these experiences are important, they have meaning and therefore value, so any negative approach on my part would be not only impolite and inconsiderate but also, quite simply, stupid.

So, in questioning the interpretations put upon these experiences, I am seeking to relate them to other human processes, to human experience as a whole. If, in order to do this, I have had to question people's sincerely held beliefs, this has been done not with a negative wish to destroy those beliefs, but from a positive wish to see them replaced by others more securely grounded.

I am not fit to determine whether a mystic like Teresa was *in some fashion* in contact with whatever may exist as the supreme force we call 'God', and will therefore not try. At that level, contact takes the form of a mystical experience, and I share Zaehner's view that 'the essence and key-note of the mystical experience is union'.[272]

Our study, however, is of *encounters*, which by definition cannot involve union: whether or not it leads to union at a later stage, an encounter is a meeting between two separate beings. Our encounter experiences may be associated with mystical experiences, may resemble them in many respects, may ultimately lead to them; but they are not the same thing.

The comparative approach
That a comparative study can be helpful even at the most superficial level is illustrated by the case of Amparo Cuevas, a Spanish visionary who in 1982 was told by the Virgin Mary, among many other things, that 'the celestial ships are already prepared which will carry the chosen ones to the promised land. They come surrounded by blue light.'[82]

To her confessor, this was *'dificil de comprender'*, but as researcher Salvador Freixedo pointed out, it was easy enough to understand for anyone who is familiar with UFO-mythology, where celestial rescue-ships, frequently accompanied by blue light, are a standard feature.

By revealing links between categories of experience which might have seemed quite disparate, the comparative approach on the one hand demonstrates the differences between them and on the other enables us to see whatever unchanging similarities underlie them. Even so, some readers may be sceptical about the validity of my bringing together experiences in many ways so different, as though I thought encounters with God were of equal value with meetings with extraterrestrial aliens, or even as though all alleged encounters with God were of equal value one with another. Some readers, particularly those with deeply held religious convictions, may be shocked, while those who reject all forms of organized religion may resent that I take the experiences of religious mystics seriously; many churchmen and many more scientists may resent that I take communication with the dead seriously; many who accept religion or spiritism will resent that I take extraterrestrial encounters seriously. Those who believe that the mystics have somehow transcended the constraints that enclose the rest of us, and had a preview of the ineffable bliss of divine contact, will not easily accept that those who believe they have spoken with the dead, or with visitors from other worlds, believe themselves to have had experiences no less rare and valuable.

And indeed, perhaps they haven't; but there are no objective yardsticks to measure by, so we have no right to assume any *a priori* limitations at the outset of our study. It may indeed be that by the time we reach the end, we shall have found that, for example, there is intrinsically greater value in the experience of a Teresa d'Avila than a private reunion with a relative on the Other Side, or a visit from a space alien. But equally we must be prepared to find that the differences are only ostensible and that these experiences have more in common than at first appears.

What is important is that, for the time being, we recognize that there exist people for whom the physical existence of the Devil is reality; people who don't doubt that the mother of Jesus revisits our Earth; millions who are convinced they have spoken with the dead; and that claims to have been visited by extraterrestrials have at least as good a right to be taken seriously as claims of saintly intervention or angelic visitation.

Pierre Janet and the well-meaning witnesses

In 1899 the French psychologist Pierre Janet was presented with the case of a young middle-class woman aged 26, who was brought to La Salpêtrière hospital by her mother and aunt because she was suffering from hallucinations. These related to a young man she had met in an office but with whom she had never had any personal relations. From dreaming about him at night she had progressed to day-dreaming of him, and then to outright hallucinations so erotic that Janet, after telling us the young man would caress her and undress her, says that what followed was so *'absolument inconvenante'* that he could not narrate it, not even in Latin, not even at a conference of psychologists.

It was evident to Janet that these hallucinations, so totally out of character with his patient's upbringing and her ostensible nature, were a symptom of hysteria. But every young person dreams of lovers, without going so far as to have hallucinations of them. Had she, he asked, a previous history of such experiences?

'There then occurred a slight family dispute; the aunt said yes, the mother said no, and when the aunt insisted, the mother said, "But that was something totally different, it doesn't concern the doctor at all."'

Naturally Janet was intrigued, and by questioning the two relatives separately he arrived at the facts. At the age of 8 his patient had seen visions of angels, in long white robes, who appeared to her even in broad daylight. At puberty, between the ages of 10 and 12, she had been subject to further visions, always religious. The angels gave her good advice and instructed her in the catechism. One angel, a female one, she identified as Saint Philomèle, and ever since then 'la petite sainte', as she called her, had played an important role in her life as guide, comforter and friend.

On attaining puberty at the age of 12, she was not troubled by hallucinations until she was 17, when the erotic experiences began. Janet comments: 'We were not surprised to find that her hallucinations, hitherto mystical, later became erotic and obscene; it is a well known fact. But why did the young woman's mother deny her daughter's earlier hallucinations?'

By discreetly questioning, Janet learnt that, following the death of the father (significantly, in an asylum where he had been sent for mental illness resulting from absinthe-drinking), the mother had become a spiritist. This had led her to believe that her daughter's early visions were truly of spirits and angels: they were not hallucinations at all, but real experiences. In her eyes, the later hallucinations weren't the same thing at all; they were pathological, needing treatment, whereas the earlier experiences were elevating and consoling, and so could not be a sign of sickness. All three women rejected Janet's suggestion that, whether nobly religious or obscenely erotic, the same kind of experience was involved. [123]

This study of ours will be worthless unless we accept at least the possibility that Janet was right. We must accept the possibility that when Teresa d'Avila distinguished between her 'true' encounters which were divine in character and her 'false' encounters which came from the devil, she was as mistaken as Janet's patient's mother. We must accept the possibility that all the encounter experiences we consider in this study, however they may ostensibly differ, are fundamentally of a kind.

Terminology
This is not the first study of people's encounter claims, but it differs from most in bringing together different kinds of such experience. This means that we need a terminology compatible with them all.

Fortunately this is not a field which has generated a highly technical jargon, and for the most part we can manage with generally understood words. However, because sometimes they are used with particular significance, it may help to avoid confusion later if we agree here at the outset what we understand by those terms.

By *contact* or *encounter* I mean an event in which a person believes himself in direct and personal contact with an entity. Generally I use *encounter* when there seems to have been a face-to-face meeting as between two persons, and *contact* where somewhat less is involved, for instance where no words are spoken, or the entity is sensed but not seen.

Reluctantly I use *witness* to indicate the person who has the experience — reluctantly, because the term is usually used of a passive observer, which hardly seems appropriate for, say, Teresa d'Avila in the intensity of her encounters with the divine. But 'percipient', likewise, implies only observation, and 'subject' is rather too clinical. 'Contactee' has acquired rather too specific connotations in the field of extraterrestrial encounters. I considered 'encounterer' and 'experient' but decided you wouldn't like either of them any better than I do.

It should go without saying, but I'd better protect myself by saying it, that when I use the term *experience* what I really mean is *alleged* experience. That is, the term relates to what the witness thinks happened, which may or may not be what really happened.

I shall not use the phrase 'he or she' throughout, because both you and I would find it irritating. If when speaking of someone whose gender is unknown or immaterial I use 'he', this has no sexist significance.

We shall sometimes need to distinguish between the entity who seems to be involved in the encounter and the being who causes the encounter to take place; for though they will often be one and the same, this isn't necessarily so. Some Catholic theologians, for instance, believe that the 'false visionaries' of Lourdes saw, not the Virgin Mary that Bernadette saw, but a counterfeit created by Satan. In such a case, though Mary is the *apparent*, it is Satan who is the *agent*. In other cases the agent may be the witness himself, projecting an image of the apparent outside himself.

Finally, the entities themselves. By *divinities* I mean any of the limitless variety of beings which mankind supposes to have created, or at any rate to rule, the cosmos, and which he therefore worships, honours, supplicates, and sometimes reproaches. Also included are *angels* to whom has been granted some part of the divine power, and *devils* who have helped themselves to it.

By *spirits* I generally mean entities who were formerly humans living on Earth but who now exist on some other plane of reality. There are also beings who never were human, but who also seem to inhabit some otherworldly plane, and these may be called spirits too unless they have a more specific label such as 'fairies'.

By *cosmic guardians* I mean beings who seem to exist on the same level of reality as you and me, but in other parts of the universe, from which they come to visit us and concern themselves with our affairs.

Contamination

Terminology is only the outer shell of ideas; each of the subject areas we shall be studying has over the years generated not only its own labels but also its own received ideas and concepts. It is important that we recognize these for what they are, which in most cases is no more than working hypotheses which we must be prepared to question.

Take a specific example: it is popularly supposed that the continued existence, on some other level of being, of spirits of the dead is somehow linked to their ability to perform paranormal feats in seance rooms, or to supply information about members of the audience in public gatherings which could come from no human source. However, no such link necessarily exists; it may perfectly well be that seance-room goings-on are nonsense, yet that survival-after-death is a fact; or alternatively, that psychic phenomena are real but life-after-death a myth.

For unfortunately each of our subject areas has been *contaminated* by beliefs which are not logically inherent. Thus all encounters with God are regarded as 'religious', and so indeed in the profoundest sense they may be; but that doesn't mean they must be interpreted in conformity with any specific religious doctrine. In the case of visions of the Virgin, for example, what the witness sees is often very different from Mary's conventional image, a discrepancy which helps to explain why so many bishops warn their flocks not to accept the claims of unapproved visionaries like Delphine.

Encounters with spirits of the dead are, as we have already noted, contaminated with confusion about 'psychic powers', which has led to a whole mythology regarding what the spirits are able to perform, what they like, and so on. Thus it is alleged that spirits operate best in the dark, and better still when the sitters join hands and sing. True, plausible explanations are offered for these allegations, but we should recognize that there may be other reasons why mediums prefer to work in the dark with a good bit of noise going on.

As for extraterrestrial encounters, though the most recent of our categories, they have already generated their own mythology. Each of the two main types of ET encounter experience, contact and abduction, tends to conform to a stereotype: thus we find that abducting aliens generally talk in a clipped, pedantic manner, reminiscent of robots in sci-fi movies, while contacting aliens are given to very long messages of a morally uplifting nature. Here again, the widespread assumption that ET encounters are part and parcel of the flying saucer/UFO phenomenon may be no more than circumstantial.

We can guard ourselves against assuming links where none necessarily exists if we take care not to mistake the *cultural context* of the encounter for an essential part of the experience. We shall of course find that the cultural context is an essential element in our understanding of the encounter experience, but we must distinguish between the core experience and the trappings which have been decked round it by commentators trying to construct a plausible hypothesis for it, or to fit it into one which already exists.

Selecting instances

Our study has a vast terrain to cover. On my shelves are literally hundreds of books about encounters with the Virgin Mary, hundreds more about encounters with spirits, hundreds more about ET encounters; and they represent only a fraction of the literature. Inevitably, therefore, selecting truly representative cases is not easy. I believe the material on which this study is based is sufficient as a basis for its conclusions, but I have supplied references to further material so that readers can see how the elements which make up the cases cited are also found elsewhere.

It may be objected that most of my examples are drawn from what is loosely called 'Western culture'. This is partly because this is what I am most familiar with, partly because it is the most fully documented. There is no equivalent in any other culture, for example, of the Society for Psychical Research's collection of apparition cases *Phantasms of the Living*. Where I have been able to draw parallels between, say, reports of European witchcraft and anthropologists' findings in Africa, I have been glad to do so; but I have found no reason for thinking that what is true in one culture doesn't apply to others. The visions of the Virgin Mary at Kibeho in Rwanda run true to form with similar experiences in Europe;[165] demon possession in China seems entirely comparable to the same phenomenon elsewhere;[186] the Chinese see the same kind of UFO-related ET-entities as everyone else.[51]

Judicious skipping

Most of you who read this book will be familiar with *some* of the material, though few with *all* of it. Since it is essential for a comparative study that everyone should have a reasonable knowledge of what is being compared with what, it is vital that those who have hitherto confined their studies to, say, mystical visions, should acquire some familiarity with what happens when a witness encounters ET entities. So in each category I have had to include sufficient examples to give the newcomer a reasonable idea of the material.

However, there is no need for the reader to plow through material with which he is already familiar. Consequently I advise — indeed, in the interests of avoiding fatigue in what is inevitably going to be an exhausting study for all of us, I *urge* — judicious skipping when you come across material already familiar to you.

Dubious sources

More than one reviewer of my earlier book, *Visions, Apparitions, Alien Visitors*, reproached me for drawing my material from dubious sources. In order to forestall any such criticism of this book, let us face the fact that *every case cited here is dubious*. Each one rests on the testimony, usually unsupported by physical evidence and often contradicted by people who did not share the experience, of individuals unknown to me in almost every case, and whose trustworthiness I am in no position to guarantee.

Sceptics, believers and open minds

Finally there is a fundamental criticism which is liable to be levelled at studies of this sort, which I may as well confront before we go any further. It is this: here am I, who have never in my life had an experience which I was remotely tempted to interpret as an encounter with God, the Devil, a spirit of the dead or a cosmic being, presuming to formulate ideas about the experience of people who *have* had such things happen to them. This raises two questions: first, by what right do I do this, and second, what use can such a study possibly be?

A simple answer is that a historian doesn't have to have taken part in the battle of Waterloo to write usefully about it. Nor would it necessarily make him a better historian if he had; what he gained in vividness he might lose in perspective. But it may be objected that we are concerned with matters not of historical fact but of inner experience. This is true, but only partially true. The experience of encountering the Virgin Mary is inward and personal; but her presence, in some form, either is or isn't a historical fact. And when many hundreds of people make similar but often discrepant claims to have met her, it is legitimate for an uninvolved person to look for objective criteria whereby the true Virgin may be distinguished from her counterfeits.

Many witnesses welcome such assistance: uncertain about what has happened to them, they are glad of guidance. Others, on the contrary, have so strong a sense of inner conviction as to feel no need to submit their experience to a more methodical and coherent examination. But there are also many others who, without having had any such experiences themselves, have come up personally against people who have, or have simply read about them and wondered what to make of their claims. It is surely helpful for society at large to have as full an understanding as possible of these matters. Even within our own lifetime, in civilized countries, encounter witnesses have been persecuted, to the point of physical attack and destruction of their homes, by neighbours reacting with primitive hostility to something they don't understand so conclude to be evil.

Yet others, while allowing the social value of our study, will nevertheless consider its down-to-earth approach trivial to the point of irrelevance when set against the higher issues involved. Compared with those who study, say, the metaphysics of the mystical experience, I will surely seem woefully literal-minded, unable to grasp the essence of the experience and preoccupied with its crude exterior.

To this I answer that for the pilgrims at Lourdes, for the sitters in the seance room, for the ET contactee, what *primarily* matters is the literal presence of the entity: all else stems from that. The rest comes later. So in this experience-based study I feel no need to reproach myself for starting where *they* start.

It is precisely because the literal experience is only the start of something much more important, that we must get that start *right*. The claims made by our witnesses, if they are true, are evidence for much greater truths.

If Teresa truly talked with God, that is proof certain that God exists. If spiritists indeed communicate with people formerly living on Earth, we can be sure that death is not necessarily the end of existence. If the contactees are truly being visited by Cosmic Guardians, then we Earthfolk can know that we are not alone in the universe.

So, in the experiences we shall be studying, may lie the answers to the most important questions that humanity has ever posed. And precisely *because* those answers are so important, the claims must be examined with openness and rigour, not only by those anxious to establish that they are true, nor by those who are concerned to expose them as false, though both believers and sceptics have a part to play in guiding us towards the truth. But that truth will be found only if the claims are examined in the light of all we know about the forces and influences which shape human behaviour. It is not a question of putting our witnesses on trial to find out if they are telling the truth or not; it is a matter of finding out what really happened to them so that they and all of us may profit to the full from their experience.

1 APPROACHING THE ENCOUNTER EXPERIENCE

When a man comes down off a mountain and tells you he has just been talking with God — or with Uncle George who died two years ago — or with a Cosmic Brother from the Pleiades, it is on the one hand very difficult for him to prove he has done so, and on the other very difficult for you to prove he has not.

Of course neither he nor you may feel the need to prove the matter either way. He for his part may be perfectly easy in his mind about what happened to him, entirely confident that he has interpreted his experience correctly. He may regard it as a matter which concerns him alone and not care twopence whether you believe him or not.

And so long as he does not seek to make any social use of his experience, or force it on others as an experience they too should try to have, and so long as he himself is none the worse, there may be no reason for the rest of us to get involved. We may, and probably should, leave him alone with his experience.

But many — perhaps most — such people *do* involve others in their encounter experiences.

This may be due to the quite understandable human impulse to share with others the traumatic excitement of what happened. But often there is more to it than that. The witness may seek reassurance that he hasn't been deceived, that he isn't going mad, that what happened to him has value and meaning. If the experience was unpleasant, he may be frightened. Even if it was pleasant, he may find it alarming to have been singled out from the rest of us.

Alternatively, he may be serenely confident both about the nature of his experience and the fact of his being chosen for it, and may now feel an urge to pass on to the rest of us what he has been told, even to encourage us to change our ways in accordance with instructions he has received.

Either way, we shall feel the need to evaluate his experience, either so that we may give him the reassurance or counsel he seeks, or so that we may decide whether to go along with what he wants us to do.

You for your part can respond to his claim in one of several ways.

You may be totally convinced by his story, especially if he is someone you know and respect. His experience may not have surprised you, because it is a predictable element in the belief system you both share. If you yourself are religious, it may seem to you on the cards that a mystic should meet God; or the event may be something you half expected, such as the long-awaited contact with Planet Earth by extraterrestrial beings.

Alternatively you may decide at once that his claim is nonsense, because you don't believe there exists a God for him to encounter, or because the Pleiades are 500 light-years from Earth and it is really not very likely their inhabitants would make so long a journey to spend half an hour in conversation with a not very distinguished Earthperson. In such a case you may not feel there is any point giving his claim serious examination. However, if he forces it on you or on others, you may feel it your duty to try to show him he is mistaken, or at least to warn others that there are grounds for doubting him.

Most likely of all, you will be somewhere between these two positions: not prepared to dismiss his claim out of hand, but at the same time reluctant to accept it without question. In which case you may feel the need to evaluate it, either for your own peace of mind, or to help him, or to protect others, or because if his story is true it could be of benefit to mankind, or from a simple and natural curiosity to know the truth of the matter.

Whether or not, when found, it turns out to be a simple truth, it is certain that the hunt for it will be anything but simple. In undertaking it, we enter a labyrinth of false paths and dead ends, of entrenched belief systems and as-yet-untested hypotheses — which is why we still don't yet know what we should think about men who come down from mountains claiming to have spoken with God, or emerge from the seance room telling us they have been speaking with the dead, or phone the newspapers to report a meeting with extraterrestrials.

Entering the labyrinth

In the study on which we are about to embark, we are going to find that many paths which seem clear and open are not as straightforward as they appear; fortunately we shall also find that some apparent obstacles are less formidable than they look. Tiresome as it will often seem, we must ask questions and test our footing every step of the way, for every path may conceal a pitfall, every barrier may contain a hidden opening.

Our first step is clear: the story told by the witness must be our starting point. We must not listen to those who tell us there's no point in listening to him because such things can't happen, or are only the symptoms of hysteria, or try to force on us any other such *a priori* assumption. They may well be right, but nevertheless we must start by listening to what the witness has to say. But as we listen we must recognize that he may be doing one of three things:

★ He may be telling the truth, and his encounter happened just the way he tells it.

★ He may be telling the truth as he sees it, but for one reason or another he may be mistaken.

★ He may be deliberately lying, for any number of reasons.

We shall not often find it easy to decide which of these options is appropriate. UFO-contactee George Adamski, for instance, will tell us things about conditions on the lunar surface which have subsequently been proved false, but we can't be sure he knew he was lying. He himself may have been suffering from some kind of mental delusion, or the entities he encountered may have fed him false information for some mysterious purpose of their own.

Because the answers we get are so often going to be ambiguous without our being able to do very much about it, at least we can do our best to see that our questions are precise and unequivocal. This means that we must free ourselves of predispositions and premises which, by limiting our question, would make the answer meaningless if it falls outside those limits.

For instance, the Roman Catholic Church has a very sensible procedure for assessing miraculous claims. It requires them to run the gauntlet of a series of questions:

1 Is it trickery?

2 Is it illusion?

3 Is it hallucination?

4 Is it of demonic origin?

5 Is it of divine origin? [25]

Given the specific belief system, the logic is impeccable, but it makes assumptions which those of us who do not subscribe to that system will not necessarily accept. For example, some of us may doubt that divine forces exist, still more that demonic forces exist. Moreover, as we shall see in the course of our study, the list by no means covers all the possible explanations, to say nothing of the complexities hidden within that one word 'hallucination' to which we shall have to devote an entire chapter.

Spiritists would come up with a different list, so would theosophists, so would Flying Saucer cultists, so would the adherents of all kinds of esoteric beings ranging from nasty elementals to serene Ascended Masters. It would be wrong of us to scratch any of these from the running, for each of them is nominated by a belief system which has won the allegiance of substantial numbers of our fellows. Equally, though, we must resist their attempts, however sincerely made, to impose their assumptions on us.

A related problem is this: what kind of person is best-fitted to evaluate these claims?

Throughout most of human history it has been taken for granted that it was a matter for priests, who claimed a divine authority which was only rarely questioned. Hence most encounters in the past, and many even today, have been assessed in the light of religious doctrine.

Perhaps the first serious misgivings about this were expressed during the witch-hunting of the sixteenth and seventeenth centuries, when it became clear that the simplistic religious yardsticks employed by the Church were inadequate. Many came to feel that just because a witness confessed to having encountered the Devil was no reason why he should be burned at the stake, the more so when it became evident that his confession, however sincerely and spontaneously made, was far from being proof that the encounter had really occurred.

Gradually, science came to seem a more effective instrument for evaluating such claims, particularly as psychology revealed the complexities and deviousness of human behaviour. Intelligent churchmen welcomed this development, but inevitably there were — and continue to be — conflicts of opinion. For instance, many of those who have made valuable and insightful contributions to the field of our study remain convinced that the actual existence of a Devil is a viable option (for example, Jean Lhermitte[157]). We have no right to say that they are mistaken, though to some options — for instance, that UFO-entities are part of a Communist plot to subvert the capitalist system[266] — we may assign a low probability-rating.

We must note also that belief systems are not confined to religions and ideologies: even within the science of psychology there are conflicting schools of thought, and too dedicated a loyalty may lead the researcher to see Jungian archeteypes or Freudian sex-symbols more widely than is justifiable. Clearly there can be no question of disqualifying assessors who possess views of their own, for which of us hasn't? Simply, we must remember, as we benefit from the massive knowledge of someone like Görres[94] on the mystical experience, or from the wayward insights of Teresa d'Avila,[250] to allow for the fact that both wrote from a specifically Catholic standpoint; and so with each of the authorities we draw on.

For one thing will become very clear as we proceed: we need to draw on a great many authorities, working in a great variety of disciplines. Theologians and psychologists, anthropologists and sociologists, will have much to tell us even if we ultimately reject either a wholly theological, a wholly psychological, a wholly anthropological or a wholly sociological view in favour of one which combines elements of all four with a seasoning of occultism, mythology and much more. If encounter experiences are still not understood after so many centuries, the fundamental reason is the inadequacy of any single-discipline approach, whether derived from a particular set of beliefs or from a particular way of looking at the world.

The process of evaluation

No encounter experience, any more than any other kind of event, occurs in isolation. *When, where*, to *whom* and *why* it occurs — establishing these facts is as likely to help us as working out *how* it occurs.

The primary account of the experience will probably come in the form of verbal testimony from the witness himself. Often, though, we shall not get it direct, but via the accounts of others, so that we must be on the lookout for contamination not only from the witness' own preconceptions but also from those of the reporters. Thus, though it has been the practice of the Roman Catholic Church to get visionaries to put into writing their own account of their experiences, we must be careful to allow for the influence, however well-meant, of guidance from a spiritual adviser.

Supplementing the first-person account we may be lucky enough to have secondary testimony. Thus in the ongoing encounters with the Virgin Mary currently being enjoyed by the children of Medjugorje in Yugoslavia, the nightly meetings are witnessed by observers, who, however, do not see what the children see.[146] We may immediately conclude that this indicates either a heightened capability on the part of the children, or a diminished capability on the part of everyone else; and by thus isolating one of its components, we have taken our first step towards establishing the nature of the process.

Relevant circumstances

When in 1846 Mélanie Calvet and Maximin Guiraud claimed to have encountered the Virgin Mary on the hillside at La Salette in southern France, it was asserted by two priests, sceptical of the children's claim, that there had been in the neighbourhood, at the time of the alleged vision, a former nun who had become something of a religious eccentric, Mlle de la Merlière; they suggested that the children might have mistaken her for the Virgin. This proposition is not generally accepted by the Church, which tends to accept the children's testimony. However, the La Salette event is so full of ambiguities and improbabilities that no suggestion, however far-fetched, can be discounted.[15,23]

Similarly, when a dozen years later Bernadette Soubirous had her famous encounters with the Virgin at Lourdes, there are many intriguing circumstances which tend not to be mentioned in the popular accounts. For one, there is the existence of a long tradition of visions of the Virgin in the neighbourhood of Lourdes; for another, there is the fact that Bernadette's vision was only one — though indeed the first — of many dozens reported at Lourdes that year. Even though we may attribute all those other claims to hysterical contagion (if we seek a psychological explanation) or to the machinations of Satan (if we prefer a theological one), these secondary phenomena make it clear that Bernadette's experience is not an isolated event, and that data of many kinds and from many sources can help us to understand what happened to her.[152]

Supporting evidence

A regrettable feature of encounter reports is that the witness testimony is generally all the direct evidence we are given. We shall see that there are virtually never any *witnesses of the witness*, and virtually never any physical traces of the event. When Elizabeth Klarer of South Africa not only met the extraterrestrial Akon of Meton but fathered his child, we might suppose that she would wish for some memento of her son, particularly since he is now living 4.2 light-years away on his father's planet, one of the Proxima Centauri system. Not only would a photo of him be a small comfort to her, but it would provide valuable confirmation of her story, which, though it has indeed been very widely accepted, has not commanded universal belief. Unfortunately, however, despite the evident technological advance of Akon's world in enabling him to travel to Earth, no such souvenirs exist; we have to be content with sketches of Akon and some sadly blurred distant views of the spaceship in which Mrs Klarer travelled.[138]

Sometimes the absence of such evidence is explained as a test of our faith. That some of us are capable of such faith is demonstrated by the loyalty with which the members of the Church of Latter Day Saints accept their founder's account of finding a sacred revelation inscribed on golden plates whose place of concealment, along with the necessary spectacles to decipher them, was revealed to him by an angel. Though eleven men signed statements affirming the books' existence, neither books nor spectacles were left with Joseph Smith. Evidently it does not bother the Mormon that his entire belief system rests on the unsupported word of a previously unknown country farmer of limited education, but one may wonder if he purchases a second-hand car with as little circumspection?

Synchronicity

Joseph Smith's discovery of the golden plates occurred at a time when there was a mania among the country people in his part of the United States for seeking buried treasure. This extraordinary synchronicity is duly mentioned by the best of his biographers[27] who, though himself a Mormon believer, is also a conscientious historian; yet he does not make what for us non-believers is likely to be the logical inference.

True, one could contrive ways of accounting for the synchronicity. Perhaps Smith's angel revealed the books in this way *because* of the prevailing craze. In the same way one could argue that the increased activity of communicating spirits during time of war is not due to the need of the bereaved to be comforted but to the desire of the dead to comfort the living. Was the vision of the Virgin Mary at Pontmain in 1870, when the Prussians were invading France, a sign of divine reassurance or a manifestation of human fear? Synchronicity does not help us assign causes and effects; but by indicating a connection, it tells us where to start looking for them. For beyond question, the *occasion* of the encounter experience is an important clue to its meaning.

Thus it can be no coincidence that UFO-related contacts began at the same time as our own first explorations of space. But which is cause, which effect? One school of thought holds that the contacts are an indication of the extraterrestrials' concern about Earth's entering the Space Age; an alternative view is that they reflect a social neurosis which has seized on space mythology as a convenient outlet for expression.

We shall of course be looking closely into the relevance of social and cultural circumstances; but even such seemingly trivial factors as meteorological phenomena and geophysical forces can be relevant. No less, of course, are the circumstances of the witness' personal life; for instance, does it mean anything, and if so, what, that the great majority of those who encounter the Virgin Mary are adolescents, or that a high proportion of UFO abductees are women in an unstable marital state?

The witness as special person

Central to the encounter experience is the witness who has that experience; central to our understanding of the experience must be our understanding of the witness. But while its external circumstances are relatively accessible, the internal circumstances — what led to, brought about, earned, enabled or resulted in his having the experience — these are far more difficult to establish.

What we would like, of course, would be a psychological portrait of the witness *before* his experience, to compare with the post-event picture which is generally pretty well documented. Needless to say a pre-event portrait is rarely available, for the simple reason that he was generally a person of no consequence before he had his experience. Usually the most we can hope for is the testimony of friends, relatives, neighbours, schoolteachers and so on.

Even what they say is likely to be distorted by hindsight, but revealing details may emerge. It is interesting, for instance, to learn that immediately prior to her 1858 encounter with the Virgin, Bernadette had been preparing for her First Communion — a sufficiently traumatic event in the spiritual development of any Catholic, how much more so in the drab and uneventful life of a sickly teenager in an impoverished family in small-town France a century ago, where such excitements were rare.

It is intriguing, too, to learn that shortly before the visions, her parish priest, speaking with the schoolteacher, compared her to two celebrated visionaries of the previous decade, remarking, 'If my mental picture of the children of La Salette is exact, this little shepherdess must resemble them.' The fact that the anecdote has been preserved implies that it was noted at the time, and so may well have come to the ears of Bernadette herself, in which case the effect of suggestion is something we should take into account. Add it to Bernadette's excited state, and bearing in mind the traditions of vision-seeing in the neighbourhood of Lourdes, we have a combination of antecedent circumstances which is, to say the least, suggestive.[145]

However, it is no more than that. Such evidence is only circumstantial. The question of what is cause, and what effect, remains unanswered. Perhaps the priest's observation was caused by some kind of premonition of Bernadette's experience? Perhaps there really is something special about visionaries, shared by both Bernadette and the children of La Salette, which the priest intuitively discerned? Perhaps the visionary tradition around Lourdes has a factual basis? We can rearrange the evidence to form any number of hypotheses.

Cause-and-effect are no easier to disentangle in the case of George Adamski, the best-known UFO-contactee of the 1950s. For many years previous to his experience, Adamski had styled himself 'Professor' and posed as guru of a vaguely exotic 'philosophy'. He had also written a naive sci-fi story in which Earthpeople visit other worlds. Was his allegedly factual encounter based on his fiction, or was his romance a mysterious prefiguring of the reality in store for him? Did a growing involvement in his career as guru lead to a megalomaniac fantasy, or did he receive the privilege of being visited by extraterrestrials because of the wisdom he had manifested as teacher and philosopher?[1,2]

Once again, the witness' own belief system must be a crucial factor. A theologian would say that an encounter with the divine is a sign of grace, bestowed as a reward on someone whose conduct has attracted favourable notice in heaven; a psychologist might see it as the exteriorized working out of the witness' predispositions; a sociologist would see in it the expression of community beliefs in one individual's experience. We shall be looking in detail at these suggestions later in our study; at this stage we merely note them as something to look out for as we consider some representative cases. But there are other possible motivating factors we should also take into account.

Material gain is an obvious one. When an encounter is claimed by a professional spirit medium, for example, we should bear in mind that it is very much in his interest to have an experience which will support his credibility and enhance his reputation. Nor should we overlook the fact that for some, fame is at least as powerful an incentive as fortune.

Political advantage is another factor. When Moses climbed Sinai and returned with two stone tablets on which ten commandments had been inscribed by the finger of God, this was politically very convenient for him, enhancing his prestige and at the same time giving a seemingly divine authority to some necessary rules and regulations. That authority might have been more lasting if the tablets had been preserved as carefully as one would expect of such unique artifacts; unfortunately this is yet another case in which the material evidence is regrettably no longer available to confirm the witness' claim. Nevertheless it served its purpose at the time, and we must take that purpose into account when evaluating Moses' experience.[20]

Detectives and Devil's Advocates

Was it raining when Bernadette had her encounter? Did George Adamski make a fortune as a result of meeting Venusians? Are the trances of spirit mediums simulated or genuine? These are the sort of questions which are asked when a crime has been committed, but is it appropriate to ask them in connection with something as private and spiritual as an encounter experience?

When the Roman Catholic Church is considering promoting someone to the rank of sainthood, it appoints an *advocatus diaboli* — the Devil's Advocate — to argue the matter with the counsel for the defence, the *advocatus dei*. His task is to present the reasons why the claimant should *not* be made a saint. His existence is a sign of reluctance on the part of the Church, not to add to the roster of the sanctified, but to have the wool pulled over its eyes by impostors, sincere or otherwise. For when a man comes down off a mountain and tells us he has been talking with God, it can be a very important matter to many others beside himself. History can be changed. The cruelties of the Crusades, the horrors of the witchcraft persecution, the continuing madness in Ireland, the mass suicides of Jonestown — these and countless other public perversities and private crimes have resulted, ultimately, from the acceptance by a sufficiently large number of people of someone else's claim to have received a divine revelation.

Most often there does not seem to be so much at stake. Bernadette's experience began as a private affair between her and the Virgin Mary. But visit her home town today, and you see the vast commercial edifice which has been constructed on a foundation which is in essence nothing more solid that the unsubstantiated claim of a teenage girl. And the Lourdes phenomenon is only the largest of many such.

If the stories of Bernadette and the others are true, then such popular fervour may be justifiable. Many people claim to have benefited from visiting Lourdes, and though not everyone would agree that the benefits outweigh the harm, it may be argued that here is something to set in the balance against the horrors resulting from other claims. But if there is a difference in kind between those experiences which have beneficial consequences and those which lead to horrors, we have the more reason to analyse every experience to learn what it is likely to lead to.

We have seen that the Roman Catholic Church recognizes the need for rigorous examination in the case of candidates for saints, and even so credulous a theologian as Ribet, a leading scholar whose 1879 study of mysticism received the episcopal blessing, wrote:

> When contemplatives affirm that the mystical experience is a free gift from God, they are referring to its subjective aspect: they do not presume to reject all knowledge acquired from the study of these phenomena. The scientific study of mysticism defines and controls the mystical experience on behalf of the church, for it is to principles and doctrine, rather than to spontaneous

happenings and experiences, that spiritual directors turn for guidance in these matters, and on them they base their judgments.[208]

What Ribet says of mystical encounters we may reasonably extend to cover all the varieties of encounter experience. We cannot afford not to subject them to scientific examination, for only by such means can we distinguish the harmful from the beneficial. If there are genuine encounters, they will stand up to such examination, while the spurious will be revealed for what they are.

The problems, as we shall see, are complex; but to a large extent they break down into simple components which can be formulated as commonsense questions. The first is:

Is the person who has an encounter experience —

   ★ an extraordinary kind of person, or

   ★ an ordinary kind of person in an extraordinary state, or

   ★ an ordinary kind of person in an ordinary state but in extraordinary circumstances?

Which leads on to the second question:

Is the experience —

   ★ the natural consequence of being such a person in such a state, or

   ★ a gift specially bestowed on such a person, or

   ★ the consequence of a conscious action on such a person's part, or

   ★ the consequence of a subconscious process occurring within such a person?

The answers to these questions will lead us inevitably to further questions, but there is no reason to fear they will lead us into rarefied fields of special knowledge. For what we are concerned with is experiences which occur to people who are in most respects like ourselves; and this being so, there is no reason why we should not be able to understand what is happening to them.

2.1 ENCOUNTERS WITH DIVINITIES

> All mystics have seen visions; their histories are made up of prodigies and marvels. The Virgin, the saints, God himself appear to the visionary; extraordinary scenes unroll before his eyes; mysterious voices encourage him, plaintive voices entreat him, menacing voices terrify him; he lives continually on the same footing as the Beyond. [182]

Whether or not divinities of any sort exist, it is a fact that a great many people believe they do. For the purpose of our study, that may be all that matters. We don't have to inquire how people started believing in divinities, nor whether those beliefs are well-founded. Except that, if we are to understand what is happening when a witness tells us he's met God, we need to share, so far as we are able, his point of view and his state of mind.

Bizarre though many religious practices may seem, ludicrous though many religious teachings may be, the primary impulse which started men believing in divinities is logical enough. Even the most atheistic of us must sense, in the chain of development from thoughtless cell struggling in featureless liquid to Beethoven composing his last string quartets, a purposeful process implying something more meaningful than mere species-survival. The fact that you and I can embark on this study is in itself a sign that that there's more to life than 'birth, copulation and death'.

If that be granted, the rest follows logically — though we may suspect some flaws in the logic which has led to the internecine struggles of the Irish Christians, the dietary regulations of the Jews or the metaphysical balancing acts of the theologians. We have to ask if encounters with divinities are a genuine manifestation of true religions, or a spurious by-product founded on false logic.

In order to understand the experience of the visionary, we must, at least provisionally, go along with the reasoning which leads to such beliefs as that the mother of a first-century Palestinian religious leader, having been taken in her physical body to some higher level of existence when her earthly life was over, can come back to earth in that same body two thousand years later; that when she does this, some people can see her and others can't; and so on. Even if these things seem to us to go against common sense, we must accept that many people believe, and believe passionately, that they are happening.

Making contact with divinities

It is understandable that some of those who believe in divinities will want
to make contact with them. It is understandable, too, that some will think
this the highest purpose in life, devoting this earthly phase of their existence
to making themselves fit for the heavenly phase they expect to follow,
like a schoolboy preparing for his university career.

Mostly, though, people expect a 'don't call us, we'll call you' situation,
where it's the divinity who makes the contact.

The distinction between *sought* and *unsought* encounters is seen by
some commentators as crucial. On the one hand are the ritual practices
of primitive sorcerers and shamans which more or less infallibly lead to
encounters of some sort; on the other are the practices of religious mystics
whose attitude is essentially passive — for whom, in Teresa d'Avila's words,
encounters are a gift given by God 'when he chooses, as he chooses, and
to whom he chooses'.

But even theologians recognize that there are certain states in which
the witness is more likely to have such experiences, and some recommend
training procedures which have proved conducive to them. In principle
the aim of the ascetic practices of the mystics is to empty the soul of worldly
clutter so that God can fill it with heavenly furnishings, rather than to
induce encounter experiences; but it is common knowledge that in practice
encounter experiences may result.

A divinity may initiate an encounter for such purposes as:

★ To bestow a gift; thus Jehovah may grant the Promised Land
   to the Jewish people, his authority overriding the claims of its
   present inhabitants.

★ To utter a warning; most recent encounters with Jesus or Mary
   embody a threat of punishment for humanity unless we amend
   our present wickedness.

★ To give instructions, such as the Ten Commandments given to
   Moses.

★ To bestow comfort or consolation, perhaps to encourage the
   believer to put up with misfortune, for which the divinity is
   ultimately responsible, or the martyr to submit to torture rather
   than abandon his belief in the divinity.

An individual may seek an encounter with the divine for such purposes as:

★ to solicit a gift, as when a magician conjures up a demon to serve
   him;

★ to solicit advice, often a professional priestly function, as
   performed for example by Shamans in tribal cultures;

★ to solicit comfort and consolation.

These purposes are not necessarily explicitly or consciously formulated. An encounter with a divinity is often seen as a privilege in itself; but then the privilege is itself a comfort and consolation. As we probe deeper into encounter experiences, we shall find that their ostensible nature and purpose frequently mask something quite different. Here at the outset of our inquiry, however, all that concerns us is what *seems* to be happening.

The powers and attributes of divinities

Divinities do not exist in a vacuum; they are related to systems of belief which describe them and define their powers. For, though most divinities are thought of as omnipotent, some are more omnipotent than others.

The fact that they can bring about the encounter experience at all is of course a manifestation of their powers; but as we have already noted, it seems that certain conditions have to be fulfilled. Even someone like Teresa d'Avila, who was privileged to enjoy so many encounters, couldn't induce them whenever she wanted.

The whole question of how reliable is our supposed knowledge of what divinities are like, what their powers and purposes are and so on, is beyond the scope of this study, yet we are going to encounter difficulties which are directly related to those questions. As an example, consider the problem of *multilocation*.

Catholic theologians have long debated whether, when Jesus is visiting Teresa, say, this means he can't be anywhere else at the same time. One of them, Suarez, seriously suggested that the reason why most encounters are so brief is because the divinity has so many such appointments to keep. Others have evaded the issue by supposing that the divinity is not in his 'real' body, but Ribet, a leading authority, insists:

Since we have no substantial evidence that the event is due to the intervention of angels, we incline to believe that the bodily apparitions of Jesus are really and personally accomplished by Jesus himself. [208]

Regarding Jesus' mother Mary, Ribet says

Most scholars rightly hold that Mary does not, from one moment to another, desert the celestial court and deprive the Chosen Ones of her presence, yet they are unable to conceive that a body can be in two different places at the same time.

Nevertheless, he decides, this is what must be happening:

Suarez admits the theoretical possibility of multilocation even for the Blessed Virgin, but he sees it as an unprecedented miracle to which we should not have recourse unless no other explanation is available. These however are scruples and exaggerations which we are not obliged to share. Bilocation is a miracle like any other, and however great it may be, we can allow the Mother of God such facilities in favour of her friends.

I quote this not to poke fun at Ribet, for whose learning I have a great respect and with whose difficulties I can sympathize. Rather I wish to illustrate the sort of dilemmas into which we get if we allow ourself to get caught up in the complexities of a belief system. And yet, if we *don't* succeed in seeing the encounter experience in the context of the witness' beliefs, we won't know what it means to him.

In practice, of course, the witness shrugs his shoulders at the contradictions entailed in his experience: what happened to him is all-important, *how* it happened is beside the point. If the theologians say that only a miracle can account for the contradictions, well, that's *their* business.

The problem of recognition
One of the practical difficulties in many encounter experiences is how to be sure who one is encountering. Though the difficulty arises most notoriously in the field of spiritist communication with the surviving dead, it is also a problem in encounters with divinities.

The ostensible entities fall into two categories:

1 Those who have formerly been incarnate in human form, such as Jesus, Mary, the saints and — outside Christianity — Buddha and others who spent a phase of their existence living as Earthpersons;

2 Those who were never incarnate, such as God the Father and the supreme deities of most religious systems.

What we think we know about either will be pieced together from whatever is on offer in the way of:

★ hard evidence, usually available, if at all, only for those divinities who have had human incarnations,

★ witness testimony, which is necessarily subjective, though sometimes strengthened by there being more than one witness, and

★ *a priori* reasoning based on logical inference, of the kind we came across when we considered multilocation.

Putting these together, we can construct a paradigm of what the divinity may be expected to be like; then if a witness encounters an entity, we can match his description against our paradigm, and that should give us a pretty good idea whether his entity really is who he thinks it is.

But if we have made a mistake in constructing the paradigm, we have only made things more difficult. For example, though the physical appearance of neither Jesus nor his mother is known, a traditional image has been achieved by a consensus, something like the identikit portraits used by the police to reconstruct the appearance of criminals from witness descriptions. When Bernadette Soubirous had her encounter experience at Lourdes, however, though she had an intuitive conviction that it was Mary who was addressing her, the image was so different from the paradigm that she was not wholly sure, and had to test it by throwing holy water at it.

Confusion between paradigms is only one of the problems. Another is the danger that, when a paradigm has been created and accepted, it may itself inspire further experiences which would, however, be only pseudo-experiences. There is an analogy here with art forgery: if a hitherto unknown painting by Vermeer comes onto the market, it can be tested by comparing it with accepted Vermeers. But suppose the paintings with which it is compared are themselves forgeries, perhaps even by the same forgers as the new one?

So with our visions; the availability of the paradigm may be the cause of the alleged encounter. This is what the Church thinks may have happened in many cases where it has not granted official approval to encounters — for example at Garabandal, Spain, in 1961, or currently at Medjugorje in Yugoslavia. These encounters are so similar to those at Lourdes and Fatima, say, which *have* received official approval, that one can understand the bewilderment and disappointment of those whose experiences are disallowed. But the same similarity which those involved find reassuring is, for others, ground for suspicion.

At the root of the problem is of course why, even if the divinity wants to encounter a human, it needs to do so by manifesting as an entity at all? Mystics of the most transcendental kind sometimes manage to experience some kind of contact with some kind of divinity so unknowable and so indescribable that they can say little more about it than that it is 'the ground of all being' or some other such phrase so all-embracing as to be ultimately useless to the rest of us, however meaningful it may be to them on a subjective, intuitive level. An encounter with such a being would hardly be an 'encounter' at all, and it is even open to question whether the entity could be termed a 'being'; Eastern philosophies, I feel sure, would be unhappy with such a label.

Leuba, an American psychologist who made a special study of the psychology of religious belief, asserted that 'one cannot enter into social relations with the Absolute',[155] so that while God might essentially be 'the infinite Absolute which is not to be moved by human needs and desires, by gifts and supplications, by thanks and praises', there would also be a need for a God who would be 'a superhuman being with whom social relations can be maintained'. The direct encounters with which we are concerned necessarily imply *accessibility* of some kind. It takes two to make an encounter: speaker *and* listener, host *and* guest, and between the two there must be sufficient compatibility for communication to take place. Which, in practice, means that the divinity must appear in more or less human form, talking a human language, sharing human ideas, understanding and responding to human thoughts and emotions.

We do not have to believe that this is the 'real' nature of the divinity, or even its everyday shape. We may, if we like, believe it takes on this appearance to put the witness at his ease; or in the case of the Devil, it may be just the reverse, with the object of frightening him.

Some of our divinities, let us not forget, are more or less human in any case. Theologians have not yet established whether Jesus had any existence *before* he came on his mission to Planet Earth; but since our knowledge of him is derived entirely from the things he did and said during his incarnation as a human, we cannot conceive of his having any other form. So with his mother: if she is at present 'living' in some kind of heaven in any shape at all, it is presumably the human one she had during her previous existence as a Palestinian carpenter's wife, since it was in that body she left our earth. Or it may be that she has relinquished that body but resumes it from time to time like a former pupil donning suitable clothes to revisit her old school.

The problem of entity recognition is quaintly illustrated by an episode in the life of Agnès de Jésus (1602–1634), who was visited and consoled in her sickness by a being she supposed to be the Virgin Mary. However,

> The consolation was changed, the very same day, to a very great trouble of the spirit, when, after she had told her confessor of her experience, he mortified her by saying he didn't believe in it. Is it likely, he asked her, that the Queen of Angels would come down from Heaven to enter a place as wretched as your room, and wish to visit a creature as miserable as yourself? This comment made her very uneasy, and revived her fears that she might be mistaken. But the Queen of Peace would not allow her servant to remain in this worried state; she sent an angel to her, who assured her that it was really and truly the Virgin who had appeared to her. [208]

Most of the difficulties presented by encounters with divinities are embodied in that story.

2.2 ENCOUNTERS WITH GOD AND OTHER GODS

Several hospital patients studied by Manchester University Psychiatry Department reported that on the threshold of sleep they had visions of Jesus Christ.

One described how 'he appeared in front of her, dressed in a long white robe. She recalled vividly his long white hair and blue eyes. He was life-sized and seemed absolutely real to her at the time, although when the experience ceased after a few moments, she knew it was a vision. This occurred when she was happy and contented in herself.'

Another, just as she was falling off to sleep, experienced a vision of 'Jesus standing at the foot of her bed. He was wearing a white robe, he had a crown on his head which seemed to glow, and he carried a staff. It was absolutely clear and real and she thought he had come as a warning to her; later she realised that it was merely a vision.'[227]

It is instructive to compare these two brief experiences with more elaborate encounters such as those which came to Madeleine Aumont in 1972.[206]

Madeleine was born in 1924 in a small village between Caen and Rouen, in western France. Hers was a modest rural working-class background. When she was 24 she married and subsequently had five children; in 1968 the family moved to nearby Dozulé to be nearer school and church, though she was not particularly devout. Indeed she said her children demanded so much of her time that she had none to spare for going to church. At the same time, as a believing Catholic, she felt guilty about her non-attendance. Later she said:

> I used to admire people who gave up their lives entirely to the service of God. In my prayers I often asked for a proof of his existence. I was like Saint Thomas: I would quite often think about God, looking at the starry sky in the evening before going to bed and reflecting that everything on this earth didn't make itself. But to have any stronger belief, I needed to see something supernatural.

On Easter Day 1970 she resolved to go to church and 'confess the faults of four years . . . Something inexplicable happened inside me.' She felt she had been possessed by 'a supernatural force', which she identified as 'the presence of Jesus'. She was astonished to have received what seemed to be a sign of grace:

Is it possible that the spirit of God acts on a being of 45, as dirtied with sin as I am, when there are so many young pure souls on whom the Lord could have bestowed his grace? . . . I felt something that was a combination of exhaustion, intoxication and happiness. This wore off after I got home, but I thought about it throughout the following week and was impatient for next Sunday, though more from curiosity than from true faith.

She took to attending Mass not only on Sundays, but also on Wednesday mornings after taking the children to school. She was reading intensively books of devotion and lives of the saints, in hope of getting to know God better, and had an increasing taste for solitude and solitary prayer.

On 28 March 1972, the Tuesday of Holy Week, she saw her husband off to work at 4.30 a.m. as usual. Before going back to bed she opened the bedroom window to admire the stars, the creation of God, and to say a prayer to the Holy Trinity. She observed a bright star near the horizon. Her first thought was that it was one of the flying saucers that people were seeing; frightened, she got back into bed. Then, about ten minutes later, when the light seemed to have gone, she got up again to look out of the window.

This time she saw a huge luminous cross in the sky, brighter than daylight, and at the same time heard words spoken in Latin, a language she didn't understand. Then another voice spoke in French: 'You will make known this cross and you will carry it.' Then the cross vanished.

In the diary she was keeping as a record of her spiritual growth she wrote down as much as she could remember, then returned to bed in tears, both dismayed and exhilarated. How, she wondered, is this cross to be made known? How is the world to be convinced that Jesus is here and that his cross dominates the world?

On 8 November she saw the cross again, accompanied by a voice urging repentance. On 7 December came a third sighting, and this time the voice instructed her that the priest should erect the Cross of Glory on the site of the vision; people would come to do penance there and find peace and joy. At the fourth sighting she was told she would see the cross three more times. At the fifth she was told the cross should be 'comparable to Jerusalem'. At the sixth, she was to tell the bishop that the priest must not leave the parish until the task of constructing the cross was completed. While her previous visions had lasted only a few minutes, this lasted more than a quarter of an hour.

Then on 27 December, during her seventh vision, the cross faded over a cloud which became the pedestal for a human figure. It leant towards her extending its hands, saying 'Don't be afraid, I'm Jesus of Nazareth, the son of man restored to life.' Then he continued in Latin, which had later to be translated for Madeleine to understand: 'O Madeleine, whom a happy destiny has made a wife, proclaim the virtues of him who has summoned you from the darkness, and his wonderful light.'

From 1972 to 1978 Madeleine enjoyed 38 apparitions of Jesus or communications from him; five of the Archangel Michael; and two of the Eucharist. Most of these occurred in Dozulé church, in the presence of the priest and two members of a religious order, and sometimes crowds of up to fifty. None of these others shared her visions.

Many of the messages related to the construction of the huge cross — *La Croix Glorieuse* — which Jesus wanted erected on the hill behind the Aumonts' house in time for Holy Year 1975. It has yet to be built, however, since neither the funds not the technology for so huge an edifice are available — Jesus has specified a height 'comparable to Jerusalem' which is calculated as 738 metres, or 624 if the height of Dozulé above sea level is included. That is roughly double the height of the Eiffel Tower.

It is quite customary for visionary entities to request that chapels or basilicas shall be constructed in their honour; it is equally usual for them to give no indication where the finance is to come from. The Dozulé request is unusual, however, in specifying a monument requiring advanced construction technology.

Apart from the Cross, the messages were chiefly the usual exhortations to penance and prophecies of catastrophe: Jesus told Madeleine she was to be his prophet, unusual for religious visions but, as we shall see, a frequent feature of encounters with extraterrestrial beings. In 1974 he warned that he would give Satan a free hand and that before the end of the century there will be a catastrophe such as not been since the Flood; but those who repent at the foot of The Cross of Glory will be saved.

Madeleine has given us detailed descriptions of Jesus. He wears a white robe with wide sleeves and a knotted cord, his hair is shoulder-length, and his face and hands are luminous. At the fifteenth vision he invited Madeleine to touch his hands. 'So I took his two hands in mine; they were warm like those of a living person.' At the seventeenth he invited her to examine his wounds. She reached out her right hand and with two fingers touched the edge of the wound in his side; she said it felt deep.

Though I have indicated some features of Madeleine's experiences being 'customary', there is no such thing as a typical encounter with God, and since her case is as unique as any other we have no right to draw any general conclusions from it. At the same time, Madeleine's experiences offer us valuable insights because, though they have not officially been accepted as authentic by the Church, they are very much the sort of thing which people all over the world are reporting, and which it is our present purpose to try to understand. So her case is as good a starting-point for that study as any.

Let us consider some features of her case:

★ *The visions were never shared with anyone else.* This is true of virtually every visionary encounter; the only exceptions are when a group of witnesses share a simultaneous experience. Theoretically it would be possible to contrive an optical device using polarization, or colour filters, or holography, to achieve selective visibility of an object, but it seems improbable that any such technical feat was performed on some fifty occasions for Madeleine's benefit, by Jesus or by anyone else. Alternatively, we may consider a temporarily enhanced capacity to see on Madeleine's part or a correspondingly diminished capacity on the part of her companions; such effects can be easily enough achieved by hypnotic suggestion, and even without hypnosis on hysterical subjects (see [123]). Even if some such process was occurring, however, it is not clear who or what could have been responsible. We have to ask what means exist for Madeleine to have an experience which clearly took place on a different level of reality from the everyday.

★ *Madeleine seems in no way abnormal.* She is a competent wife and mother who enjoys the respect of her neighbours. Her parish priest and others who have met her, though some may have thought her deluded, have not thought her mad. True, no psychiatric study was carried out; but nothing we know of her — apart from her experiences themselves — indicates any exceptional departure from the norm.

Nor is there any apparent reason why she should have been selected for such an experience. We cannot claim to understand what hidden motives may influence a divinity to bestow its gifts on one person rather than another, but neither Madeleine's personal merits nor her circumstances seem to distinguish her from millions of other candidates. We have to ask whether whatever was 'special' about Madeleine was something in her spiritual make-up which caused her to be selected, or something in her psychological make-up which made her particularly liable to have such an experience.

★ *The requests made by the divinity discourage credibility.* The construction of such a cross, while impressive by human standards, would be no great shakes to a divinity who had created the universe; but if Jesus was looking at the matter from a human viewpoint, why didn't he suggest something more practicable? We have to ask whether this does not suggest a human rather than a divine origin for the request.

★ *Madeleine's spiritual state* is of crucial importance. It is evident that she had been passing through a spiritual crisis, and equally evident that her encounters were associated with that crisis. We have to ask what precipitates a crisis of this kind, and what causes it to lead to an encounter experience.

Some of these difficulties recur in the following case, very different yet equally representative of the experiences claimed by a surprisingly large number of people, who thereby bring on themselves the suspicion and even the hostility of their neighbours, the disapproval of the authorities, and just occasionally, the fervent devotion of a handful of friends. To the individual himself the experience may bring delight or dismay, peace of mind or anxiety, self-doubt or self-satisfaction, according to his temperament, his cultural background, and the support or lack of support he receives from others.

Michel Potay, who now calls himself 'Frère Michel', is a self-appointed apostle who dispenses from his 'house of the Revelation', near Bordeaux in south-west France, a teaching which is more like group psychotherapy than orthodox religion, but which he claims was revealed to him by Jesus Christ in person.

Previously an industrialist, with a wife and three children, Potay's interest in the occult led him to give up his work and set up as a professional psychic in Lyon. In 1968 he became a priest in the Orthodox Church; a meeting with the anti-Pope Clement XV inspired him to quit the Church and set up his own semi-collectivist religious community in January 1974. On the night of 15 January a female voice woke him from sleep and told him to make his way to a particular room, where

> I saw the Christ! I shan't attempt to describe my feelings at that moment, for they are incommunicable to anyone who has not experienced such a meeting. He was standing, dressed in a shapeless garment quite unlike those in which he is usually depicted, so tight-fitting it was as though he wore it only because Christ would not wish to manifest naked. His hair was long and gathered at the back of his head, as though in a pony tail. His hands were beautiful, manly like his face. He had stigmata on his wrists and on just one of his feet. One night as I was looking at this single stigmatised foot he told me, I was the last to be crucified. They were short of a nail, so only one of my feet had a nail through it. [30]

Over the ensuing forty nights Jesus, obligingly speaking in French, dictated a new gospel whose object was the reunion of Christianity with Judaism and Islam, superseding the Bible, the Koran and the Talmud, along with all the theological commentaries of the three religions. Sometimes the dictation stopped while Jesus spoke of personal matters, or answered questions he read in Michel's mind — for Michel never spoke to Jesus in words.

It wasn't long before the Evil One found out what was happening and did its best to interfere:

> To go into details about the torments and temptations he inflicted on me would be out of place. But though God abandoned me for long periods, to be tested by Satan, he knew the limits of my endurance; every evening towards 10 p.m., whether or not Christ visited me that night, the demon left me. On 6 April, incensed by my resistance to his wishes, the demon lifted me off the ground and threw me head-first to the floor; the following night Christ placed his hand on my wound, which at once disappeared.

God — that is to say, God the Father — also appeared to Michel, in the form of a rod of light, and gave him obscure messages in a language he found difficult to understand.

Because of Michel's previous career, and the implausible nature of his account, we may well be tempted to dismiss it as spurious, the product of some mental derangement. But it is precisely because Michel's experience may indeed be spurious that I have chosen to quote it. For our study will achieve nothing if it does not provide us with criteria which will enable us to distinguish between the genuine and the spurious — having first, of course, decided what we mean by those two terms. It is not enough to *believe* that Michel's was a pseudo-encounter; we must have *grounds* for our belief. And if we cannot find any grounds, we have no right to reject it.

Clearly there is a substantial difference between the experiences of these two French visionaries and those of the two English psychiatric patients with which we started this chapter. But is it an *essential* difference?

The theological view would be, I suppose, that the two English cases were simply morbid symptoms of disturbed minds, while the two French, though they may not have been what the witnesses thought them, were on an altogether different level. If it was not God who was responsible, it was very likely Satan the deceiver.

For those who are not subscribers to a religious belief system there is, however, a viable alternative. We may suppose that initially a more or less similar event happened to each of our four witnesses. The difference in what subsequently happened was due to the difference in the cultural background of the witnesses and the social context of the event. In the culturally rich, socially supportive French context, the experience received encouragement to develop. In England, on the other hand, where such phenomena are more generally regarded as pathological, no nourishment was forthcoming from the socio-cultural context, and consequently the experiences had no encouragement to develop.

There is probably some truth in this hypothesis, but it is clearly inadequate as a total explanation. What it shows, though, is how, by varying just one parameter — in this case, the socio-cultural parameter — the total character of an encounter experience may be changed. From which it follows that we must learn to distinguish the secondary parameters, which give the experience its outward form and direct its subsequent course, from the primary factors which are the essence of the experience, and perhaps do not greatly vary from one experience to another. Established religious organizations are always wary of those who claim direct contact with divinities, rather than working through regular channels involving priests or otherwise authorized persons. While there is always the possibility that some of these may indeed have been privileged to meet God face to face, it is certain that many others are deluded, not to mention the deliberate charlatans. If the claims of such people are admitted without question, all manner of dubious and even dangerous teachings may be set loose on society.

But what questions are to be asked? How are such claims to be tested? And who is qualified to ask the questions and test the claims?

The priestly experience

For many professional religious persons, encounters with God are part of their function. In primitive societies, tribal priests and shamans undergo rituals which result in what they believe to be divine encounters; thus, among the Manasi of South America, 'the god comes down to Earth, converses with the shaman, and finally carries him to the sky with him, letting him fall to Earth a few moments later',[55] while Eskimos believe that their shaman dives to the bottom of the sea to make personal contact with the deity.

However great our respect for folk tradition and popular belief, few of us would hold that such experiences involve real encounters with real gods. If a real encounter with the divine is concealed beneath the formality of the ritual, it is similar to those mystical experiences which we have set aside as beyond the scope of our study.

Virtually every religious belief system presupposes a God who started the cosmos off in the first place and keeps it going for obscure purposes of his own. Inevitably, this God is conceived in more or less anthropomorphic terms; even the most learned theologian will use phrases like 'God wills that . . .' or 'God will not allow . . .' turning the observed facts about the universe into personal directions.

We may say that God must be either:

1 perfectly describable, because he exists in more or less human form and created us in his image; or

2 fundamentally beyond description, but presenting himself to us in quasi-human form for the purpose of communication; or

3 utterly beyond description.

As religions develop, so do their notions of God. As Robertson puts it,

A God becomes more respectable precisely as he gets less to do. When he was the near God, meddling in everything, he was more obviously made in the image of his worshippers, more 'mythological' in the sense of having many more stories told about him . . . It is when Zeus is put over others in the position of Supreme Judge that he begins to lend himself to higher ethical ideals; and the highest of all were those formed when the God-idea became so remote as to elude form, and was resolved into the idea of a universal Mind of which men's minds were portions.[213]

Personal encounters with divinities, then, seem something of a throwback. What actually happens when the Catholic Pope receives new instructions from God? Does he enjoy a face-to-face encounter, or is it more of a mind-to-mind affair? High priests in all religions tend to play with their cards close to their chests, so we can only speculate; yet the question is not a trivial one, for the consequences of divine revelation, as transmitted by a Muhammad, a Joseph Smith or a Pope, can affect millions of lives and change the course of history.

It is understandable, then, that the priesthood should be cautious when an individual bypasses the system, when a Frère Michel proposes to supersede the great religious books of the world with a new gospel allegedly dictated to him by Jesus. But some illuminati offer such valuable teachings that their claims to have received them directly from God cannot be easily set aside: Saint Teresa of Avila is the classic example. Somehow a place had to be found within the system for experiences such as hers:

> Confessors began to keep careful records of such experiences in the lives of people under their charge, gradually accumulating a rich treasure of authentic materials. The ecstatics were entrusted to vigilant guardians who kept them company at all times, so that whatever escaped the confessor would be known by some other means. Often, the superior would require those whom God had chosen for these extraordinary experiences to write a full account; on other occasions it was God himself who ordered it. An experienced confessor would not hesitate to devote his whole life, or a large proportion of it, to the direction of one single person. [94]

So far as the Church is concerned, such safeguards justify it in distinguishing between the experiences of a Teresa who was, so to speak, on the payroll, and those of a freelance like Madeleine Aumont:

> Monastic mystics are exempt from the temptations to which secular ecstatics in the outside world are liable to succumb. These latter find themselves in a region totally unfamiliar to them, where they see no beaten track, no guide to direct their steps; whereas the mystics tread a road trodden by many others before them. Even in their sublimest transports they do not lose their footing. Directed by their confessors, they benefit from all that has been learnt in the past.

But working within a system also has its dangers. There are, for instance the incentives to have such encounters — the privileged social position which is likely to result; the exciting distraction from the humdrum tenor of monastic life; and for those with strong individual characters, a way of acquiring divine sanction for their wishes — all these could, as Teresa herself recognized, result in pseudo-experiences. 'Natural weakness is very great, especially in women; we should not immediately take it for granted that every little fancy we may have is a vision . . . There are souls so absorbed in their own ideas as to feel certain they see whatever their fancy imagines.'[250] With her customary common sense she advised distractions, plenty to eat and plenty of sleep, and not too much praying.

A further danger is that the witness, or his counsellors, will unconsciously modify the account of the experience to conform to the authorized stereotype. If A's experience has been accepted as genuine, then there is a temptation for B to stress the way in which his experience resembles A's, and play down any differences, so that his too may be found acceptable. As a result, we find stereotypes imposing themselves on all kinds of encounter experience — with spirits and extraterrestrials just as much as with divinities.

But the greatest danger is that the individual aspect of the experience will be lost in the communal, and we must recognize this as the great shortcoming of all establishment attitudes to the encounter experience.

The scientific alternative

This is what American psychologist Arthur Deikman has to say:

> A mystic experience is the production of an unusual state of consciousness. This state is brought about by a de-automisation of hierarchically ordered structures that ordinarily conserve attentional energy for maximum efficiency in achieving the basic goals of the individual: biological survival as an organism and psychological survival as a personality . . . Under special conditions of dysfunction . . . or under special goal conditions such as exist in religious mystics, the pragmatic systems of automatic selection are set aside or break down, in favour of alternate modes of consciousness whose stimulus processing may be less efficient from a biological point of view but whose very inefficiency may permit the experience of aspects of the real world formerly excluded or ignored. The extent to which such a shift takes place is a function of the motivation of the individual, his particular neurophysiological state, and the environmental conditions encouraging or discouraging such a change.[43]

If Saint Teresa had been able to disentangle the underlying meaning of that passage from its cloak of academic jargon, she would first have felt an amused pity for the poor scientist struggling to fit her experiences into his ordered paradigm of what makes people do what they do. Secondly, though, she would have applauded Deikman's concession that mystical experiences result from the fact that some people have needs higher than wondering where their next meal is coming from or who's after their job, their wife or their worldly goods.

What we shall want to question is the narrow concept of what constitutes 'biological efficiency', which ignores what we, in this study, are going to see as possibly the crucial factor in bringing about and shaping the encounter experience: *the possibility that these experiences occur because for that person, at that particular time, such an experience was the best thing that could happen to him*. It may present itself as a solution, as an escape, as an opportunity, as a therapy, or as a best option — the function will vary according to the individual and according to his need. (And we must not lose sight of the possibility that it may be not the witness but some other agency who decides.) But whatever its purpose, it is —

taking the widest view of what constitutes biological efficiency — the most biologically efficient thing that could happen to him.

The Swedish mystic Swedenborg said:

> I am well aware that many will say that no-one can possibly speak with spirits and angels so long as he is living in the body; many will say it is all fancy, others that I recount such things to win credence, while others will make other kinds of objection. But I am deterred by none of these: for I have seen, I have heard, I have felt. [248]

The most impressive feature of encounters with divinities is the sense of conviction of the witness — a sense of conviction which is often in conflict with the beliefs prevalent in his cultural milieu. Hence the difficulty Church authorities have always experienced in handling such cases. It is tempting for us today with our newly rediscovered respect for the rights of the individual to interpret this conflict in fashionable 'individual = right, establishment = wrong' terms, but this is clearly too simplistic. It is well-nigh certain, for instance, that our witness Michel Potay was 'wrong' in so far as his experience is seen as a religious one; I incline to agree with the Church authorities that it is highly unlikely that this new gospel he has for us derives from Jesus. But that does not give us the right to dismiss his experience, only the need to re-label it.

Nor is it clear that orthodox science has sorted things out so satisfactorily that we can forget what the theologians have to say altogether. Whether or not we believe that any divinity is involved, the encounter experience surely has a greater significance than is confined in any narrow interpretation of 'biological efficiency'.

2.3   ENCOUNTERS WITH ANGELS

> Judging from those with whom I have worked and interacted, it seems that the angelic entities which manifest to us often appear as one of the religious figures which we esteem highly — such as a particular saint, guru, holy figure, master. [240]

Francie Steiger's angels may seem more typical of contemporary 'New Age' thinking than of religious tradition; but in fact her suggestion that angels take on the form of other beings in order to visit us is one that many Catholic theologians have considered, though few have ended by accepting it.

The suggestion has the merit of accounting for one essential characteristic of angels, their human appearance, which could be because:

- ★ they *are* human; or

- ★ they *look* human; or

- ★ they *assume* human appearance temporarily.

The distinguished anthropologist M.J. Field is one of the few to have based a serious hypothesis on the first of these options. Drawing on her experiences as a doctor in Africa, she proposed that the angels of the Bible were really stewards or messengers acting on behalf of terrestrial landlords, transformed by the processes of folklore, powered by the fearfulness of primitive peoples, into instruments of divine authority. [76]

Novel, ingenious and plausible though this culture-based hypothesis may be, it certainly cannot account for the entire range of angelic contact. The second option, that angels look human because that is indeed their natural appearance, may be favoured by primitive peoples for whom angels are virtually a kind of spirit, but it is too literal for most commentators, who have tended to prefer the third option. Thomas Aquinas was expressing a widely held view when he suggested that 'angels are composed of the ambient air of the place where they appear, which they arrange and condense into an appropriate form'. [208] Such an hypothesis accounts for the variations in their appearance while explaining why it is so realistic.

Virtually every religious system incorporates the idea of angels in some form. Since God is generally conceived anthropomorphically as a king ruling his subjects, it follows that he will need ministers, ambassadors and messengers, and it is in such roles that angels generally appear, especially during the more naive early stages of a religion's development. Many religions recognize specific angels by name: Christians have Gabriel, Michael and so on, as well as Satan who was an angel prior to his defection. Several of these are shared with Islam, whose Jabril is the Christian's Gabriel and whose Mikail is the Michael who visited Jeanne d'Arc and who rather confusingly is both archangel and saint. In addition Muslims have several of their own, such as Azrail, the angel of death, whom at first Allah concealed from the others. When Azrail was at last displayed to them, they all fell into a thousand-year swoon.

Though angels no longer play a prominent part in the official activities of the major religions, they continue to manifest on a more popular level. The most dramatic appearances occur when angels appear in support of soldiers at war. During the early weeks of World War One, when the Allies in Belgium were in danger of being overrun by the Germans, the 'Angels of Mons' were widely reported. Together with saints like George and Michael and mysterious entities such as 'the Comrade in White', they inspired a substantial body of reports. These are generally dismissed as folklore but the fact that such reports continue to be made is testimony to the enduring force of beliefs which one might have thought long discarded. Not long ago, American evangelist Billy Graham published a book entitled *Angels, God's Secret Agents*,[97] and the quotation from Francie Steiger with which this chapter opened is a further indication that angels are still part of popular culture, though performing roles somewhat different from those they performed in the Old Testament.

Guardian angels

The Islamic belief system recognizes three sorts of angels. One group do nothing but worship Allah; another group have specific tasks such as controlling the operations of nature or inflicting death; while the third, the *hafaza*, protect the individual from their evil opposites, the *djinns*, and also monitor his conduct in preparation for the final judgment.

The concept of personally assigned angelic guardians is widespread and long-standing. The classical Greek writer Menander tells us that 'by every man at birth a good demon takes his stand, to initiate him in the mysteries of life'.[103] By this Greek term 'demon' we must evidently understand not an evil spirit but a benevolent, if stern, guardian and guide.

It is natural that as religions become more personal, so angels appear less often as divine agents, more frequently as private counsellors. Wartime appearances apart, most recent encounters with angels take the form of personal experiences with beings who take a direct interest in the individual. A particularly interesting account is that given by the scientist Humphry Davy:

I expose myself to your ridicule in the statement I am about to make, yet

I mention nothing but simple fact. Almost a quarter of a century ago I
contracted that terrible form of typhus fever known as jail fever, whilst
engaged in a plan for ventilating one of the great prisons. My illness was
severe and dangerous; as long as the fever continued, my dreams or deliriums
were painful and oppressive; but when the weakness consequent to exhaustion
came on, and when the probability of death seemed to my physicians greater
than that of life, there was an entire change. I remained in an apparently
senseless state, but in fact my mind was peculiarly active; there was always
before me the form of a beautiful woman with whom I was engaged in the
most interesting and intellectual conversation.

I was passionately in love at the time, but the object of my admiration
was a lady with black hair, dark eyes and pale complexion; this spirit of my
vision on the contrary had brown hair, blue eyes, and a bright rosy
complexion, and was, as far as I can recollect, unlike any of the amatory
forms which in early youth had haunted my imagination. Her figure for many
days was so distinct in my mind as to form almost a visual image: as I gained
strength the visits of my good angel, for so I called it, became less frequent,
and when I was restored to health they were altogether discontinued.

Ten years later, when I had almost lost the recollection of the vision, it
was recalled by a very blooming and graceful maiden 14 or 15 years old that
I accidentally met during my travels in Illyria; but I cannot say that the
impression made upon my mind by this female was very strong.

Now comes the extraordinary part; ten years later, twenty years after my
first illness, being in a course of travels ordered by my medical advisers when
I was exceedingly weak from a severe and dangerous malady which for many
weeks had threatened my life, *I again met the person who was the representative
of my visionary female*; and to her kindness and care I believe I owe what
remains to me of existence. My despondency gradually disappeared, and
though my health still continued weak, life began to possess charms which
I had thought were forever gone; and I could not help identifying the living
angel with the vision which appeared as my guardian genius during the illness
of my youth.[41]

Davy is no fool, and pictures an objector saying:

I really see nothing at all in this fact beyond the influence of an imagination
excited by disease. From youth, even to age, women are our guardian angels,
our comforters; and I dare say any other handsome young female, who had
been your nurse in your last illness, would have coincided with your
remembrance of the vision, even though her eyes had been hazel and her
hair flaxen . . . almost any agreeable form would have become the
representative of your imaginary guardian genius.

We may well feel that the objections that Davy so scientifically puts into
the mouth of an imaginary sceptic come somewhere close to the truth,
but they fall far short of a complete account of the matter. His inability
to relate his original 'angel' to anyone he had actually known can indeed
be ascribed to defective or unconscious memory, and the later supposed
resemblance to the workings of his imagination. But the coincidence of
re-encountering the young person who played so crucial a role is surely

remarkable, and while indeed we *could* ascribe it all to chance and fancy, I think it not unreasonable to retain the option that some deeper and more meaningful process was at work.

It is significant that Davy's 'guardian angel' is removed from any religious connotation; not once does he suggest that his experience inspired any religious reflections. We must indeed ask ourselves whether the traditional religious character of such beings is anything more than the trappings imposed by the witness' cultural circumstances. Consider, in contrast to Davy's, the experience of Soeur Jeanne des Anges, one of the central figures in the tragic outbreak of convent hysteria at Loudun, France, in the 1630s. She claimed to be in continual contact with her angel, whom she described to her confessor thus:

> I will tell you, my Father, that for more than two years my good Angel has appeared to me usually visibly and externally to my bodily eyes. He takes the form of a very handsome young man, about 15 years old, just over a metre tall. His clothes seem white, very bright; his two eyes seem to me like two suns; a great light surrounds him, his face is serious but nonetheless very friendly. When he wishes to renew the marks [of her stigmata] he takes my hand in a very gentle manner; I feel a light warmth on my hand, gentle, not uncomfortable. [153]

From all we know of Soeur Jeanne's career, in which the chief question is to what extent her lies, dissimulations, scheming and paranoia were voluntary, to what extent the product of her delusions, we have no reason to believe one word she tells us. Her angel could be a figment of her imagination along with so much else that she reported. Later in this study we shall be looking more closely at what is really meant by such phrases as 'a figment of imagination'; for the moment, let us simply recognize that to give an experience such a label, just as to attribute Davy's experience to the work of the imagination or to relegate the Angels of Mons to 'folklore', is in no way to dismiss them or to deny them importance.

Soeur Jeanne's communications with her angel were part of the total experience whch led her to play a leading role in the tragedy of Loudun. Whether or not we believe her angelic visions to have been delusory, we must recognize that they were purposeful; and so we must suppose that they were part of a process which had meaning, for herself if for nobody else. The same is true, more explicitly and more privately, of Davy's experiences with an angel who, imagination or not, appears to have helped save his life; and no less true, though now on a public scale, of those who claimed to see the Angels of Mons and were thereby immensely encouraged. Delusion, imagination, folklore they may have been, but they had tangible and visible consequences. Each must therefore be seen, once we have stripped it of its trappings, as the expression of a purposeful process. It will be our task, later in this study, to consider what that process and what that purpose may have been.

Angels at the threshold of death

There is one specific function of angels which may turn out to be especially significant for our study: their traditional association with death, and particularly its approach.

In the year 304, after being appallingly tortured by the Roman authorities for his Christian beliefs, Saint Vincent was thrown into Zaragoza prison to die. There he was visited by a multitude of angels who congratulated him on his spiritual victory, telling him 'Your struggle is over, and the moment has come for you to lay aside the burden of mortality and rejoin the choir of the blessed.' His prison was transformed into a bright and beautiful place, and the broken pots which had been strewn on the floor to hurt his body were transformed into a bed of roses. Soon afterwards he died.[208]

The current renewed interest in NDEs (near-death experiences) has brought to light a number of cases in which people who find themselves at the point of death encounter beings which they identify as angels. Some reports come from people who are able to give us a description before they die, others from people who recover from what was seemingly a fatal condition. Here is an extract from a case in the latter category:

> Again I felt this presence, but I didn't see any light this time, and thoughts or words came to me, and he said Jack, why are you crying? I thought you would be pleased to be with me. I thought, Yes, I am, I want to go very much . . . Then why are you crying? (The subject explained that he was worried about his nephew) Then the thoughts came to me from this presence, Since you are asking for someone else, and thinking of others, not Jack (himself), I will grant you what you want. You will live until you see your nephew become a man.[212]

While Jack makes no specific identification of his 'presence' with a guardian angel, his experience is similar to scores of incidents in which the entity *is* so identified. Many of these involve angels of traditional appearance, who seem to be acting as a kind of reception committee to help the dying person through his ordeal.

Angels also act as messengers of death to others. The mother of Hélène Smith, whom we shall be meeting in Part Four, occasionally had psychic experiences of her own. About the year 1870, when Hélène's three-year-old younger sister was sick, her mother, waking during the night to attend the child, saw a shining angel standing beside the child's bed with arms stretched over it. After a few moments the apparition vanished like a dispersing cloud. Mme Smith woke her husband, but not in time for him to see anything, so he mocked her fears and reproved her for reading a fatal significance into what she had seen. However, next day, against the expectation of the doctor, the child died.[77]

For Flournoy, who heard of the incident when attending Hélène, this was 'a splendid example of accurate maternal presentiment, felt subconsciously and translating itself into ordinary consciousness by means of a visual hallucination, which borrows its symbolic content from an appropriate popular image'. Such a view of the case places it in the same category as the Angels of Mons, as an instance of folklore in action, and the postponement of Jack's death on compassionate grounds can be accounted for in the same way.

But even if we accept that these incidents relate to a subconscious thought or purpose, we must take seriously the overwhelming sense felt by each of these witnesses that some other being was involved. Flournoy's explanation is certainly intelligent and plausible, and we may feel that it is adequate to account for Mme Smith's fairly straightforward apparition experience; but could we explain our other and infinitely more complex cases in the same way? Humphry Davy pictured his imaginary sceptic making a very similar suggestion, but evidently found it insufficient to account for his experience.

At this stage of our inquiry, certainly, it would be premature for us to reject the possibility that the entities involved in these cases have some kind of autonomous existence, and are something more than projections from the witness' own mind. We must be able to answer the question which encounters with angels so dramatically pose: Is it possible for the individual to create for himself experiences so vivid, so meaningful and often with such practical consequences?

2.4 ENCOUNTERS WITH MARY AND OTHER SAINTLY BEINGS

My tongue preaches Mary; I will not miss an occasion to speak of Mary and I will try my best to introduce the subject in every conversation, recalling her mercy and privileges . . . My hand writes of Mary; Mary's name will head my notebooks . . . My works will praise Mary, for I will exhibit her picture everywhere I can; I will care for altars and churches in her honour, and statues, images and medals spreading her devotion. [6]

No encounter case can be evaluated without taking into account its cultural context; no category illustrates this more notably than encounters with the mother of Jesus of Nazareth, the Virgin Mary. The continuing recurrence of such experiences on the one hand, and on the other the widespread cult of Mary typified by the lines just quoted, pose vividly a question which we shall find raised by many kinds of experience: which causes which, the belief or the encounter?

What can hardly be questioned is that the Mary to whom such pious devotion is directed is an artefact of human belief. Thomas of Villanova writes of her:

Let us pass on to her virtues: but what can we say except that God gave to Mary all that a creature can possibly receive? He enclosed in Mary the perfection of all the saints and of the whole Church. All that is remarkable in any saint you will find in Mary; the patience of Job, the meekness of Moses, the faith of Abraham, the chastity of Joseph, the humility of David, the wisdom of Solomon, the zeal of Elias; in her is the purity of virgins, the courage of martyrs, the piety of confessors, the knowledge of doctors, the contempt of hermits for the things of this world . . . [194]

In fact there is no historic basis whatever for such statements. We cannot even be sure that Mary existed: if Jesus lived as a human we may suppose he had a mother, but the circumstances of his birth have made the question of her motherhood a uniquely curious matter.

There is no need for us to get involved in these questions; but it *is* important that we recognize that an encounter with Mary is an encounter with a being about whom precious little is known, far less than might warrant Thomas of Villanova's adulation. Yet from that little has been evolved a being who on the one hand has provided the subject for endless theological debate, and on the other has become the focal point of unprecedented popular piety.

To many who dedicate themselves to the cult of the Virgin, this discrepancy is irrelevant; they derive their faith not from human history but from divine revelation. Such an attitude of mind is not one we can refute; but we can and should explore alternative ways of interpreting alleged encounters with a being whose nature is so largely a construct of human belief, even though that belief may be divinely inspired.

The durable image

There is evidence, from graffiti in the Roman catacombs, that Mary was the subject of special attention even in the earliest days of Christianity. Throughout the period of the early Fathers and into the age of medieval theological disputation, however, studies of Mary were largely academic. The mystical apprehension of Mary's role, which led to the widespread popular cult, didn't really take off until the seventeenth century, when writers like Grignon de Montfort encouraged the faithful to direct their devotions to Mary, rather than directly to God, on the grounds that God 'wishes to be glorified through her and praised on earth by the living through her'.[194]

Judging by the subsequent response, all people needed was such encouragement from official sources. Synchronistically, encounters with the Virgin, infrequent hitherto, became a periodic manifestation eventually establishing their own traditions. Each major incident tends to create its own cult: the site where it occurs becomes a place of pilgrimage; there is lobbying to get the visionaries officially recognized by the Church authorities. At the same time, each succeeding event has the effect of reinforcing the image of the Virgin. As a result of encounters like those of Bernadette Soubirous at Lourdes, Mary has acquired a distinct and recognizable character: a benevolent but stern being, willing to intercede with Jesus on our behalf but in no way inclined to relax standards of human behaviour.

Bearing in mind that Mary is, after all, basically a human being like ourselves, albeit with the added experience gained by spending 2,000 years in Heaven, we should not perhaps be surprised to find her revealing a distinctly human nature; but there are times, for instance when she requests more honours, or espouses a specific political ideology (she is resolutely opposed to Communism) when her actions encourage us to wonder whether an alternative explanation would not make better sense.

Catholics themselves are by no means blind to these difficulties, nor united in their attitude to encounter claims. Church authorities recognize only a tiny proportion as genuine: others are given a kind of provisional status, or simply ignored, or specifically discouraged.

The result, inevitably, is a divergence between official and popular attitudes: over and over again there are incidents in which people flock in their thousands to the site of an encounter despite the explicit discouragement of the local bishop. Robert Pannet, a French religious writer who champions 'popular' as against 'academic' religion, holds that the Church establishment has lost touch with the simple faith of ordinary people. Faced with the difficulties raised by apparitions of Mary, he uses reasoning which is very relevant to our studies:

> If the character of the observations is so detailed, this is undoubtedly because the Virgin imposes her presence on her devotees with such exceptional impact. The mother of God is truly there where they see her, and is truly 'the blessed among all women'. She is not a ghost nor an ectoplasmic materialisation. And since the witness has got to give a confident and exact account of his experience, the Holy Spirit makes use of the visionary's imagination to create a precise image, employing elements from his own cultural store: thus Bernadette sees the Virgin in the costume of the 'Enfants de Marie' of her own parish. [191]

This, of course, is nothing short of a miracle. And while it is an ingenious way of accounting for those elements which discourage a face-value interpretation of the encounter, we have to ask, once again, whether we need go to such lengths? Do we really need the help of the Holy Spirit? Couldn't the visionary manage by himself?

Ambiguities and contradictions

Because encounters with the Virgin Mary have been so much more fully documented than other kinds, there is a temptation to take them as representative of encounters as a whole. We must be cautious, though, of taking them or any other category of encounter as typical, without also making allowance for what is specific to each category. The Mary of the encounter experiences is in several respects a unique entity:

★ She is an element in a specific belief system, within which she plays a historic role as an intermediary between humanity and the divine. We may see this as the 'official' Mary.

★ Because she embodies qualities which answer profound human needs, Mary has become the focus of an immense and unquestioning popular devotion, losing all resemblance to the Palestinian carpenter's wife she is supposed to be. The attributes popularly ascribed to her, though they may be accepted by theologians in their individual capacity, are not part of official doctrine. An accretion of folklore (e.g. such concepts as 'the Seven Sorrows of Mary', 'the Seven Joys', etc) has formed round her; she is invested with names signifying specific functions ('Our Lady of Sorrow', etc.). We may see this as the 'popular' Mary.

★ Despite the foregoing, because Mary is supposed to have once been a living person, encounters with her tend to have a uniquely intimate character. Witnesses speak of her taking a personal interest in their affairs, she is a source of comfort and counsel. We may see this as the 'private' Mary.

How does this ambiguity work out in practice? It is instructive to examine, not one of the widely publicized cases such as Lourdes or Fatima, whose very popularity renders them atypical, but one more characteristic of those many hundreds of encounters which often achieve no more than a local and short-lived popularity.

The apparitions of Vallensanges

The events at Vallensanges, a small village not far from St Etienne in central France, occurred in 1888, achieved a momentary fame, then sank into oblivion until in 1978 a new book[16] re-drew attention to them. Interestingly, instead of being a modern reappraisal of the events, the book confines itself to narrating them from contemporary records, with a minimum of comment or question. As a result we are in a position to approach the events without having to accept or reject other people's evaluations of what is to all intents and purposes a virgin case.

The inhabitants of Vallensanges were, like most French peasants of the period, extremely poor, barely scraping a meagre living from the land. They were all nominally pious. Jean Bernard was at 13 the eldest of five children. It is said that rather than play with the other boys, he preferred to spend his time at a little 'chapel' he had built and in which he had placed a crude statuette of the Virgin.

At 7 in the morning of 19 July 1888, Jean's mother sent him to collect firewood. Seeing a lizard, he immediately looked round for a stone with which to kill it; turning back, his eyes still lowered to the ground, he saw there was a foot on the lizard. Raising his eyes he saw that the foot was that of a 'grande dame' who made a sign with her finger that he should kill the lizard, which he did forthwith. She smiled, then rose into the air and disappeared. She was wearing a white dress, a blue cloak spangled with stars, a veil and a golden crown: she was extremely beautiful. Jean went home and told his family; the news spread rapidly.

Six days later he saw her again at the same place. He was accompanied by his brother and sisters and a large crowd, but they saw nothing. He asked a private favour which he did not reveal to others; Mary granted it.

At the next encounter he was followed by a light to the 'grotto' (I take this to refer to the little chapel he had built) and he asked the Virgin to cure a neighbour's child, 13-year-old Antoinette Genebrier, who had been deaf since birth. The girl did eventually regain her hearing, and it was no doubt in recognition of this supposed miracle that she subsequently became a nun.

Jean asked Mary if the people of his village were good; she said some were good, but others awful ('affreux'). They should go to mass more often and say prayers for her son. She said she would henceforward appear twice a week, on Wednesdays and Saturdays, and at the more convenient hour of 11 a.m. She also agreed to appear in a more convenient location, a field belonging to his own family.

A sizeable crowd was present at each encounter, and the Virgin agreed to bless their rosaries (praying beads). On later occasions, though, when the crowds grew larger, she refused to bless any more of them. When Jean asked her to perform a miracle, she said maybe. At the eighth encounter she said that she had been all set to perform a miracle, but the crowd had been pushing too much. At the ninth she was weeping; when Jean asked why, she explained that she could no longer restrain the wrathful hand of her son, and unless people amended their ways he would punish them with afflictions. The potato crop would be ruined and the vines wither.

At the tenth she told him secrets which he never revealed. At the eleventh he said, 'If you are the mother of the Lord, step forward, if you are the devil, step back' (a traditional folklore test). She stepped forward, and when he threw holy water (another traditional test, which Bernadette also employed at Lourdes) she didn't disappear as she would have done if she had been a demon, but just smiled.

At the nineteenth encounter she gave an equivocal answer to his request that she create a sacred spring (another standard folklore item); she never did so. The twentieth encounter was, as she had herself announced, the final one; more than 800 people (another account says 8,000!) were present. Even if we accept the more modest figure, this is impressive for an isolated country village.

That was the end of the apparitions at Vallensanges. Though the Church throughout refused to officially acknowledge them, the local clergy took an interest in Jean. He was given an education, and became an emissary of the church, serving it in many capacities and eventually becoming a priest before his death in 1932. His childhood experiences were virtually forgotten.

Even this brief summary of what is in fact a very brief record invites us to note several interesting points:

★ The previous exceptional piety of the witness.

★ The improbability, in our eyes but perhaps not in those of a 13-year-old boy, that the Virgin would approve the killing of a lizard.

★ The conventional appearance of the entity.

★ The warning that Jesus would punish those who did not repent. The specific punishments mentioned were such as would seem catastrophic to a peasant boy — crop failure is the ultimate disaster in a farming community. Precisely the same disasters were threatened by the Virgin to the visionaries of La Salette in 1846, an incident with which a pious boy would certainly have been familiar.

★ The willingness of the entity to re-time and re-locate its visits to suit the witness.

★ The hesitancy of the entity to meet Jean's requests for a miracle, and what seems suspiciously like a convenient evasion by blaming the crowd.

★ The miracle cures, which such entities have been expected to perform since pre-Christian times, [223] are in this case as in so many others open to less-than-miracle explanation; four were claimed:

— a girl of 13 cured of deafness since birth;

— a girl of 11 cured of a crippled arm;

— a woman of 24 cured of a crippled leg, who was able to leave her crutch behind at the scene;

— a man in his 50s, paralysed for 18 years but able to walk home afterwards.

No medical testimony is available for any of these cures, which are all of a kind where spontaneous remission is known to occur; we may acknowledge that had there been no apparitions, there might have been no cures, but we do not have to presume that anything miraculous occurred.

★ Jean's test of the Virgin at so late a stage in the proceedings is curious. Possibly what happened is that someone told him of similar tests having been carried out elsewhere (for example, four years previously at St Colombin where nine-year old Marie Lordeau had tested *her* entity in just this way) and Jean saw it as a way of validating his own experience. We note again how obligingly the Queen of Heaven submits to being ordered about by a child.

★ Though initially the entity was happy to bless rosaries, as the crowds increased she refused. Have we the right to speculate that Jean himself was growing bored with the practice? And could this also be the reason why the entity decided to limit her appearances to twenty?

In its contradictions, ambiguities and illogicalities, the encounter experience of Jean Bernard is typical of many, perhaps most, encounters with Mary. Those who cannot bring themselves to accept such implausible experiences as genuine visitations by Mary are compelled either to reject *all* such experiences, or find a way to distinguish the genuine from the spurious. By and large, non-believers do the one, believers the other.

But is it necessarily a question of one or the other? On the face of it, it seems it must be. Either the Virgin was there or she wasn't. Either Jean really saw her or he didn't. So long as the entity is presumed to be some kind of objectively real being, these choices are forced on us.

If, on the other hand, we start to explore models in which the entity, while possessing *some kind of reality*, is partially or even wholly composed of *subjective* elements, many of the contradictions disperse. Inconsistencies in the entities become inconsistencies in the witnesses.

This doesn't dispense with the difficulties, it merely shifts them. We still have to cope with the problem of which comes first, the belief or the experience. It is clear that the Mary-entity, as it manifests in the encounter experience, is just what people are hoping to see. The Church would say this is because the 'real' Mary answers people's needs in a way nobody else does; psychologists would say it is because people have created a fantasy-figure who answers their needs. To say that folklore elements are undeniably present in the encounter is to explain nothing, for folklore may derive from reality just as much as it may embody and keep alive a myth.

Encounters with the Virgin Mary demonstrate more clearly than any other category the interaction of reality with fantasy, the interplay of popular myth-making with individual experience. Implicit in cases like the Vallensanges apparitions are all the paradoxes we are going to have to solve. No less implicit, I believe, are the clues whereby we can resolve those paradoxes.

Encounters with other saints

Mary is not of course the only saint who features in encounter experiences; but she is the only one who, if the theologians are correct, was taken up to heaven in her physical body at the time of her death. Some Old Testament prophets are also reputed to have enjoyed this privilege. Saints on the other hand return as a rule to dust like the rest of us, except that their bodies are often preserved from decomposition in what is often regarded as a miraculous manner, and in former times their bones and other bits of their bodies were liable to be preserved as relics. (To read the account of how chunks of Teresa of Avila were hacked off her body before it was hardly cold is to discover a gruesome ambiguity in the phrase 'respect for the dead'.)

Strictly speaking, then, encounters with saints belong in the same category as encounters with spirits of the formerly living, rather than with divinities. However, it is more convenient to include them here, since saints, once dead, tend to be assigned the same sort of jobs as angels, serving as messengers, counsellors and intermediaries between humanity and divinity.

Like Mary, saints are generally regarded as relatively accessible. When Vesuvius erupted in 1872, the people of Napoli attacked the statues of their patron San Gennaro because he had failed to protect them. It is the same state of mind as prompts television viewers to suppose that the characters in their favourite soap opera are living people. A mind thus incapable of distinguishing between shades of reality would have not the slightest doubt that an encounter experience was exactly what it seemed to be.

For the purpose of our study, encounters with saints are no different from the other categories of encounter which derive their force from an unquestioned belief system.

2.5 ENCOUNTERS WITH SATAN AND OTHER DEMONIC BEINGS

The devil works on man by *temptation*, through the faculties of the mind, above all the imagination. With images and suggestions he inflames men's passions and drives them to sin. Nobody escapes these everyday assaults.

Less frequently, he reveals his presence by unpleasant irritations, more frightening than dangerous; sounds are heard, objects are moved and sometimes broken: we call this *infestation*.

In other cases he attacks people, striking and wounding them; sometimes he lets himself be seen, sometimes he is invisible: this is *external obsession*. Alternatively, he seizes control of the faculties, though without depriving them of all action; he clouds the intelligence, and in the lower instincts (the only ones he can reach) he instils false ideas, unhealthy appetites, monstrous feelings, which disgust the higher instincts; this is *internal obsession*. Finally, he takes hold of the human organism and controls the limbs, the tongue, the whole body, activating them at his will, while generally depriving his victim of all awareness of what is happening; this is *possession*.[225]

Saudreau's catalogue of the various ways in which the evil power afflicts us is representative of the way the problem presented by these phenomena tends to be approached from within the Christian belief system.

What to the believer is the thing they all have in common — that all are the handiwork of the devil — has resulted in a number of experiences being lumped together which may not necessarily be all of a kind. Those who work outside a belief system, such as psychologists and parapsychologists, while they give the phenomena different labels and reject the idea that they are caused by an external agent, have to cope with the fact that these experiences are presented to them as though they form a distinct and specific category. That is how they have traditionally been regarded, that is how the witnesses themselves interpret them, and that is how we must start by approaching them in this study.

Alternative approaches are of course available. To a considerable extent psychologists have been able to account for these experiences in terms of human behaviour. The French psychologist Pierre Janet, in particular, demonstrated the extraordinary 'data-processing' abilities of the human mind in special states such as hypnosis and hysteria, and no intelligent theologian questions that such processes are operating in a great many cases.

Where the behavioural scientists have hitherto shown themselves inadequate is precisely where the believers, who are prepared to invoke supernatural forces, are not at a loss: in accounting for those features of the phenomena which appear to be paranormal, that is, seem to go beyond what is generally thought scientifically possible. For instance, as Saudreau indicates, Christian teaching offers a plausible and coherent explanation for what he terms *infestation*, more popularly termed *poltergeist activity* or more scientifically *recurrent spontaneous psychokinesis*, in which events occur which seem to go beyond the known capabilities of the human mind. If we want to avoid the idea of an external agent, we must either go along with the parapsychologists and accept that hitherto unknown human faculties are involved, or we are forced to fall back on questioning whether the facts occurred as reported.

Certainly that is often the case, and the belief system is generally to blame. Anxious to relieve his anxiety about what has happened to him, the witness will not only interpret his experiences in terms of the prevalent belief system, but is likely to subconsciously work his account to conform to it. We can be fairly sure that the greater number of seemingly paranormal events recorded in the *Legende Dorée* and other medieval chronicles either never took place, or did not take place as reported.

But to dismiss every 'supernatural' encounter with the Devil, simply because it is improbable, is more than we have the right to do. At this stage of our study we must accept that phenomena which are ostensibly paranormal do indeed occur. The question is whether the psychologists and the parapsychologists can come up with better ways of accounting for them than those who attribute them to the operations of an evil power?

A force of evil, embodied in a malevolent divinity, is a staple ingredient of virtually every religious belief system. Generally it is conceived as a counter-balance to the positive, benevolent force which created the cosmos. Sometimes, as in the official Christian and Islamic systems, evil comes to a cosmos which is fundamentally good when Satan is driven by some obscure purpose to defect and set up a rival establishment; sometimes, as in the scenarios of the Gnostic heretics and the Zoroastrians of Persia, evil is seen as implicit in the order of things on the philosophic ground that you can't have good without its opposite, evil.

Most of us will see this as no more than academic game-playing, for there is no way we can know what the ground rules for constructing a cosmos may be. Unfortunately, academic game-playing can lead to very practical consequences: disputes about whether the Devil exists, and whether certain activities are his work or not, have probably led to more intolerance, cruelty and bloodshed than any other idea that has exercised men's thoughts.

Most belief systems are inherently intolerant: *their* god and *their* values are good; everyone else's are evil. From which it is logical, if you happen to believe in a force of evil embodied in a specific entity, that this entity is responsible for the creeds, beliefs and ideologies which you do not happen to hold. Monsignor Cristiani, a leading Catholic scholar, admits:

'It is certain that the first Christians considered the idol-worship of the pagans to be diabolical. In their eyes, the pagan gods were demons.'[35]

When Christian missionaries went to China in the nineteenth century, they did not hesitate to label the indigenous divinities as demons, though clearly the Chinese did not think of them as malevolent[186] In our own day, many fundamentalist Christians believe in all sincerity that Communism is the work of the devil, and in times of war even the kindliest churchman will not hesitate to suggest that the devil is in league with the enemy.

The same process occurs on a more personal level. People who believe in the devil attribute to him anything they find reprehensible — whether it be smoking, dancing, sexual pleasure, alcohol, astrology, theatre-going or playing tip-cat on Sunday. Fundamentalist and Catholic Christians alike are convinced that anything which savours of occultism — which can be anything from spiritism to black magic, from ouija games to serious research (no doubt including the writing and even the reading of this book) — constitutes 'dabbling in the occult' and 'doing Satan's work for him'.

Encounters with the devil demonstrate the importance of taking into account the cultural context within which the experience occurs. When someone tells us he has met the devil, our first step must be to learn what the devil means to him. For when the devil is equated with anything from which an individual wishes to dissociate himself, the witness may have a personal motive for such an encounter — to cast the devil in the role of whipping-boy, to take the blame for what may in fact be the witness' own deeds or thoughts.

For we must recognize that notions of good and evil are only relative: the Chinese didn't think their gods were demons; Communists don't think their beliefs come from the devil. In the same way, we must beware of thinking that an adolescent who proclaims himself a devil-worshipper has necessarily given himself over to evil ways; if he is having difficulty adjusting to society, the devil which for others is a negative force may seem to him to symbolize a very positive freedom from authority — whether that of parents, school or the prevailing political establishment.

The witches who met the Devil

The consequences of good-evil polarization in connection with the devil are seen at their most appalling in the witchcraft mania which plagued Europe from the fourteenth through to the seventeenth centuries (though with a long previous history and with echoes which continue to our own day). Though the origins, extent and nature of witchcraft continue to be matters on which historians cannot agree, it is at least evident that witchcraft *persecutions* resulted from the religious establishment's conviction that any belief system which was not Christian must be diabolical. This meant that people who held contrary views were stigmatized as heretics, which — according to the perverse notions of Christian mercy and justice evolved by the theologians — meant that they could and should be persecuted.

As a result, a great many sensible and intelligent Christians found themselves more or less reluctantly committed to inflicting appalling punishments on people who may have been weak or deluded, but were technically guilty of sin. For by their own admission — and not every admission was wrung out of the witnesses by torture — the accused witches had sought and achieved encounters with the devil.

Not everyone took at face value the witches' claims to have taken part in meetings with the devil:

> Those in charge of these inquiries had of course before anything else to establish with their own eyes whether these excursions were real or only imaginary. The theologians, particularly concerned to learn the truth of the matter, were also the first to conduct tests. Nider, in his *Formicarius*, has preserved for us the result of a test of this kind carried out towards the end of the fourteenth century. A Dominican divine learnt of an old village woman who believed she went travelling at night with others of her kind. All his efforts to shake her out of this belief were useless; she insisted she trusted her experience more than his words. 'Very well,' he said, 'let me be present at your next excursion.' She consented, adding, 'Bring several witnesses with you, and you will all see me leave.'
>
> In their presence she placed herself in a kneading trough which was on a bench, and began to anoint herself while uttering magic formulas. After a while her head slumped and she fell asleep. She then started to have visions where she saw Venus and other such things, so that she began to rejoice aloud. Her violent movements shook the trough until eventually it fell off the bench, injuring her head. When she awoke, the priest said to her, 'Well, will you still maintain that you really went off with the wild horde? Everyone here will witness that you never left the trough.' This, together with his exhortations, finally led the old woman to recognise and abandon her error.[94]

This was by no means an isolated case, but not all had a happy end. At Nantes in 1604 seven alleged sorcerers claimed that thanks to their relationship with the devil, they had the ability to go on a journey and return with news of what they had seen while travelling:

> Soon after, they dropped as if dead, and stayed about three hours in this state; after which they got up and narrated everything they had seen at Nantes and in the surrounding countryside, indicating places, occurrences and the person involved. Their claims were immediately checked and it was found that all they had recounted was true.[21]

Since, true or not, this was the work of the devil, all seven were executed. The display of psi-abilities in this case is particularly significant, as it indicates that the witnesses were in one of those special states of consciousness which appear to favour the exercise of these abilities (and which we shall look at in more detail in 5.2). Further intimations of what was happening to the witness on these occasions emerge from this Italian case:

At Firenze a woman was brought before the judge, accused of practising magic. She admitted the charge, and said that she would attend a sabbat that very night if they would let her go home and anoint herself with ointment. This the judge allowed her to do. She rubbed herself with the revolting grease, lay down, and fell asleep right away. They tied her securely in her bed; they pricked her, struck her, burned her; but nothing could disturb her sleep. The following day they had great difficulty in waking her; she then told them she had been at the sabbat. From her account, it was evident that the pain they had inflicted on her in striking and burning her was mixed in her mind with the things she believed she had seen and experienced.[94]

This case not only suggests a special state of consciousness, but also gives clues as to how that state was achieved. Clive Harper, writing in *Folklore*, has alleged that the traditional recipe — a blend of atropa belladonna, aconite, sweet flag, cinquefoil, smallage, bats' blood and young children's fat — would in fact have psychotropic effects, and rubbed all over the body would easily give rise to hallucinations. In experiments with belladonna, subjects had the illusion of changing location, which is consistent with the witches' belief that they had travelled. Harper adds:

> The bat's blood and child fat would not have added to the unguent's effects; though the bat's blood may have been thought to aid nocturnal flight by means of 'sympathetic magic'. We should not however dismiss the gruesome additives sometimes mentioned in connection with the flying-ointment. 'Skin of Toad', for example holds interesting possibilities. From the skin of one species of toad the powerful hallucinogen Bufotenine has been extracted.[101]

There is, indeed, abundant evidence to show that the claims made by witches to have encountered the devil were not founded in fact. How they came to believe they had such encounters is not always clear, but what we learn in the course of this study will indicate the process that probably led to the delusion. For the moment, we may reasonably proceed on the basis that for this category of encounters with the devil, at least, alternative explanations are available.

Personal persecution

According to church doctrine, the devil is continually on the hunt for souls that he can lure to damnation. Like any hunter, he values most the quarry that is most elusive; particularly pious people are particularly at risk.

Such a one was Jean-Marie Vianney, better known as the Curé d'Ars, a village near Lyon in central France. Appointed to the parish in 1817, at the age of 32, he at once set about eradicating what he believed to be the devil-inspired behaviour of his parishioners, in particular dancing, which for him was nothing but an incitement to evil. It took him a quarter of a century to root dancing out of Ars, but he managed it in the end, along with immodest dress and working on Sunday.

It was only to be expected that the devil would fight back; and very significantly, it was Vianney himself who expected it. For 35 years he was plagued by an entity he named *le grappin* (which literally means 'hook') and engaged with him in a contest which at times seemed to take on the character of a not altogether unfriendly rivalry.

The *grappin* would wake Vianney up with strange noises at night, and startle him with strange lights by day; it shook the curtains of the priest's bed, sometimes shifted it, and on one occasion set it alight though the door was locked. It would shout 'Vianney, Vianney, potato-eater, not dead yet? I'll get you, though!' It imitated the roar of a bear, the howling of a dog, the trampling of cattle, and a sound like a carthorse being lifted to the ceiling and dropped to the floor. Once it made a noise like an army of Cossacks or Austrians marching through the village, but next morning when Vianney looked, the snow in the street was unmarked. It caused bits of meat to appear in the orphanage soup on a fast day, and materialized once as a bat flying round the bedroom, once as a big black dog who scratched the soil where a man was buried who had died without confessing his sins. [257]

These and other such anecdotes are solemnly recounted in all the books I have consulted about Vianney, including Trochu's standard life, with never a suggestion that they might be anything other than what Vianney thought them to be, the devil's handiwork. Neither he nor his commentators ask themselves why the devil, with supposedly infinite forces of harassment at its disposal, should limit itself to such puerile phenomena.

Vianney was evidently a remarkable man, universally respected and admired except by those of his fellow-villagers whose dreary lives he sought to make more dreary still. Nor is there reason to doubt his sincerity, even though the great majority of the stories rest solely on his say-so. Nonetheless, we must recognize that they can be accounted for without invoking the devil. Vianney was clearly obsessed with the mission to reform his fellow villagers; he practised all kinds of austerities, living mainly on potatoes; it is evident that he led an emotionally isolated and introspective existence despite being the parish priest. These circumstances could well have led to consequences both psychological and parapsychological: on the one hand, hallucinations and paranoid delusions, and on the other, psi-manifestations of the poltergeist type which he would naturally have attributed to the devil, and which would have confirmed him in his delusions.

Vianney was made a saint in 1925 and Ars today is a place of worldwide pilgrimage. Visiting his home, one cannot fail to be impressed by the simple circumstances of a life so totally dedicated to what he believed was right. But respect for the man does not require that we go along with his interpretation of what happened to him without considering alternative explanations.

Since the devil is so universal a being, the question of identification seldom arises. By its appearance and by its intentions, the entity conforms to the image that the witness has acquired from his cultural background. It can even manifest where belief is ostensibly absent:

> In 1915 I was living in a flat in Curzon Street. I cannot say I was happy at this period, as I had been undergoing a more or less severe strain, but my life apart from this was uneventful. I was not devoting any time to occultism, much as it has always interested me.
>
> I went to bed, fell asleep and then commenced to dream 'waking', or so it seemed. I always sleep with a light in my room, and I thought I suddenly opened my eyes and saw a young man standing at the foot of my bed — slight, tall, with a grave, dark face, something like the youths of the Italian Renaissance. He was so 'real' that I said Who are you, and what are you doing here? He answered, I am the Devil, and I am come to bargain with you for the souls of two women who have injured you, and who are now spiritually in your hands. I answered, I am dreaming, and you are only a creature of my imagination. There is no Devil, no Spirit who can bargain for souls.
>
> You are wrong, he answered, I *am* the Devil, and I can assume the likeness of a human being.
>
> I then seemed to drift again into sleep, and next morning I regarded my experience merely as an interesting dream.
>
> On Saturday the whole thing was repeated . . . Again the dark youth disclosed his identity, again he wished to traffic in souls, and again I obstinately refused to allow that he was actually a Presence in my room. 'I know I am dreaming, you are not really here, you are only a dream.'
>
> The young man looked at me steadily, leaning over the low end of the bedstead. I am here, and tomorrow you *must* and *will* believe in my existence.
>
> Once more I seemed to drift into a sleep within a sleep. I woke in the morning, had my early tea, and when my maid gave me my dressing-gown preparatory to my bath, she exclaimed, Oh Madam, what have you done to your shoulder?
>
> My nightdress was square-necked and short-sleeved. On my shoulder was the distinct imprint of a man's hand, discoloured, as it bruised into the flesh! The mark was visible for three or four days. [75]

Personal persecution by the devil is a widespread phenomenon today, to judge by the flow of books and pamphlets emanating from fundamentalist Christian sources. I have no reason to question the sincerity of those who write these publications, and a few of them display common sense as well as sincerity. But for all these authors, as for the protagonists of the stories they tell, there is no question that it is the devil who is involved.

To take one example from hundreds, we read of an American girl named Vail Hamilton who had been attracted by the promised benefits of Transcendental Meditation. At first she was pleased with 'a calming of my mind and an altering of awareness' just like the advertisements said, but then 'as my consciousness changed, I began to become aware of the presence of spirit beings sitting on either side of me when I was meditating. I did not consider the possibility of Satan or his demons at the time, but just accepted it as a really weird trip.'

However, after she had been meditating for four years,

> I awoke one night with a sense of fear and apprehension, because a spirit was putting pressure all over my body and head in an attempt to enter and take possession of my body. I commanded it to leave, and resisted it until it left. I did not fully realize the implications of this oppression until later. I began to experience other supernatural sensations — ESP and clairvoyance, telepathy, and the beginnings of astral travel.

Then she was converted to Christianity:

> Since becoming a Christian I have encountered the same kind of spirits I used to experience during TM. The Lord has given me discernment, and I now see that they are demons. Before I became a Christian the demons seldom bothered me, and I even mistook them for guardian angels at times. But after I was born again to Christ, they became very hostile and tried to overpower me on several occasions. [98]

The writer of the book in which that story is reprinted evidently accepts this interpretation without question. But the story is rich in suggestive details:

★ The fact that the witness was meditating at the time suggests that in all probability she was in an altered state when she had the experience.

★ That she had previously thought the entities might be 'guardian angels' and only subsequently determined they must be demons could be an example of fiendish deceit on the devil's part, but equally it might suggest a hallucination, created in the course of her altered state of meditation, to which for personal psychological reasons she ascribed a specific identity.

★ That the entities were not identified as demons until she had become a Christian could be, as Vail suggests, a tribute to new 'discernment' bestowed on her by the Lord as a reward for conversion, but equally it might suggest a reinterpretation imposed by her newly acquired belief system.

If the stories are true, then thousands of individuals are being harassed as Vail was, and often much more dramatically. But we do not have to regard the two facets of the experience — first, the encounter with an entity, and second, the identification of that entity with the demon — as inseparable. That many people believe they have had encounters is beyond question; that those encounters are brought about by demons, on the other hand, is very much open to question.

But we have also to consider yet another possibility, that some, if not all such encounters are in fact pseudo-encounters, inspired by a belief that such encounters can and do take place.

Professional exorcists

To judge again by the fundamentalist Christian publications, a large part of the time of many ministers is taken up with repelling the attacks of the devil and his assistants. Such persons claim to have acquired an extensive knowledge of the devil and his ways: the American 'internationally known leader of the Charismatic Movement', Reverend Derek Prince, once cleared a woman of a shoal of demons who named themselves Hate, Pride, Jealousy, Self-Pity, Infidelity and Death.[192] Along with dozens of his colleagues who have made a speciality of detecting and dealing with demons, he has no doubt that it is the devil he is up against, and not some psychological trouble which takes this form in certain individuals, nor does it cross his mind that it might be the teachings of people like himself which cause an individual's trouble to take this particular form.

A minority, however, are more cautious in their approach; and it was a relief to me, ploughing my way through a heap of these terrifyingly self-confident accounts, to find one minister who was prepared to be open-minded. It is significant that he is one of the rare Catholic ministers I came across in this connection: Father Alphonsus Trabold, Professor of Comparative Religion of St Bonaventure University in the United States:

Only on very rare occasions have I ever performed an exorcism of any kind. Even in those cases, I am not absolutely sure, even to this present day, whether or not these *were* cases of true possession, or if there was some other explanation.

However, at the time of this particular case, I felt there was an emergency situation. Since I did not have time to try other means of helping this girl, I felt there was sufficient reason to perform an exorcism. The girl had experienced a period of infestation in her apartment, which was witnessed also by the girl who roomed with her. She had reached the stage of obsession where she believed Satan was appearing to her and talking to her, threatening to take her over completely, and stressing the fact that there was no escape from him.

I tried to talk to the girl. I tried to use psychological methods such as suggestion, counselling, etc. This went on for quite some time. But I could not make any headway. She became more and more restless, more and more irritated by my efforts.

The story I learned was this: She had quite some time ago sold herself completely to the devil. Her father had been very cruel to her and her mother, and the girl wanted to get revenge and punish him. She felt she could not ask God to do this, so she invoked the Devil to do it. For quite some period of time she had been worshipping and serving him. Then the consequences began — poltergeist or infestation phenomena, visions or hallucinations of the Devil or demons.

The only action I felt would help her would be some form of prayer and exorcism. Let me stress again that I considered this an emergency situation. I felt if the girl did not receive help immediately, she could very likely have tried suicide. Or, even if it were a case of purely psychological ailment, she could have become psychologically unbalanced if I did not act immediately.

We are dealing here, of course, with a person in great need. Whether or not we are dealing with a true diabolical being or whether we are dealing with a demon created by the mind of the person, it is extremely real for the person. So if an exorcism helps in any way, either in a supernatural way of actually driving out a real demon, or psychologically, simply by removing the demon from their mind, it is for me an act of healing.

When performing the exorcism, I did have a feeling of an evil presence. The opposition of the demon was very strong; the battle continued for quite some time. Finally the girl opened her eyes and a beautiful smile came on her face. 'Is he gone? Is he really gone?' I assured her he was. It seemed to be over. She experienced the first perfect night's sleep she had had in many, many months. No further evil manifestations took place. While I have no absolute proof the exorcism was successful, the indication is that it was.

I must in all honesty call attention to a possible alternate explanation from the point of view of psychology. If she were suffering from merely a psychological delusion, and there was a deep suggestion within her that she was possessed by the devil, you could overcome this through a counter-suggestion. If the person is so convinced the Devil is real and his influence is real, the only way you can help her, even on a purely psychological level, is to come down to her level of belief. Even if we are dealing with a case purely of a psychological state, the exorcism becomes a form of healing.[192]

The pragmatic argument is unanswerable; to save this girl, it was exorcism or nothing. And if it be objected that exorcism of a non-existent devil can be at best only a short-lived expedient, it can be answered that nothing more may be necessary, since the trouble which the devil symbolizes is itself likely to be only short-lived. The individual has been overwhelmed by a temporary state of mind to the extent that he cannot regain his balance without outside help; it doesn't much matter what form that help takes if it sets him on his feet again. Once back on his feet, with any luck he should be able to take care of himself.

In so far as the individual is concerned, pragmatism clearly pays off. But there is a wider issue involved, which is that those who act in accordance with a belief system, whether or not they accept that system, contribute to reinforce it. The wisest thing ever said about the devil was this axiom of Alphonse Louis Constant, the nineteenth-century French occultist who wrote under the nom de plume Eliphas Lévi: 'He who affirms the devil, creates the devil.'[156]

2.6 ENCOUNTERS WITH FOLKLORE ENTITIES

If you visit a holy well and see a mysterious female figure who vanishes or in some other way reveals that she is not a fellow human, there are many things she could be instead. She could be a nature spirit of some kind, who may be simply mischievous like the German *nixy*, or more kindly, credited with the well's traditional healing powers; or a Christian saint whose origins go back to pre-Christian days, a water spirit taken over by the new faith; or the ghost of a girl who drowned herself in these waters after being romantically betrayed — in Eastern Europe she becomes a *rusalka* who seeks revenge by luring male passers-by to drown in the water; or she may be a swan-maiden using the well as a bird-bath, discarding her swan feathers and assuming human form for the moment; or she may be a fairy or a *huldra* from Norway with whom human shape is habitual, who may either flee human contact or deliberately seek it in order, like the *rusalka*, to entice her victims to a watery death.

Every corner of our planet is as full of folklore figures as it is of natural species. These are not divinities in the same sense as the other entities we have been looking at, but they possess attributes which put them above or beside humanity. Many are no more than the animistic creatures of primitive religion, which assigned to every manifestation of nature its appropriate resident entity; but belief in many others has survived the onset of higher religions, and encounters with them continue to be reported to this day, and not only within primitive cultures. In 1920 a Mrs Celia Alleyne wrote to the distinguished scientist Sir Oliver Lodge:

You ask me to tell you about the 'Fairies' I saw in my childhood. I have always been conscious of other forms of spirit life besides our own. I can remember when I was five, before I could read fairy tales (and we were not told any), slipping out of bed at dawn and going into the garden to talk with the fairies; it was when I could be alone and away from my brothers and sisters that I felt and saw them. They were always beautiful, never old, not very young, just without age.

Sometimes I would at night suddenly awake feeling rigid with fright, and I used at once to send a call to the fairies to come to me, and first I would hear faint music growing louder and louder till my room was filled with music, and from every side little fairies came and glided along the coverlet and all my fear was turned to joy, and they put me to sleep again.

Since I have grown up I have still seen the fairies, but the conditions must be right. A short time ago I was on the Downs in the morning and it was very still and quiet and no one about, and as I sat in the grass I felt the conditions change — I became aware of faculties which normally I have not at all. I could hear each blade of grass vibrating and there was harmony in every note, I could see an aura to every flower and the fairies were there in colours like the auras. My material body was forgotten, I seemed to be in a new, inner world of colour, music, and scent, and perfect peace and happiness.

I did not talk much about the fairies, I never realised other people didn't see them. I thought my brothers and sisters too noisy to see them. I have often known them come to my aid when in childish difficulties, but I never mixed the fairies up with the human spirits which I often saw.

Another thing which may interest you is that as a child I could see in the dark; there was no darkness for me, I could see a blue light which showed things to me, not a diffused light, but a guiding light which I thought the fairies brought for me.

You ask about size. My impression is from four to six inches (15 cm). Concerning clothing — not any; they appeared to me iridescent, instead of being a solid whole they were visible vibrating particles, without the appearance of any actual sex. I have never noticed any wings.

I am really rather an active sort of person and not in the least inclined to sleep or doze during the daytime. All my friends call me extremely practical![231]

Though fairies do not have the support of religious doctrine, as do the other entities we have looked at in this section of our inquiry, they make up for it in the support they get from popular belief. In all parts of the world, at all periods, there are people who claim experiences like Mrs Alleyne's. There is little point in quoting other examples, since all are equally believable or unbelievable, though some have the advantage of having more than a single witness.

Lodge was sympathetic but sceptical:

I do not for a moment question your possession of unusual psychic faculties; it seems to me quite likely that you are occasionally in touch with other intelligences, and can be made the channel for genuine information derived from them, either telepathically or in some other way. But these intelligences will not usually be bodily dwellers on this planet. Scepticism becomes pronounced when a race of creatures living on this planet but quite unknown to biology are asserted to have a real and not a visionary existence.

Scepticism as to the physical existence of these creatures does seem to be the most appropriate response; no naturalist considers the possibility that water spirits could have any existence other than a misinterpretation of some real living creature. In 1926 a book was published purporting to contain 'sundry records from the Proceedings of the Society for the Investigation of Faery Fact and Fallacy', but reluctantly I suspect it is a leg-pull and not a brave attempt at scientific research into fairy existence.[229]

There is, however, something like a 'science of folklore' which seeks to establish paths through the tangled thickets of popular belief. The first step is to recognize that this belief can take different forms:

★ *Myth*, which comprises traditional concepts, generally preserved in story form, usually seeking to account for phenomena or happenings such as how the world was made or fire discovered.

★ *Legend*, which comprises traditional stories about people and events which are more or less historic fact, such as the belief in 'sleeping deliverers' like the emperor Friedrich Barbarossa who sleeps with six of his knights beneath the Kyffhäuserberg in Thuringia until Germany shall have need of him.

★ *Folktale*, which comprises stories embodying popular attitudes and responses, without historical pretensions, such as the story of Cinderella which embodies the concepts of incest and of deliverance by a fairy godmother.

Needless to say, folklorists are not agreed as to where precisely the lines should be drawn between these categories, not that this matters too much since it is often impossible to assign a story to one category or another. Our uncertainty whether there was ever a historical King Arthur, for instance, means that we can't confidently pigeonhole Arthurian chronicles as myth, legend or folktale.

What is more important for the purpose of this study is that folklore figures often have features in common with other entities. The healing springs which the Virgin Mary has often revealed, notably at Lourdes, put her right alongside the various entities we noted at the beginning of this chapter. There is little to choose between a tempting *huldra* and a tempting demon. And many entities perform the same protective functions as guardian angels, such as the 'Comrade in White' from the World War One trenches:

One of our men fell. He tried to hide in a hollow of the ground, and as he lay helpless, not daring to lift his head under the hail of fire, he saw One in White coming to him. For the moment he thought it must be a hospital attendant or a stretcher-bearer, but no, it could not be; the bullets were flying all round. The White-robed came near and bent over him. The man lost consciousness for a moment, and when he came round he seemed to be out of danger. The White-robed still stood by him, and the man, looking at his hand, said 'You are wounded in your hand.' He answered, 'Yes, that is an old wound that has opened again lately.' The soldier says that in spite of the peril and his wounds he felt a joy he has never experienced in his life before.[32]

By contrast with Mrs Alleyne's fairies, this entity is identified as an individual, the Comrade in White. In fact, we are evidently expected to identify him with Jesus, whose hand-wound from the crucifixion has reopened as a result of the horror of the war. But whatever his label, he is just one of many crisis helpers who appear to guide travellers who have lost their way or to encourage exhausted climbers, to warn people in danger of making a fatal mistake or to provide lonely children with companionship.[58] The Jesus-wound is no more than a local variation which confirms that these entities adapt to their immediate circumstances, while remaining essentially archetypes.

In Albacete, Spain, in the depths of the winter of 1981, a 4-year-old country boy disappeared. Despite intensive search he was not found until six days later, several kilometres from his home; yet though scantily dressed against the winter weather, he was in fine health. He told how he had been cared for by a very beautiful lady, carrying a light, who had vanished when the searchers approached.[82]

While simple kidnapping suggests itself, the searchers must have taken into account this and other natural explanations. Without fuller investigation, the story as we have it is of no evidential value. On the other hand, similar stories have been told throughout the centuries and in all parts of the world. For example, just as I am in the course of writing this, I read of a case in June 1986 in which a 5-year-old child, climbing out of a 30-metre gully into which her mother had crashed their van (in which the mother still lay unconscious) was comforted by a young boy holding a black puppy.[68]

The fact that stories like this continue to be told can, if you like, be taken as indication of the endurance of the guardian entity as universal folklore; but that leaves open the question of how folklore came to take that particular form. Was the young boy an angel in disguise? Was he a forgotten memory from the girl's own past, summoned up now to give comfort in a moment of crisis? Something of the sort, evidently; but exactly *what*?

Jung, in his study of archetypes[125] offers a greater wealth of interpretation for the mother-archetype than for any other. 'The loving and terrible mother', possessing both positive and negative aspects, can represent such benefits as fertility and wisdom or such sinister forces as devouring fate and secret lore. From such a diversity, popular consensus will choose the stereotypes which best meet its needs and preferences.

Those needs will not always be positive and benevolent. Though we crave the protection, comfort and security of the benevolent mother, we also need to be able to give our fears a name and form, and so the malevolent aspects of the mother-figure have also a function to perform.

In folklore figures we can see, more clearly because they are free from the fetters of a formal belief system, how encounters with otherworldly entities are related to our needs, fears, hopes and expectations.

2.7 COMMENTS ON PART TWO

Our brief overview of people's claims to have made personal contact with divine, demonic and folklore entities has given us little more than a general notion of the sort of experiences people are having. We are certainly not yet in a position to say either that Teresa d'Avila unquestionably met Jesus or that she unquestionably didn't. We have seen that almost without exception our witnesses are sincere people whose word we have no reason to doubt, particularly since they had the experience and we didn't. At the same time, we have seen that there are often good grounds for questioning whether their interpretation of what happened to them is the correct one.

The question of evidence
The first difficulty that confronted us is the lack of hard evidence in virtually every case, or, when evidence is offered, its ambiguous and even dubious character. There is scarcely one of these experiences which has any other foundation than the unsupported word of an individual, who was alone when it happened.

If these beings are who they claim to be, and if they wished to leave tangible evidence of their visit, clearly they could do so. Theological commentators sometimes suggest reasons why they don't, such as that they wish to test our faith; but this is only hindsight speculation. We don't find Jesus saying 'I know you'd like me to leave behind a tangible sign which would be so convincing that the entire world would have no option but to believe henceforth in my existence, but it's more important for me to test your faith, so I shan't do it.'

Consequently our evaluation of the witness' experience will have to be based only on whether we find his account convincing in itself.

The question of perception
We have seen that an encounter experience differs in many ways from a meeting between two humans. In particular, apart from co-witnesses, anyone else who happens to be present neither sees nor hears the entity. (There have been a few claims to the contrary, but none that offers convincing testimony.)

Thus if Mary appeared in physical form to Bernadette, she must possess some means of arranging, either that only Bernadette saw her, or that

Bernadette's companions did *not* see her.

That problem doesn't arise if the entity is *not* physical, but then we have the difficulty of deciding in just what form it is appearing. Most psychologists would opt for some kind of hallucination, and at the risk of spoiling the story for you I may as well say we are going to find they are almost certainly right; but we are also going to find that to label an experience 'hallucination' takes us only a very short way towards understanding the experience.

The question of the *process* whereby the experience is able to take place, irrespective of whether it is a miraculous event effected by the divinity or is something more prosaic, is one to which we must direct some of our attention.

The question of identity

We have seen that while some entities are clearly identifiable as Jesus, Mary, Satan, etc, others are largely undifferentiated, so that it is only with the benefit of hindsight that they can be labelled angels, demons and so on.

Even when the entity announces its identity, it doesn't follow that we can accept that announcement. It could be an angel appearing in a familiar form so as not to alarm the witness, or it could be Satan pretending to be an angel appearing in a familiar form — in other words, once we acknowledge that the entity may not be what it seems to be, we are committed to acknowledging that there are no limits to what it might be.

What about the witness' own conviction? We have seen how often a witness may be totally convinced by his experience, and yet be mistaken; we must conclude that *any* witness, no matter how sincere, no matter how sure, may none the less be deluded. The question of how our witnesses may have been led to mistake the identity of the being they encountered is another line we must pursue.

The question of motivation

We have seen that some encounters, at least, came about ostensibly because the entity wished for them — God with a set of commandments for Moses to give his people, Mary with a warning for two little shepherds to pass on to the rest of mankind. But even in such cases we must remember that we have only the word of the witness. We must consider whether Moses, for example, may have had a political motive in saying that God wanted to speak to him.

Certainly human motivation seems evident in some cases. No doubt divinities are not to be constrained by mere humans, but prayer may, one supposes, be answered: so that when a Catherine Labouré ardently yearns to meet Mary, her devotion is rewarded. But again it is not beside the point to ask *cui bono*, who benefits?

Mary may of course have had the best of reasons for appearing to Catherine; we have no means of knowing. But it seems unfair that religious visionaries like her, living in relative security and comfort diminished only by self-denials which are, after all, voluntary and ultimately self-serving, should be favoured when so many are not. If Mary is so concerned for suffering humanity, wouldn't her attentions be better bestowed on an Ethiopian mother watching her starving child die in a refugee camp?

The question of personal motivation, and the part it may play in determining whether the witness shall have an encounter experience, and what form it may take, is clearly another important aspect for us to study.

The question of cultural context
We have noted a marked tendency for witnesses to encounter the entities they might expect to encounter. Mary appears to Catholics, the devil to fundamentalist Christians, and so on. The witness doesn't necessarily have to subscribe to a belief system to have it affect his ideas; awareness of it may well be enough. Both the fact that the experience occurs, and the form it takes, will reflect his cultural background. The children at Medjugorje in Yugoslavia, who are currently meeting the Virgin Mary every evening, did not question, from the first far from detailed sighting, the identity of the entity; it is only reasonable to ask if their certainty indicates a degree of pre-conditioning.

The question of state
We have seen that many of our witnesses were in something of a special state at the time, which leads us to speculate that perhaps the same is true of the others. If so, then the question of what can happen to people in special states, and what they themselves then become capable of, opens another promising line of inquiry.

These are some of the questions raised by our first group of encounter experiences. We shall find the same questions raised by other kinds of experience, and as similar difficulties occur in different settings, we shall find this helps us to define the kind of answers we need and points us in the most useful directions.

But while we must not be content with any explanation which does not account for these difficulties, we must not concentrate on these negative aspects to the point where we forget that they are fundamentally *positive* events. For most of our witnesses their encounter experiences, no matter what they 'really' were, were important and meaningful, and conferred a positive and practical benefit. Whatever explanation we come up with has got to account for that just as surely as it must resolve the contradictions.

3.1 ENCOUNTERS WITH SPIRITS

Few of mankind's beliefs have been held so long, so widely, and on evidence so slender, as that when we finish our life on Earth we in some form proceed to a further life on some other plane of existence.

Since survival is a possibility which vitally concerns us all, it is not surprising that opinions on the matter come from all kinds of people, and that many different kinds of specialist have deployed their expertise in regard to it. Religious leaders have built their scenarios into their teachings, and theologians have subsequently argued about what they meant. Philosophers and anthropologists in their fashion have speculated as to *how* the idea came into being, while psychologists have sought to demonstrate *why* it did. Only a very few people, though, have undertaken a serious search for empirical evidence as opposed to divine revelation or metaphysical reasoning.

Not that this apparent lack of evidence seems to have inhibited belief in the least. People believe in survival because they *feel* it to be a fact, and though the psychologists would substitute 'wish' for 'feel', it remains none the less a matter of sentiment rather than sense.

Ironically, though very little scientific research has been done, that little has shown that evidence *does* exist, and even in considerable abundance. You might think this would encourage a more substantial research effort into a subject which concerns us all, but this has not been the response. All but a few scientists, theologians, philosophers and psychologists have steered clear of the subject, for reasons which do not appear to be logical but to be dictated by some kind of taboo.[61] Again, sentiment rules. Consequently most investigation has been carried out by amateurs — as, indeed, has this present study.

Just as we can evaluate encounters with divinities only if we relate them to the belief systems current in the witness' cultural milieu, so, now that we turn to encounters with spirits, we must consider how they will be affected by this remarkable public attitude to methodical research. Though in private a surprisingly large proportion of people will admit to experiences which are hard to account for except on the supposition that we survive death, in public they will greet the mention of ghosts and ghouls with affectionate amusement, while the mention of seance room spirits will arouse something more like contempt.

Encounters between the living and spirits of the dead are of two sorts:

1   Visits paid by the dead to Earth, usually for the purpose of conveying a message or a warning to the living; these are *apparitions*. In some cases, the dead seem never to have left the Earth, but remain earthbound either because there was a hitch in the transit operation, or because they are detained by notions of guilt, revenge or 'unfinished business'; these are *hauntings*.

2   Contact via a specially gifted 'medium' who acts as a channel of communication, enabling messages to be passed to and fro, and occasionally permitting the dead to materialize in a form visible to the living; this is *spiritism* or, in its specifically 'religious' form, *spiritualism*.

For both these kinds of encounter there is an enormous quantity of testimony, albeit largely consisting, like the accounts of encounters with divinities, of unsupported statements by individual witnesses. Unfortunately there is very little agreement as to what is taking place either when an apparition is seen or when a spirit manifests, since there is nothing in our scientific knowledge which corresponds to it.

It is also unfortunately the case that much of the alleged evidence is patently false. Apart from conscious cheating, which is encouraged by the understandable but regrettable professionalization of mediumship, there is no lack of instances where the spirit fails so lamentably to substantiate his claim to be the person he claims to have been that only the most credulous will take his word for it.

If this is true of so many cases, argue the sceptics, is it not reasonable to suppose that some kind of deception, not necessarily deliberate, is involved in *every* case?

Popular misconceptions
Before we consider the evidence that the living have encountered the surviving dead, it will be helpful if we ensure our minds are not contaminated by certain popular misconceptions:

★ *An apparent encounter with someone who is supposed to be dead is not necessarily evidence of survival.* Some other process may be involved. Those who believe that mischievous entities sometimes masquerade as saints and angels may equally suppose they can assume the likeness of the dead. Or thinking along quite other lines, we may suppose that a 'trace' of some kind is 'left behind' by a dying person which, for a limited time, may give the illusion that he is still active, just as parts of his body continue to function for a while after death.

★ *Knowledge of information supposedly known only to a dead person is not necessarily evidence of survival.* It is certainly evidence that there exists some other means of passing on information than those with which our science is familiar; but that's another matter. Certainly, the simplest explanation is that it is the dead person who is supplying the information, but we must consider alternative explanations however improbable. It is conceivable, for instance, that a *living* mind could, given certain conditions, have access to:

— an information store in which *all* information is stored *forever*;
— the *formerly living* mind of the dead person, by means of some kind of retro time-travel;
— the dead person's memory store, which may remain accessible for a limited period even when the body which houses it is no longer functioning, just as someone might leave behind him a video-film of himself alive, for his friends to screen when he is dead.

I leave you to think up yet more alternatives.

★ *Paranormal phenomena in the seance room are not necessarily evidence of survival.* The tradition whereby the spirits of even the most intelligent dead give proof of their survival by making luminous trumpets dance round the room and other such child's play came about from an understandable desire on the part of sitters in the early days of spiritism for 'miracles' which would prove that otherworldly forces were at work. Unfortunately, these vulgar displays became a standard feature of mediumship.

It may indeed be the case that paranormal powers are involved in some of the phenomena, and the subject rightly has its own intrinsic interest; but the correlation with survival is not a necessary one. A gifted psychic may give the spirits the credit for the amazing feats he executes by his own unconscious abilities, without our having to come to the same conclusion.

If none of these things is proof of survival, what *would* constitute such proof? If it could be shown that genuine communication does take place between the living and the dead, that would be proof. But it is perfectly legitimate to believe in survival *without* believing that communication occurs between the living and the dead; indeed, this is what Christian teaching officially maintains.

In short, we can believe in survival without believing in encounters with the dead; but if we accept encounters with the dead, we accept survival of some kind.

The obvious explanation
Why, you may object, am I going to all this trouble to avoid the most obvious explanation? Am I not shying away from the subject of survival as ignominiously as the theologians and the scientists whose evasions I was earlier deploring?

My reply in regard to claims to have encountered the dead, as with claims to have encountered divinities, is this: it is *certain* that many of these claims are false. So, if we are to learn the truth of the matter, we must first learn how to distinguish the true from the false, which means establishing what criteria a genuine encounter would have to fulfil.

Our task is made yet more complicated by the fact that there is no single belief in survival to which people either do or don't subscribe: different races and different cultures favour different versions of survival. But this complication works to our advantage; for these differences raise questions which are relevant to our study:

★ Do we *all* survive death, or only a select few? And if the latter, what is the basis for selection?

★ *How much of us* survives? Shall we be conscious individuals with the power to, for example, communicate with the living?

★ If a spirit of the dead revisits earth, does something physical come from 'there' to 'here'? Or is it more a question of something which now has no time/space dimension, but which for the purpose of the visit is temporarily relocated in time and place? Or is the visit a purely mental event performed by the mind of the survivor in the mind of the medium?

★ Can *any* dead person revisit the living, or is it a special dispensation? If the latter, what does one do to qualify?

★ Can *any* living person receive visits from the dead, or only a special kind of person, or a person in a special kind of state or in special circumstances?

To many of these questions we shall return at a later stage. For now, as a sobering reminder that both conviction and doubt in these matters have a long history, let us recall a conversation which took place more than 2,000 years ago, when the Athenian philosopher Socrates, prior to drinking the poison he had been ordered by the state to drink, sat with his friends discussing his immediate prospects. His friend Cebes said to him:

> In what concerns the soul, men are apt to be sceptical. They fear that when it leaves the body it may have nowhere to go, and that on the day of death it will perish as it is released from the body, to disperse like smoke into nothingness. Surely much argument and many proofs are needed to convince a man that his dead spirit will continue to exist, and possess force or intelligence?

Socrates, as ever, was equal to the occasion, and offered logical arguments to support his conviction that the end, for him now only a few minutes off, would be only apparent:

> I am confident there is such a thing as living again, and that the living spring from the dead, and that the spirits of the dead continue to exist. [197]

But listening to his friends' polite acceptance of the abstract logic he was, even at such a time, supremely able to deploy, it is hard not to feel that though out of respect, affection and perhaps pity they declared themselves persuaded, they would have been happier with something more tangible, more evidential.

That 'something' is what the spiritists, and to some extent the psychical researchers, claim to be able to offer. But before spiritism was invented, before there was any such thing as psychical research, people were reporting encounters with the supposedly dead; indeed, it was because of these encounters that spiritism and psychical research came into being.

So we start with ghost stories.

3.2 ENCOUNTERS WITH CRISIS APPARITIONS, REVENANTS, HAUNTERS

Ghost stories are among the oldest stories in the world; they are to be found in the popular literature, written or oral, of virtually every culture. Yet even after thousands of years we do not know whether these stories are founded on fact or fantasy.

Clearly there is fact *of a sort*. It is a fact that people have experiences which lead them to think they have encountered other people once but no longer living. Whatever causes them to think so must possess some kind of reality.

The choice is not so much between fact and fantasy, as between subjective and objective reality; is a ghost something which forms *inside* the mind, or something which exists *outside* it? And if the latter, is it what it appears to be?

In short, the traditional question 'Do you believe in ghosts?' is meaningless as it stands. It makes sense only if it is understood — as indeed I suppose it is generally understood — to mean 'Do you believe the experience known as "seeing a ghost" involves an encounter with a spirit of the surviving dead?'

Even then we have to distinguish between the different ways in which ghosts may survive. Such differences were crucial for Christian theologians, because the manner of survival had profound implications for church doctrine. For instance, the question whether there exists a state called 'purgatory', from which the dead can return with relative ease, was answered one way by the Catholics, a contrary way by the Protestants, and this led to a controversy of a kind fascinating to scholars but of only academic relevance for this study.

In practical terms, a ghost of the dead may be one of three things:

1   A dead person who — usually close to the time of his death — manifests — usually to someone known to him — in a way which suggests he is trying to communicate the fact that something has happened to him: this is therefore known as a *crisis apparition*.

2   A dead person who has gone on to some other plane of existence where he seems to retain intelligence and personal identity, and from where he seems able, under appropriate circumstances, to revisit Earth and make contact with the living: the most appropriate label is the French *revenant*.

3   A dead person who for some reason is unable or unwilling to proceed to the next phase of his existence, but remains earthbound in some form. Because such entities usually confine their appearances to a specific location, their activities are known as haunting, but the word *haunter* is not widely used; I propose, none the less, to use it.

Crisis apparitions

It is quite probable that crisis apparitions are not spirits of the dead at all, but phenomena associated with the event of death; so, interesting as they are, we could set them aside as irrelevant to our study. However, we do not know if this is so, and in any case there are features of crisis apparitions which *do* have a bearing on our inquiry. Here is a typical case, reported by a Swiss witness whom I shall call Anna:

> My friend Trudy and I attended a horticultural college in England in 1936. One of our fellow-pupils, Patricia, was at first rather reserved towards us foreigners, but later our mutual love for animals and plants drew us together. Two years later, back in Zurich, I met Trudy at Pfauen Square at midday on February 14. Suddenly in the crowd I caught sight of Pat, our English friend. In spite of the warm weather she was wearing her old raincoat and hat. 'Trudy,' I cried, 'Look, there's Pat! I'll call her'. I ran across to the tram-stop where Pat was just getting into a No. 5 tram. I saw her take her seat but before I could reach the tram it started off. Trudy had not seen Pat. Some days later I received a letter from Pat's mother telling me that her daughter had been thrown from her horse and broken her neck at midday on February 14. [121]

In accounting for this incident, we have somehow to reconcile the following facts:

★ Anna could not have known in any 'normal' way what had happened to Pat.

★ Pat could not know where Anna was.

★ Some kind of communication occurred between Pat and Anna.

★ Pat's fall was the occasion for it.

★ The possibility of chance coincidence is so remote that we can reasonably ignore it.

There is no accepted scientific explanation for such an event, but of course psychical researchers have proposed various models. My own preference is for a co-production between the subconscious minds of both Pat and Anna, whereby each contributed towards staging a kind of 'psychodrama'. (This hypothesis is developed in greater detail in my previous study. [58])

This still leaves many unresolved questions. Why wasn't Pat able to tell Anna what had happened to her? Did Anna see an apparition of Pat, or did she impose her image onto a stranger who was really present? But it does account for most of the awkward elements.

On the other hand it is pure speculation; we have no evidence that such a capability exists in the subconscious mind — indeed, for that matter, the subconscious mind is itself very much an unknown quantity.

The possibility exists that crisis apparitions are an automatic process, a response to a traumatic event like an alarm set off by a burglar. The alarm analogy can be extended to those sci-fi movies in which, after the Bomb has fallen and destroyed all life, certain automatic processes — like alarm clocks — continue to function.

There is also another way of looking at the crisis apparition, not as the *last* despairing gesture of a being at the termination of its existence, but as the *first* manifestation of existence on a new level, a level on which the being is capable of things it could never do while alive. Pat's effort at communication with her living friend may seem futile and unsatisfactory, but if it was her first effort as a just-graduated spirit, maybe we shouldn't judge it too severely.

Revenants

The most obvious reason a spirit of the dead might have to revisit earth is to help and comfort those it has left behind. We are not surprised, then, that recently bereaved widows report experiences such as these:

> On many occasions following her husband's death she experienced a complex hallucination of him lying beside her in bed. The first thing she was aware of was the heat of his body, she would turn over and see him and feel him lying next to her in bed, just as he always used to. He would say comforting words to her such as 'Don't be frightened, I'm not far away'. She often saw him immediately on waking, passing her window, apparently fully dressed, wearing his usual clothes, as if he was going shopping. Often on these occasions he would also speak and say 'Don't worry, because I'm always near you — I've not left you'. These experiences were always fully projected, life-sized, in natural colour, and always for the moment she thought he had really come back to her. His presence always afforded her great comfort.[227]

From the same source we hear of another witness who saw her husband standing at the foot of the bed, dressed to go to work, for about five minutes. She reported it as being 'as real as seeing a real person'. Another, who saw her husband while she was in a half-awake state, said 'He appeared quite real. I thought he had come back in the flesh.' Another, who saw her husband the night following his death, reported that his appearance seemed to have altered: 'I saw Jim standing in the doorway dressed as he was in his coffin — he didn't look English to me, he looked foreign — dark skinned.' Nevertheless she saw him with her eyes, and he appeared perfectly real though she knew it was a vision.

The ambiguity of revenant cases is well illustrated in the following case, chosen because it is comparatively recent, because the persons involved are well-known and respected, and because it is about as uncomplicated as such a case can be. The very simplicity of the incident increases our bafflement at not being able to explain it:

Canon J. B. Phillips, a theological writer, described in one of his books a paranormal encounter he had experienced. This came to the notice of two leading members of the Society for Psychical Research, Andrew Mackenzie and Mollie Goldney; my account is made up from his original account and from his replies to their questions. [231]

Phillips describes himself as 'incredulous' and 'as unsuperstitious as they come'. At the time of the event, in spring 1964, though in good health he was 'mentally tired, as I had been working at full capacity for several years . . . mental and spiritual depletion . . . depressed'.

One light spring evening, in full daylight, he was sitting watching television when he was suddenly aware that the religious writer C. S. Lewis was 'sitting in a chair within a few feet of me, and spoke a few words which were particularly relevant to the difficult circumstances through which I was passing. He said "It's not as difficult as you think, you know".'

Phillips had by no means been intimate with Lewis, though they had corresponded, and had met on one occasion. He had no doubt as to the apparition's identity: Lewis was 'ruddier in complexion than ever, grinning all over his face, and positively glowing with health. I cannot emphasize too strongly that he was solid and in no way transparent.' He was wearing the 'rather rough, well-worn brown tweeds' characteristic of him, though on the one occasion they had met Lewis had been wearing a cassock.

A week later, this time when he was in bed reading before going to sleep, Lewis appeared again, 'even more rosily radiant than before' and repeated the same message. This visit, like the first, lasted no more than half a minute. On both occasions, Phillips' wife was in the house. During the first apparition she was in the next room preparing supper, on the second occasion she was watching a latish programme on TV.

Phillips insists that he had not been thinking about Lewis, and though he was well aware of his death a few months earlier, he was 'neither alarmed nor surprised'.

This seemingly simple case confronts us with many of the difficulties of apparition cases. Consider some of its features:

★ The event seems to have met a 'need' on Phillips' part: Lewis' words 'helped and encouraged' him. Though the two men were not close acquaintances, Lewis was well-suited to bring comfort to his fellow writer and fellow Christian, and his high reputation would give his words greater authority than if they had come from someone Phillips respected less.

It seems reasonable to infer that Phillips' need was what brought about the event, but this leaves open the question of which of the two was responsible for initiating it.

★ Paranormally acquired knowledge seems to be involved, in that Phillips saw Lewis in clothes which he did not know at the time were characteristic of him; however we can't rule out the possibility that Phillips may have seen Lewis dressed thus on television or in a photograph.

★ Though helpful, Lewis's message seems curiously thin. Surely, after going to the trouble of appearing, there was much more he could have said, not to speak of imparting interesting information about the experience of death and conditions in the afterlife.

★ Lewis' natural behaviour and lifelike appearance suggest a planned illusion of reality, while his ability to make himself at home in a room he had never visited during his lifetime, like Pat's natural behaviour in the Zurich tram-station, suggests that the witness must have contributed at least part of the necessary information.

Revenant cases, of which the Phillips case is typical, confront us with a choice of two basic scenarios:

1   Lewis did in some form visit Phillips, for the purpose of helping and encouraging him. The visit was realistically staged so as to convince Phillips of its reality and at the same time not to alarm him. Phillips' subconscious mind assisted in the staging by supplying information not only about Phillips' state of mind, but also where Lewis could expect to find him, when would be a suitable time with his wife out of the room, where to sit and so on.

2   Phillips imagined the incident, using Lewis as a suitable spokesperson to express his own subconscious thoughts, and projecting the imagined encounter in the form of a seemingly external scene to give it added force, drawing on subconsciously retained knowledge of Lewis' appearance.

While it is hard to account for crisis apparitions without assigning at least part of the responsibility to the apparent, many revenant cases, such as this one, seem to relate only to the need of the witness. Quite the reverse seems to be true of our next category.

Haunters

Here is a thumping classic case of haunting, which I choose because it contains most of the features which suggest that haunters are real entities with autonomous existence independent from the witness.

In the year 1665, John Rudall, a parson of Launceston in Cornwall and headmaster of its grammar school, heard from a 16-year-old boy of his alarming experience on the way to his daily lessons at the home of a local clergyman:

> In the course of his daily walk, always in one and the same place, he encountered every day a woman with a pale and troubled face, clothed in a long loose garment, with one hand always stretched forth and the other pressed against her side. Her name, he said, was Dorothy Dinglet, for he had known her well from his childhood, and she often used to come to his parents' house; but that which troubled him was, that she had now been dead three years, and he himself had been with the neighbours at her burial; so that, as the youth alleged with great simplicity, since he had seen her body laid in the grave, this that he saw every day must needs be her soul or ghost.

After hearing young Bligh's account, next morning Rudall went with him to the place:

> We had hardly reached the accustomed spot, when we both saw her at once gliding towards us; she floated along the field like a sail upon a stream, and glided past the spot where we stood. So deep was the awe that overcame me, as I stood there in the light of day, face to face with a human soul separate from her bones and flesh, that my heart and purpose both failed me. I had resolved to address the spectre, but I stood like one amazed and speechless until she had passed clean out of sight. A spaniel dog, the favourite of Master Bligh, when the woman drew nigh, began to yell and bark piteously, and ran backward and away, like a thing dismayed and appalled.

After consulting his books, Rudall decided on action, and applied to his bishop for permission to carry out an exorcism. He went alone to the field, and prepared a circle like those used by magicians. When the spectre appeared, he persuaded it to enter the circle, where he questioned it and found that it was 'unquiet, because of a certain sin'; the spectre indicated what, and by whom. When Rudall asked the entity why it so terrified the boy, it replied 'It is the law; we must seek a youth or a maiden of clean life, and under age, to receive messages and admonitions.'

Rudall asked the spectre 'what sign she could give that she was a true spirit and not a false fiend?' It replied that 'before next Yule-tide a fearful pestilence would lay waste the land and myriads of souls would be loosened from their flesh, until, as she piteously said, "our valleys will be full".' — a seemingly impressive forecast of the Great Plague which afflicted England that same year.

After evensong that night, Rudall had 'a long discourse with that ancient transgressor, Mr B', the boy's father. Though Rudall's account is reticent about details, we may guess that the elder Bligh had enjoyed clandestine intimacies with Dorothy, whom we know to have been a frequent visitor at the house, perhaps with unfortunate consequences.

Next day Rudall again waited for the spectre, and this time had no difficulty entering into communication:

I rehearsed the penitent words of the man she had come up to denounce, and the satisfaction he would perform. Then said she, 'Peace in our midst'. Then with certain fixed rites I did dismiss that troubled ghost, until she peacefully withdrew, gliding towards the west. Neither did she ever afterward appear, but was allayed until she shall come in her second flesh to the valley of Armageddon on the last day. [104]

I suppose this story could be a total fabrication, though it is taken from Rudall's own diaries written down at the time for his own use rather than publication. But there seems to be no middle course between rejecting it utterly or accepting that something very close to his account did really occur; such circumstantial happenings aren't to be rationalized into anything like a misperception of a natural phenomenon, or a clever hoax.

To reject Rudall's story on the grounds that after three centuries we have no means of verifying his statements or assessing the witnesses would be the prudent and in many ways a justifiable course. But thousands of such cases have been reported: are we to reject each and every one on the same grounds? That would be tantamount to asserting that thousands of people, in all parts of the world and at all periods of history, have been fooled — or have fooled others — in the same way.

This could indeed be the case. But we have no right to make such an assertion unless we cannot provide a reasonable alternative account of what happened to make first young Bligh and then Rudall believe so firmly they had had a real experience. We do not have to prove that our version is what actually happened, because we can't; the same factors that prevent us from checking on Rudall's story also prevent us from testing our rival version. But our scenario must at least plausibly account for the boy behaving as he did and Rudall behaving as he did; moreover, since to explain away a single case would get us nowhere, it must be an explanation which, suitably adapted, will serve as a model for the thousands of other such cases.

Even though we may set crisis apparitions on one side as not necessarily involving the dead, and though we might conceivably find an explanation for revenants in terms of some subjective process, it is hard at first sight to see how hauntings can be anything else but encounters with spirits of the dead. However, there are some suggestive factors to be considered.

Hauntings seem to be located in space. Dorothy Dinglet might, one thinks, have revisited the house where her wrong occurred, to trouble the conscience of the man who had wronged her; instead she haunts a particular field, where she can be encountered by anyone passing by. But the passer-by isn't just 'anyone', it is the man's son. Though she plausibly accounts for her choice by saying that haunters are required to pick on a young and innocent child, an alternative explanation suggests itself.

A recurrent theme of our study will be the probability that encounters occur only to certain kinds of people, or to people in certain kinds of state. Mr Bligh might have been put into such a state by remorse for having wronged Dorothy, but that doesn't seem to have been the case. His son, on the other hand, was in the throes of adolescence, with all the emotional instability that state implies: he might well have been upset if he learnt of his father's extramarital carryings-on. In short, we have every indication that something more than chance was involved in the selection of the witness. If so, then we may infer that the mind of that witness played at least a contributory part in the encounter process.

But what of haunting cases in which the witness does not know the apparent? Here is such a case:

> In June 1881 we went to live in a detached villa just out of the town of C——. We had been there about three weeks when about 11 o'clock one morning, as I was playing the piano in the drawing room, I was suddenly aware of a figure peeping round the corner of the door; thinking it must be a visitor, I jumped up and went into the passage, but no one was there. I only saw the top half of the figure, which was that of a tall man, with a very pale face and dark hair and moustaches. The impression lasted only a second or so, but I saw the face so distinctly that to this day I should recognise it if I met it in a crowd. It had a sorrowful expression. It was impossible for anyone to come into the house without being seen or heard.
>
> In the following August I saw the same face. I again saw only the top half of the figure, which seemed to be in a somewhat crouching posture. Later in the same month I was playing cricket in the garden with my little boys. From my position at the wickets I could see right into the house. I distinctly saw the same face peeping round at me out of the kitchen door. I threw down the bat and ran in. No one was in the kitchen.
>
> A little later in the year, about 8 oclock one evening, I was coming down the stairs alone, when I heard a voice from the direction, apparently, of my little boys' bedroom. It distinctly said, in a deep sorrowful tone, 'I can't find it.' My step-daughter, who was downstairs, also heard the voice, and thinking it was me calling, cried out 'What are you looking for?' The voice could not by any possibility have belonged to any member of the household. [232]

After comparing notes, the stepdaughter not only confirmed hearing the voice, but revealed that she had seen the figure four times in July. No formal investigation was carried out, and the identity of the apparent was never learnt. It did however emerge that the row of villas shared the reputation of being haunted.

There does not seem to be much one can do about a case like that, with so little to go on. But I chose it for that very reason: the very fact that there is so little to go on is in itself significant. For the apparent arbitrariness in this instance, by comparison with the strongly motivated and purposefully logical Bligh case, means there's no use our coming up with a clever across-the-board explanation which, having established that some hauntings are witness-based, concludes that all are ultimately subjective.

It may be that the witnesses played a role in the case just quoted, but it can only have been a very minor one. Anyone, it seems, might have had the encounter, or at any rate anyone who was 'tuned to the right psychic wavelength', for want of a more scientific term to define whatever determines that some people see what others don't. But only in that respect does it seem as though a 'witness-based' explanation could be viable. The overwhelming implication is that the entity, whoever or whatever it was, played the major part. If so, could the difference between the two cases be, quite simply, that Dorothy Dinglet made a better job of her encounter than this unknown being?

A distinguishing characteristic of hauntings is that frequently more than one witness is involved: the fact that Rudall as well as young Bligh met Dorothy, that the stepdaughter as well as the mother saw their mysterious haunter, implies a degree of objective reality. But this too is something which is open to question:

Mr B, aged 32, shared a house with his sister; another sister, married, lived 300 metres away in the same street. After the death of their mother, Mr B experienced symptoms both mental, including depression, and physical, including an ulcer (notoriously stress-induced), and some psychic experiences. In 1958 he stated:

> Since my mother died, her apparition comes usually twice a week through the closed door of my bedroom and stops at the foot of my bed. She stands there for a while and stares at me. I always have the impression that she wants to tell me something but can't.

He admitted to being very afraid of the apparition, hiding his head under the bedclothes till she had gone.

The sister he lived with reported:

> At night I have seen her in my room, standing near my bed, or near the fireplace. She has also appeared to walk through the locked door. Sometimes she was crying, sometimes calling my name. These visions have occurred a short time before sleep, perhaps ten minutes; I only know that I have felt drowsy.
>
> Upon waking I have seen her, standing at my bed, just looking at me. Always I have tried to keep her out of my room, trying to push her away. But I have not felt anything to touch. I have wakened and felt her gripping my arm, I have also felt her sitting on my bed. The last time I saw her, she was dressed in a red dress, which she often wore in life. She looked happy, and I spoke to her. I asked her where she was, and if she was happy. She assured me that she was very happy, nodding her head and saying 'yes'. This time I was not afraid, and I tried to keep her with me. But she disappeared through the window.

Brother and sister compared notes, but only later learnt that the sister down the street was having similar experiences; nor did she know of theirs:

> I have seen my mother very often, but I wouldn't tell anybody but my

husband. But he just laughed and said, Rubbish. But I saw her many times, usually just when I was falling asleep. She would come in, right through the panels in the door, and then would stop at my bed and gaze. I got frightened and hid my head under the pillow till she went. And do you know what's the funniest part of it? That I could see her with my eyes closed. Twice I waked up my husband, but he is no use. He never could see her, though she was there, just at the foot of my bed, staring at me. Then Frank said I was just as mad as my poor mother was, and the next minute he snored again. I was quite disgusted. Men, quite useless they are.[163]

Lukianowicz, the doctor concerned, classifies this as a 'hallucination à trois'. All three had tended their mother during her final illness, which included mental symptoms (hence Frank's reference): Lukianowicz surmises that guilt for wishing she would die may be the motivating force. The fact that all three had similar experiences he attributes to their relationship, their physical proximity and the shared experience of nursing their mother.

Predictably, he does not even consider the possibility that any external agency — the mother herself or some spirit in her guise — was involved: hallucination is for him a sufficient explanation. That hallucination was the *process*, we need not doubt, nor that they were of the kind known as hypnagogic, which occur on the threshold of sleep; but the question, why some people should hallucinate an encounter and others not, demands an answer if we are to construct a general model rather than a one-off explanation.

Further light on what may be happening in hauntings is thrown by the experience of Matthew Manning, a noted psychic, in his own home. For some three years between 1971 and 1974, Manning had ostensible encounters with former occupiers of the house, particularly Robert Webbe, an eighteenth-century owner. Much information was provided, chiefly through automatic writing, all of which when checked proved correct.

In this case, identity was clearly established. There was no specific motive: the impression given was that Robert was in a sense still inhabiting the house. He was inclined to be resentful of the new occupiers, and puzzled how he and they could be sharing the house; he was also puzzled by modern appliances and other changes. Evidently he was living in the house as it was in the 1970s; at the same time he was 'living' in the eighteenth century, engaging in such activities as dining with neighbours, suffering illness and so on. Manning comments:

I hold the view that a part of the consciousness of Robert Webbe survived his physical death, and continued to exist — I do not say 'live' because I cannot regard it as a life — in my house . . . I could only conclude that he must be trapped in some kind of postmortal nightmare, unable to leave the house on which he had spent so much money and of which he was so proud. Sometimes he remembered that he was no longer physically alive, and at other times he was still trapped in the time at which he died . . . I visualised time as a record being played on a gramophone; with Webbe it was as though there was an obstruction at the point of his death which caused the needle to jump back across the grooves through which it had previously played. Thus Webbe was somehow reliving the final years of his physical life over and over. Sometimes I seemed to communicate with him as the needle reached the obstruction on the surface of the record, and he would be aware that he was now dead, and at other times I would communicate with him after the needle had jumped back again.

The more I thought about it, the more convinced I became that Webbe's 'spirit' was like some kind of incandescent light. A bulb will only light up when connected to a source of electricity, like a battery; I was the battery for Robert Webbe. I could not help thinking of how he had looked wax-like and lifeless until I had spoken to him. He had almost come back to life then.[166]

We must respect Manning's own interpretation, that he performed — no doubt, thanks to his psychic gifts — some kind of 'enabling' role which made it possible for Webbe to make his presence known. Nevertheless, we must also consider an alternative explanation, that by virtue of those same gifts he *created* the entire episode. How such a process might be effected is a question we shall consider in detail later in the course of this study.

Ostensibly, haunting cases present impressive grounds for thinking that *some* encounter experiences, at least, originate with an external agency. We have seen that the witness plays a part, and sometimes an essential one, but it seems still to be the external agent that is primarily responsible.

But haunting cases are also ambiguous and contradictory in ways that are hard to understand so long as we hold an external agent responsible. We have seen, too, that they contain many elements which call for more detailed study: witness state and witness motivation are two obvious themes to follow up, while the question of just how the interaction between the living and the dead takes place is an intriguing one. Only when we have looked into these and other aspects of the matter will we know if we have the raw materials for a model that will resolve the contradictions while accounting for the apparent participation of otherworldly entities.

3.3   ENCOUNTERS WITH SEANCE-ROOM SPIRITS

She was a high-class medium — which meant an honest and peculiarly simple woman who was yet capable, in certain abnormal or trance states, of ingenious and sustained deceptions. That was it — or that was it in uncompromisingly rational terms. Mrs Nurse was just the type: a shallow pool until the water parted and sundry problematical depths were revealed. Mrs Nurse would sit in a darkened room with bereaved mothers and sensation-seekers and inquiring Fellows of the Royal Society. Strange voices would come from her; voices voluble, hesitant, coherent, fragmentary, pathetic, pompous, fishing, shuffling. And people would listen as they had listened ever since the days of the Witch of Endor. One hears his wife speaking. One makes a verbatim report. One weeps. One smuggles a microphone. One offers bank-notes. One plans tests with a manometer, a sphygmograph, a thermoscope . . . in other words, Mrs Nurse was a steady selling line. [118]

Every night, in countless public halls and private sitting-rooms, encounters purportedly take place between the living and the dead. Specially gifted individuals offer to put us in contact with the spirits of those who have departed this life for some other level of existence.

If this is indeed happening, it would be an encouragement for us to believe that our other encounter experiences are likewise genuine contacts with otherworldly beings; for spiritism is simply a methodical system for putting encounters on an organized basis.

The idea came to mankind at a very early date. The medium was a recognized institution even in Old Testament times; Saul, though previously he had sought to abolish witchcraft, found it convenient at a moment of crisis to consult 'a woman that hath a familiar spirit' who claimed to be able to put him in touch with the dead. In all essentials, this is what is done by our present-day mediums. [20]

In eighteenth-century France a young Parisienne named Marie-Anne de la Ville, after running away from her convent, set herself up as a sorceress with a modus operandi just like that of mediums in all periods and cultures. Clients visited her to question her Spirit, who would answer with the traditional one rap for 'yes', two for 'no'. [34] That Marie-Anne was probably no better than an opportunistic adventuress only confirms the popular belief in spirit communication, as a circling predator reveals the presence of prey.

What had hitherto been a covert activity became institutionalized as a result of incidents at the home of the Fox sisters, at Rochester in New York State. In 1848 disturbances of a poltergeist type inspired the girls to see if they could make contact with whatever force was producing the phenomena. To their surprise, they received an intelligible reply, and further experiments seemed to confirm that they were in touch with the dead.

With hindsight we can see that this was not the only way the phenomena might be explained. But given the cultural climate of America at that date, the Fox sisters can hardly be blamed if they jumped to the conclusion that they had hit upon a technique for making controlled communication with the dead. The birth of spiritualism provides us with an exemplary object-lesson in the importance of taking into account the cultural context in which an experience occurs. Americans, always hospitable to new spiritual notions however extreme, were at that time eagerly embracing all manner of harmonial philosophies and transcendental pantheisms, fourierist utopias and latter-day saintliness; they easily found room for one more, spiritism.

But spiritism had a quality which the more high-flying belief systems lacked, and one which made a strong appeal to the other side of the American character: it was *practical*. Spiritism was, if not do-it-yourself, something your friendly neighbourhood spirit medium could bring for you to enjoy in the intimacy of your own home.

Marvels and materialization
The simple marvel of spiritism was that it opened a regular channel of communication between the living and the dead. Emma Hardinge Britten, writing in 1869, explained:

> From the first working of the spiritual telegraph by which invisible beings were enabled to spell out consecutive messages, they ['the spirits'] claimed that this method of communion was organised by scientific minds in the spirit spheres; that it depended mainly upon the conditions of human and atmospheric magnetisms, and pointed to the ultimation of a science whereby spirits, operating upon and through matter, could connect in the most intimate relations the worlds of material and spiritual existence.[22]

Predictably, there were doubting minds who questioned whether the 'spiritual telegraph' might be more of an echo, reflecting the minds of medium and/or sitter. So just as the religious visionaries had called on the Virgin Mary for miracles with which to confound the sceptics, the spiritists called upon their contacts in the other world for marvels. And indeed marvels duly occurred, for which the spirits claimed the credit; whereupon the sceptics, as is their wont, upped their demands, and the spirits were constrained to provide greater and greater marvels. From simple raps and table-lifting, which could be too easily effected by deliberate cheating or unconscious muscular action, the phenomena escalated via floating trumpets and vocal prodigies, anomalous lights and mysterious apports, to culminate in materialization. Thanks to a substance called ectoplasm, the spirits are able to fabricate short-lived facsimiles of themselves, capable of being seen, touched and photographed by the witness.

The evidence for materialization, as a phenomenon, is very strong. Though by its nature it is the most tempting for a charlatan to fake, it has also been among the most thoroughly investigated; the weight of accumulated testimony, often given by eminent scientists who thereby place their reputations at risk, cannot easily be set aside, and I certainly do not intend to try — partly because I am not competent to do so, but also because even if materialization is a fact, it does not necessarily testify to any kind of activity on the part of the spirits, still less to their actual appearance amongst us.

We have seen that those entities which have the best claim to be the returning dead, the revenants, are so lifelike in their appearance that often it is only in retrospect that the witness realizes he has been communing with the dead. Seance-room materializations, on the other hand, though they manifest for no other purpose than to establish their identity, persist in appearing in long loose robes and veils which, unbecoming as they are, may, I suppose, be the uniform fashion in the next world, but also have the quality of being mighty convenient for the fake medium in this world.

Needless to say, this does not have the result of inhibiting recognition by tearful relatives. But the impartial observer must be dismayed by the discrepancy between what the sitter presumably expects to see and what he *does* see. As revealed by the camera (in photographs taken and published by the spiritists themselves), materialized spirits are so ludicrously unlifelike that even the fondest relative would turn away in disgust were his reality-testing faculties not sabotaged by emotion.[39]

That materialization, as a phenomenon, offers interesting territory for the psychical researcher, is something else. Dubious though many of the experiments have been, some at least must be taken seriously. But as evidence for survival, and more immediately for our purpose, as evidence that the living can communicate with the dead, seance-room materialization seems of no value. Fortunately, not all encounters with spirits of the dead are of this pathetic quality.

The question of information
The best evidence that through mediums the living can contact the dead is the content of the communication between them.

That some mediums on some occasions produce information they could not have acquired by conventional means is something I propose to take for granted. Only a sceptic determined to the point of bigotry will refuse to accept the evidence that mediums like Eileen Garrett and Leonore Piper possess an ability which, for the time being, we must classify as paranormal.

If we label such a person 'psychic', however, this does not imply that he is controlled by higher or occult forces, nor, specifically, that it is the dead who provide him with the information. That is what a medium generally claims, and he may be correct. But it may equally be his way of explaining to himself what might otherwise be an inexplicable and somewhat alarming faculty.

At the same time we must give reasonable consideration to the hypothesis that it is the dead we have to thank for this paranormally acquired information, which has been a traditional feature of ghost stories for as long as those stories have been told. For as long, too, as serious research has been directed at these matters, this has been the most impressive indication of otherworldly involvement. In 1848 Dr Haddock, of Bolton in Yorkshire, was experimenting with a young female subject:

> Emma frequently went, spontaneously and without any warning, into a state of exstasis. She sometimes retained a recollection of the place she was in, and the persons around her; but her mind was chiefly occupied with visions, apparently of another state of existence, and of what appeared to be spiritual beings.
>
> She could, when asked, perceive any concealed object by clairvoyance, but was usually too much engrossed with her spiritual perceptions to attend to such matters. On one occasion when in her usual magnetic (i.e. hypnotic) state she told Dr Haddock that next night a person long dead would come to her and show her a book which she was to take to him.

The following night she did indeed find the book 'while in a kind of somnambulistic exstasis', and though she was unable to read she located the correct passage, and when the book was dropped was able to find the passage again.

> It is evident that while her exstatic vision somehow directed her to the book, she, who could not read, and was besides in the dark, had some means by which she saw and recognised the passage. When light was present, she never attempted to use her eyes, which were moreover turned up and closed, but always placed the book upon her head, and there turned over the leaves. This vision was evidently connected with her states of spontaneous exstasis, because the person was one who had always appeared to her in that state.[99]

The explanation that the information was given her by 'a person long dead' is not only that given by the subject herself, who is in a better position than anyone to know, but is also the most economical. However, paranormally acquired information of this kind occurs in a great many instances where no attribution to the dead is made, for example in connection with the hysterical patients studied by Janet and other French psychologists of the late nineteenth century. While recognizing the paranormal character of the phenomenon, they tended to regard it as a side-effect which affects certain individuals when in an altered state, whether it be one into which they fall spontaneously due to their unbalanced mental condition, or a hypnotic state into which they have been experimentally induced.[122,123]

Janet and his colleagues regarded it as out of their province to speculate how their subjects acquired the information. Others could not bear to leave the question unresolved, and in the absence of any convincing alternative, the spiritists' claim that the information was supplied by the dead has achieved wide acceptance.

One who accepted it was the distinguished scientist Sir Oliver Lodge. Previously critical of spiritist claims, he was ultimately persuaded by personal experience that intervention by the dead was the most logical explanation. During World War One he received a series of communications relating to his son Raymond. The involved case fills a bulky volume, and the comments on it would fill another, so I can hardly pretend to do it justice here. However, some characteristic incidents will give an idea of the evidence which convinced Lodge.

On 8 August 1915 the American medium Leonore Piper receives a message via an entity naming itself 'Richard Hodgson' (who may or may not be the surviving spirit of a leading psychical researcher who when living had been known to Lodge) addressed to Lodge (whom she knows) on behalf of Myers (another dead researcher known to Lodge). The message is obscure, but says among other things that Myers will 'act as Faunus' while Lodge would 'take the part of the poet'; the word 'protect' also occurs.

Lodge can make nothing of the message, but, as 'Hodgson' suggests, he consults Mrs Verrall, a fellow psychical researcher and also a classical scholar. On 8 September she explains that the reference is to a poem by Horace, in which the poet is protected by Faunus from a falling tree. The implication is that 'Myers' will protect Lodge from some disaster. Lodge thinks it might be of a financial nature.

On 14 September Lodge's 26-year-old son Raymond is killed in action near Ypres, in Belgium. Lodge learns of this three days later.

A friend, the Revd Bayfield, gives Lodge his interpretation of the Piper message, that 'Myers', who had known what was going to happen, plans to help his old friend weather the tragedy. Later in September Lodge receives further messages from various mediums, including the respected Mrs Leonard and A. V. Peters. On 27 September a message from Peters contains a reference to a photograph, adding some specific details.

On 29 November Lady Lodge receives a letter from a Mrs Cheves, a total stranger, saying that her son, a doctor at the Front, has a group photo including Raymond, and offers to send it. On 3 December the medium Mrs Leonard, in a sitting with Lodge, gives a detailed description of the photograph, purportedly in Raymond's own words.

On 7 December the Lodges receive the photo, which precisely matches the description given via Mrs Leonard.

This is probably the most impressive single incident of the case, but it is one of many. It came as the ultimate confirmation to Lodge, who was already 'convinced, after more than thirty years of study, not only that persistent individual existence is a fact, but that occasional communication across the chasm is possible'.[232] Feeling an obligation to pass on to others this impressive reassurance, he rapidly prepared a detailed account of the case; his book[162] was rushed into print and was predictably an instant bestseller; there were six editions in November/December 1916 alone.

Reviewing the book for the SPR, however, the tough-minded Mrs Sidgwick noted that even Lodge, as a methodical scientist, had recognized alternative explanations:

> We must admit with Sir Oliver Lodge that it does not completely exclude explanation by telepathy between living minds. A considerable number of the communications purporting to come from Raymond Lodge show knowledge which, while it can hardly have reached the medium in any normal manner, may without improbability be accounted for by telepathy from the sitter or other living person.[232]

The difficulty is one which researchers continually face. To convince us that it comes from the communicator and from no other source, a message must contain information

★ which is not known to anyone living, for in that case it could have been acquired by telepathy;

★ which is not recorded in any place, for in that case it could have been acquired by clairvoyance;

★ but which is verifiable, thus proving that the communicator had access to true information.

The answer is, of course, to announce something that hasn't yet happened. It could be argued that this happened in the Raymond case; Mrs Piper seems to have had forewarning of Lodge's tragedy, and it is possible that this came to her from dead-Hodgson or dead-Myers. However, there is the possibility that Mrs Piper's psychic abilities included precognition, and she may simply have attributed her own perception to 'Hodgson' to give it authority.

What encourages us to think it may have been precognition on the medium's part is the imprecise character of the warning. This is typical of human premonitions, whereas we might think that Myers and Hodgson, if really anxious to help their friend, would forget about silly word-games and come out with something more explicitly helpful. Such a view was taken by one of Lodge's most thoughtful and sympathetic critics, Paul Hookham, who reviewing the case in 1917, thought it yet another testimony to 'the unexplored, unknown and limitless faculties of the human mind':

> It is shown again and again that mind communicates, certainly with mind

and possibly with matter, in a way which is incomprehensible to our normal senses and capacity of reasoning. In the presence of this unknown extension of mental faculties, any test of human survival by the display of knowledge and identity on the part of a dead person is impossible. The knowledge and characteristics may come from powers exerted by the medium to which, as they are to us incomprehensible, we have no justification in setting any limit.[111]

Everything we have learned since has confirmed our ignorance of what limits there may be to the powers of the human mind. But don't let us forget that even if we agree that it was *possible* for the information about Raymond to come from a source other than the dead, that doesn't mean it didn't: it means only that we have a choice.

The question of identity

There is very little about the 'Raymond' case which argues *against* the survival hypothesis. The worst we can say of it is that ultimately it fails to convince us. We shall find most other cases of spirit/medium communication, though they have satisfied spiritists aplenty, to be even less convincing.

Stainton Moses was one of the leading exponents of spiritism in England towards the end of the nineteenth century. His sincerity and integrity, to say nothing of his energy, are hardly to be questioned: what is less easy to admire is his uncritical acceptance — an acceptance shared by the thousands who read his classic *Spirit Teachings*, published under his *nom de plume* of 'M. A. Oxon' — of the marvels that happened to him.

Moses worked chiefly through automatic writing. His entranced hand was borrowed by Bible prophets (Elijah, Daniel, John the Baptist), sages and scholars (Plato, Aristotle, Linacre), musicians (Beethoven, Mendelssohn) and many more, including people he had known personally such as Bishop Samuel Wilberforce.[183] With such a galaxy of distinguished collaborators, as the not unsympathetic but hard-headed Father Thurston observed,

> we should expect passages of striking literary merit, or at least here and there some gem of inspired teaching which would satisfy the reader that he was in contact with intelligences of the highest order . . . The extracts seem to me to be characterised by a drab mediocrity which nowhere rises above the level which Moses himself turned out week after week in his leading articles.[252]

which leads him to question the improbability of the whole thing:

> Stainton Moses was, no doubt, an upright and honourable man of good education, but there was nothing remarkable about his intelligence or personal character. He inspired no enthusiasms. No one pretends that he left any perceptible stamp upon his pupils during his eighteen years as English Master at University College School. He must surely have been a little surprised that

the prophets and sages of antiquity were so interested in his spiritual development. The faith of the believer must be very robust who can persuade himself that for ten years a whole galaxy of Hebrew prophets, and sages both pagan and Christian, who have since then completely vanished from the Spiritualist horizon, concentrated their efforts upon the task of regenerating mankind through the mediumship of 'M. A. Oxon'.

Thurston's feelings are ones we shall frequently have occasion to share in the course of this study, for Moses was just one of many individuals who seem to be in no way specially qualified for their encounter with the Queen of Heaven, with the spirits of the eminent dead, or with the Supreme Beings of Inter-Galactic Parliament.

Communications from the famous dead would clearly be, if genuine, of special interest, so messages of this kind call for special scrutiny. The fact that the ostensible communicator is well-known should make it easier to evaluate the content and style of a message purporting to come from him; but the difficulties are well illustrated by the scripts which came allegedly from Oscar Wilde via a group of British psychics in 1923. Here is a characteristic passage:

> Being dead is the most boring experience in life; that is, if one excepts being married or dining with a schoolmaster. Do you doubt my identity? I am not surprised, since sometimes I doubt it myself. I might retaliate by doubting yours. I have always admired the Society for Psychical Research. They are the most magnificent doubters in the world. They are never happy until they have explained away their spectres; one suspects a genuine ghost would make them exquisitely uncomfortable.
>
> I have sometimes thought of founding an academy of celestial doubters, which might be a sort of Society for Psychical Research among the living. Our first object might well be to insist on investigating at once the reality of the existence of, say, Mr Dingwall [a leading British investigator and Research Officer for the S.P.R. about this time]. Mr Dingwall, is he romance or reality? Fact or fiction? Fortunately there are no facts over here. On earth we could scarcely escape them. Their dead carcasses were strewn everywhere on the rose path of life. One could not pick up a newspaper without learning something useful.[230]

If this is Wilde speaking, I think most of us would agree that he has carried with him beyond the grave both his personality and his manner of expression. If it is pastiche on the part of the psychics, it presupposes a notable combination of skills:

★ *cryptomnesia* (unconscious memory) of Wilde's way of speaking and use of words and mannerisms and choice of words. Inquiries established that though the psychics were naturally acquainted with Wilde's writings, they were not particularly fond of or interested in them. However, one of the psychics concerned was the noted researcher G. S. Soal, who 'took every prize for literature at school'.[252a]

> ★ the *creative ability* not only to rework the remembered material
> in a new form, but to do so in words and ideas appropriate to
> the circumstances. If Eric Dingwall was an unexpected visitor,
> then the extemporization is even more remarkable.

If all messages purporting to be from the eminent dead were of this
quality, the case for the survival hypothesis would be stronger.
Unfortunately, the Wilde scripts are some of the few of which their alleged
authors would not have been ashamed. We shall see most such claims
reveal little more than the ability to say extraordinarily little in an
extrordinarily large number of words, in no style whatever.

In some instances, we are puzzled by something worse still; the
information given is demonstrably *false*. The classic Conner case occurred
not in connection with an obscure or dubious medium, but the one who
perhaps of all mediums has earned the greatest respect, Leonore Piper,
whom William James described as 'my own white crow' who proved to
his satisfaction that not all crows need be black, that the psychic faculty
is a fact.

In 1894 a young American, Dean Bridgman Conner, went to Mexico
City. In March 1895 he died there of typhoid fever; his death and
subsequent burial in the American Cemetery were reported to his family
by the American consul.

Some months later, Conner appeared to his father in a dream, claiming
to be still alive, a captive being held for ransom by Mexican kidnappers.
Friends of the family arranged a sitting with Mrs Piper, taking some of
the young man's possessions. Her 'controls' confirmed the dream, even
indicating where he was being held prisoner, describing the building and
his captor. A succession of investigators was sent to investigate. One of
them eventually located the nurse who had been with Conner when he
died, and who confirmed the accuracy of the Consul's original report. [109]

It seems clear that Mrs Piper had psychically picked up the kidnap
story; it is equally clear that her 'controls' were either unable to distinguish
dream from reality, or were unscrupulous in allowing Conner's father
to nourish false hopes that his son was still alive.

If this were an isolated instance, we might overlook it as a momentary
'breakdown in communication'; but even spiritists accept that in every
seance there is an admixture of incorrect information. They have of course
found ways of accounting for this, just as Stainton Moses found ways
of stifling any doubts he may have felt that he was in touch with Beethoven
or as Victor Hugo allowed himself to be convinced that he was receiving
fresh material from Goethe and Shakespeare. [184]

The frequent untruthfulness of the spirits is good reason to doubt the
authenticity of any communication purporting to come from beyond the
grave. But we must not forget that alongside the false statements are many
that contain *true* information. Any alternative explanation must account
for both the true and the false.

A case occurred in 1921 which throws some light on what is really happening when a psychic claims to be in contact with the spirits. Blanche Cooper, a well-known medium, had in the course of a seance made some factual statements which were capable of being checked. Dr Soal of the Society for Psychical Research (who, incidentally, had been involved in the Wilde scripts) went to the area indicated, and returned with further information, which was confirmed by Cooper at the next seance. After this had happened three times, Soal noted that Cooper was doing little more than confirming his findings or reflecting his own ideas.

He decided to test this by inventing some wholly imaginary findings, choosing at random a house in the indicated district and giving its owner a fictitious name. At the next seance, Cooper's communications made it clear that her spirits had been quite taken in by Soal's inventions, feeding his fabrications back to him. He adds:

> The stories which the sitter suggests to his unconscious mind should be plausible and not such as would conflict with the statements given by the communicator at the previous sittings. In my own case I actually came to half believe the things I had supposed, and had a sort of desperate hope that they might turn out to be facts after all. [232]

Note that though the spirits come badly out of this case, the medium emerges with honour, for she certainly demonstrated her ability to acquire information from Soal's mind by psychic means. That the information was false does not diminish her feat, rather the contrary, for it shows that she could not have obtained the information by any other means.

The abilities required to bring about a seeming encounter with the dead, whether the spirits are responsible or those abilities are subconsciously possessed by the medium himself, have never been more remarkably displayed than in the Cummins/Willett case, known — from one of its more picturesque images — as the 'Swan on a Black Sea' case.

Geraldine Cummins was a private medium of high reputation, who worked through automatic writing. In 1957 she was asked if she would try to obtain messages on behalf of a son who wished to contact his mother (who had died the previous year); she was given no further details.

She soon found herself receiving messages from an entity who after a few sessions could be clearly identified as a Mrs Coombe-Tennant (1874–1956), who had been a noted public figure as well as having a wide circle of friends among the social and political establishment. This meant that her character, views, attitudes and mannerisms were widely known, not simply — as is usually the case — to members of her own family.

In addition, she had been connected by marriage to the psychical researcher Myers, and through him had been in contact with a wide circle of people such as the Balfours and Lytteltons who were involved in psychical research early in the twentieth century. She herself had taken up automatic writing, and had been one of the group through whom the obscurely impressive 'cross-correspondence' communications were obtained.

The messages which Cummins received purportedly from Mrs Coombe-Tennant are remarkable in many respects:

★ they are coherent and intelligent;

★ they contain not the usual vague ambiguities but many checkable facts such as names and dates;

★ they contain no demonstrably untrue statements beyond the casual errors we might reasonably expect;

★ they are consistently in the manner of the alleged speaker, and express her views, as family and friends testify;

★ they mix thoughtful reminiscence about the past with perceptive comment on the present, implying an up-to-date view of events which cannot be explained by dredging from the communicator's memory at the time of her death.

It is virtually impossible to provide a representative sample, because it is the overall effect which is so impressive. This quotation illustrates the personal quality of the messages:

> A friend was telling me that I was very French in my manner and appearance. I took it as a pretty compliment — she meant it as the reverse of one — and warmly embraced her. Oh! she was so taken aback . . . But the intended gibe temporarily gave real reassurance, as I was painfully conscious of the disfigurement of being very stout! But Frenchwomen have an air, a *je ne sais quoi*, that has always seemed to me admirable. If you would know me, Geraldine Cummins, you have to be introduced to this *vain* young lady, however trivial now seems to me her self-conscious concern about the redundancy of her figure.[36]

In his preface to the published scripts, the philosopher C. D. Broad considered the possibility that Cummins might have 'created' the communicator: 'There is, undoubtedly, some independent evidence for the existence, in some few persons, of remarkable creative and dramatizing powers, which reveal themselves *only* when their possessor is in a dissociated state.' But Cummins would have had to possess not only the telepathic and clairvoyant powers necessary to obtain the information, but the creative and dramatic abilities necessary to present it in the style and manner of the communicator. And because he doubted whether there was evidence that anyone had ever combined those gifts, he concluded:

> Much the simplest and most plausible hypothesis *prima facie* is that Mrs Coombe-Tennant, or some part or aspect of her, survived the death of her

body on August 31, 1956; that she was still actively in existence as late as March 6, 1960; and that during that period she from time to time controlled, directly or indirectly, the pen of the automatist Geraldine Cummins.

In principle we cannot quarrel with this tentative and balanced judgment. However, I think it possible that our comparative study, by widening the range of cases examined, may show that remarkable powers of information-retrieval on the one hand, and of creative dramatization on the other, are less rare than Broad supposed.

Finally, we should note that Cummins herself was by no means committed to the survival hypothesis. 'I have never been controlled by an alien mind,' she wrote. 'Mine has never been a case of *possession* by another mind. I am as a stenographer taking down words from dictation and employing as it were an inner hearing . . . Whether the contents of my scripts are transmitted to me by a subconscious or unconscious mind or a discarnate communicator, that is for others than myself to judge.'

Though most spiritists accept the phenomena at face value, a few mediums, like Geraldine Cummins, have questioned the source of their communications, while the more intelligent researchers have recognized that commitment to belief would be premature; thus Lodge, commenting on Mrs Piper, considered that her 'control' might be either:

★ merely a personation of Mrs Piper's subliminal consciousness; or

★ a telepathic influence from living persons acting upon that consciousness; or

★ really some surviving influence of the departed intelligence who is the ostensible communicator.[232]

Another researcher who agonized over the alternatives was Professor William James, who accepted the memory and dramatization skills displayed by a Mrs Piper, but could not bring himself to accept 'that such an immense current of experience should spell out absolutely nothing but the words "intentional humbug".'[232]

It seems to me, though, that James is here rather begging the question with his 'intentional humbug', for it is surely possible that intentions rather more obscure than those which show on the surface may be at work; and what is 'humbug' to one man may convey a concealed meaning to another. The content of most mediumistic utterances, while rubbishy enough, is no more so than that of, say, the dream I had last night. Yet that dream was the creation of my subconscious mind. If that mind, which I believe to be a highly sophisticated instrument regulating my life in ways my conscious mind can't begin to understand, can occupy itself with the production of nonsense in the bedroom, surely it can also do so in the seance room?

So Professor James, unwilling to believe that it is all 'humbug' feels constrained to conclude: 'The notion that so many men and women in all other respects honest enough, should have this preposterous monkeying self annexed to their personality seems to me so weird that the spirit-theory immediately takes on a more probable appearance.' Amusingly enough, somewhat similar reflections impelled his fellow countryman, the author Nathaniel Hawthorne, towards a contrary conclusion. Commenting on the most celebrated of all spirit mediums, Daniel Dunglass Home, he wrote in 1858:

> Spirits, I suppose, like earthly people, are obliged to use such instruments as will answer their purposes; but rather than receive a message from a dead friend through the organism of a rogue or charlatan, methinks I would choose to wait until we meet. But what astonishes me most is the indifference with which I listen to these marvels. They throw old ghost-stories quite into the shade; they bring the whole world of spirits down amongst us, visibly and audibly; they are absolutely proved to be sober facts by evidence that would satisfy us of any other alleged realities; and yet I cannot force my mind to interest myself in them. They are facts to my understanding, but not to my intuitions and deeper perceptions. My inner soul does not in the least admit them; there is a mistake somewhere. [105]

If I am accused of scrabbling desperately to find a reason, *any* reason, not to accept the spiritist's claims, I could reply that I am in good company. It is evident that Lodge and James, despite their ultimate acceptance, were bothered by many aspects of the survival evidence. We have seen that Father Thurston was disinclined to accept Stainton Moses' communications, not on the doctrinal grounds we might have expected of a Jesuit, but on commonsense grounds. We have seen that Geraldine Cummins was anything but sure where her communications came from, and another most respected medium, Eileen Garrett, was equally uncertain 'whether the controls are the separate entities they profess to be, or whether they are "splits" of my own personality. They may well be parts of my own mind, but raised to a level where they operate outside the laws of cause and effect that dominate normal daily existence.' [90]

The evidence that something paranormal occurs in many cases of alleged spirit communication is, I would say, beyond question. But even those who accept this, even those who are most sympathetic to the spiritist claims, even those who allow themselves to be convinced by them, will never quite lose Hawthorne's feeling that 'there is a mistake somewhere'.

I hope that, before we reach the end of our inquiry, we shall have a clearer idea where and what that mistake may be.

3.4 ENCOUNTERS WITH DARK FORCES

We see that many, despite what the mediums and the alleged communicators themselves say, are reluctant to take alleged encounters with spirits of the dead at face value. Mostly their reluctance reflects commonsense doubts, but there are others who reject the claims because they conflict with their beliefs. These go further than simple doubt, for their beliefs also enable them to specify alternative explanations of what is happening.

Since the entities themselves claim to be spirits of the dead, it follows that if they are *not* spirits of the dead, they are lying. So every one of these alternative models presupposes entities which are deceitful, if not downright malevolent. If they agree on nothing else, the various religious and occultist approaches are unanimous in attributing these phenomena to 'Dark Forces' of one kind or another.

We have already seen that most religious systems embody the notion of an evil force, and most versions of Christianity have opposed spiritism as nothing more than parleying with the devil. However, the notion of some kind of autonomous malevolent entity spreads wider than formal religious doctrine.

Ralph Allison, an American psychiatrist who has been particularly involved with multiple personality cases, recently stated his belief that at least some of the secondary (he employs the term 'alter') personalities into which the patient's personality fragments may be *not* part of the patient himself, but invading entities:

> The alter personality serves a definite and practical purpose — it is a means of coping with an emotion or situation that the patient cannot handle. The discovery of an entity who doesn't serve any recognisable purpose presents a diagnostic problem. Interestingly enough, such entities often refer to themselves as spirits. Over the years I've encountered too many such cases to dismiss the possibility of spirit possession completely.[7]

He identifies a series of grades of possession: apart from two 'subjective' grades . . .

> Grade III possession occurs when the controlling influence seems to be the mind of another living human being. Grade IV possession is control by the spirit of another human being. Grade V possession is control by a spirit that

has never had its own life history and identifies itself as an agent of evil.

Allison cites cases from his own professional experience which seem to belong in each of his categories, and his experience-based logic is irrefutable. But as we shall see when later we examine it in more detail, the process of personality dissociation offers well-nigh unlimited scope for precisely the qualities of creative dramatization and improvization which we have seen may be involved in encounters with the dead. So if for no other reason, we must, while respecting Dr Allison's experience, entertain the possibility that the same forces which may have helped Geraldine Cummins in her apparent communication with Mrs Coombe-Tennant are at work in these apparent cases of spirit possession.

Are these forces the 'Dark Forces' of the theologians and occultists? In a 1906 book entitled *The Dangers of Spiritualism*, [205] J. Godfrey Raupert gives us a detailed and alarming account of how he came across a young man who possessed 'psychic' powers, which led to ostensible communication with a former acquaintance of the young man's, now dead through suicide after some shady business dealings.

Despite many corroborative details and a personality presentation almost in the Coombe-Tennant class, Raupert found sufficient contradictions to conclude that the communicating entity was *not* the spirit of the dead businessman. Forcing the issue, he courageously confronted the entity with these contradictions. This led initially to an apparent retreat, but the entity returned to plague the young man with paranormal events of an alarming character, described with remarkable precision by Raupert who had invited his friend to take refuge in his own home:

> I retired about twelve o'clock and must have been asleep quite an hour and a half when I was suddenly startled by a noise like that of hammering. Slipping into my dressing gown and hurrying downstairs, I found my friend partially dressed, pacing up and down his bedroom. I became the witness of a scene such as I have never witnessed before, and as will not be effaced from my memory for many a day.
>
> A hundred hands seemed to be hammering away on walls and doors and table and bed, and every now and then there was the sound of feet tramping along the floor. Nothing that we said or did seemed to have the slightest effect upon the authors or causes of the strange phenomenon, and both my companion and myself simply sat on the bed in a state of helplessness and bewilderment.
>
> When I had explained matters to my wife, and had offered some sort of explanation to the female servants, who were sleeping on the same floor and who had been startled by the noises, I returned to spend the rest of the night with my distracted friend.
>
> Sitting in that spirit-haunted room, and listening to the noises which were disturbing the household and which we could not control, there seemed at that moment nothing so ludicrous as the sceptical attitude of the conventional man of science, who denied the objectivity of the phenomenon. Ten minutes

in that little bedroom would infallibly have blown his scientific theories to the winds. It seemed as though the very rabble of the unseen world had been let loose in order to exhibit the power of its malice and its impotent rage.

Raupert found the inference that some masquerading and malevolent entity was responsible as hard to avoid as Allison finds in his multiple personality cases. Raupert is intelligent enough to give serious consideration to the sceptical view, that such phenomena 'may be attributed to the action of his own submerged and hitherto but very little understood personality', but finds it inadequate.

And indeed we must ask, is there any more adequate way of accounting for such phenomena than attributing them to encounters with malevolent discarnate spirits? After all, every religious and occultist belief system in every culture has found it necessary to presume their existence. I have a shelf full of books by churchmen warning me of the dangers of trafficking with these dark forces, and as many books by occultists who don't always take such a negative view. Is it simply a question of choosing between the two — on the one hand, evil entities who will pounce on us if we give them half a chance, and on the other, some hidden, primitive force within ourselves which, when something dislodges the lid, escapes our control and runs amok?

I propose that we entertain the possibility that these two scenarios are not so distinct as they seem.

I suggest we consider that there may be a part of each one of us which, if it gets the chance and feels the inclination, can break loose and run wild, thumbing its nose at the rest of us. The chance to escape may come directly from a physical cause, as Dr Jekyll's potion gave Mr Hyde a chance to dissociate himself from his inhibiting companion; or it may result from a breakdown in our normal power of control, due to some conflict or crisis which fragments our holistic self. Either way, it manifests in the apparent form of a more or less autonomous being, whose motivations are so different from ours as to explain Ralph Allison's entity who doesn't serve any recognizable purpose', and whose behaviour is so primitive as to occasion displays such as plagued Raupert's friend.

Such a model seems to account plausibly enough for the many thousands of such cases, without requiring us to subscribe to any specific belief system. But it does not eliminate the question of belief altogether. For one feature recurs in all these cases, which is of the greatest significance for our study: *these manifestations rarely, if ever, occur unless the individual believes they can occur.*

Provisionally, then, we are faced with a choice between these two scenarios:

1   Certain discarnate entities do actually exist, permanently and autonomously. However, being parasites with no means of upkeep of their own, they are not able to manifest unless they can obtain the support

of the subconscious mind of an individual. Such support is of course not usually forthcoming; but if the mind's normal healthy state is unbalanced by a personal crisis, or by drugs or some such physical cause, it is powerless to prevent the entity borrowing or creating a secondary personality and drawing from the individual the energy it needs to work with. These entities are not necessarily malevolent, but are sufficiently primitive in their desires and motives to appear malevolent to the dismayed host, who watches the entity's actions with unrecognizing alarm, quite unaware that he is indirectly responsible for providing the entity with the means of existence.

2   The subconscious mind of the individual, if unbalanced by personal crisis or some physical cause such as drugs, uses its creative and dramatic powers to create imaginary encounters with an imaginary entity. These encounters express his fears and worries, and the entities are derived from his beliefs (which are not necessarily consciously held; they could equally well be a hangover from childhood which he thinks he has totally outgrown). As a civilized being, he fails to recognize these hidden aspects of himself, and finds it easier to believe that the entity he encounters originates outside himself.

If we consider only the kind of phenomena encountered by Dr Allison in his consulting room or Mr Raupert in that terrifying bedroom, I dare say we might regard the first of these options as most consistent with the events. But when we set them alongside other cases of different kinds, we shall find that the second option is not only viable but consistent with a wider spectrum of human experience.

Instead of hypothesizing malevolent entities for whose existence the evidence is only circumstantial, we may find it easier to believe that the only 'Dark Forces' are those which exist within ourselves.

3.5 COMMENTS ON PART THREE

The long-standing and widely held belief that the dead not only survive on some other level of reality but also contact the living and occasionally revisit us is a seemingly logical inference from certain events. Of these, the most impressive are the alleged encounters with spirits of the dead.

If these experiences are what they seem to be, it would be proof certain that survival is a fact. This is so very much what many people *wish*, that we must take that wish into account when evaluating the evidence they accept in support of that belief. At the same time, it is so very much what another large class of people wish *not* to believe, that we must also take *their* wish into account. In short, if we hope to arrive at a balanced estimate of the matter, we must contend not only with the inherent difficulties of the subject, but also with the efforts (not necessarily deliberate) of those who seek to influence our judgement by:

★ using irrelevant evidence which supports their position;

★ ignoring or dismissing evidence which argues against their position;

★ misinterpreting evidence in favour of their position;

★ offering unverifiable explanations for the negative evidence.

Irrelevant evidence
Much of the evidence regarded as supporting the survival hypothesis is in the form of physical feats and marvels, but in fact these are irrelevant to the survival claim, whether or not they occur. While it is possible that they are caused by the spirits, understandably anxious to demonstrate their existence, they could equally well be attributed to human powers, albeit powers such as psychokinesis which are as yet not recognized by science. (In many cases, of course, more mundane explanations will suffice.)

Another category of evidence, the seemingly paranormal acquisition of information, is similarly irrelevant so long as we are willing to accept the existence of psi-communication (ESP). Often, indeed, there is no need to invoke even ESP, since cryptomnesia and other known psychological processes may be responsible for the seemingly remarkable feats.

Ignoring and dismissing evidence

Many a witness who claims to have encountered the dead is able to produce information which it does not seem possible he could have obtained by any means recognized by science; for example, he may be able to describe correctly what someone whose apparition appeared to him simultaneously with her death was wearing at the time.

Those who favour a purely psychological model for the encounter experience will question, and rightly, the evidence that such information has been obtained paranormally. Often they show it to be dubious, sometimes downright false. But where the evidence stands up to rigorous investigation, we have no right to set it aside. Our doubts do not relieve us of the responsibility of accounting for what seems to the witness, rightly or wrongly, to be a good reason for believing he had an encounter with the dead.

Misinterpreting evidence

Anyone who has attended a 'psychic demonstration' is familiar with the ambiguity which arises when more than one witness claims an entity as their own, or reads into the medium's words their own interpretation. These are the most blatant examples of wish-to-believe at work.

We shall see later in this study, when we consider the question of motivation, how complex a part may be played on many levels by the witness' hopes, fears and expectations. In the case of encounters with the dead, there are also the motivations of the medium to be taken into account, and sometimes also those of the investigator.

Unverifiable explanations

Just as theologians recognize with regret the occurrence of false visions, but ascribe them to Satan, so spiritists acknowledge the manifestation of 'false communicators' but explain them as 'lying spirits'. They may be right, but this has the feel of an *ad hoc* explanation, conjured up to account for an awkward phenomenon. In the absence of any independent evidence we must regard the existence of 'lying spirits' as no more than speculative.

Unfortunately, spiritism is plagued with awkwardnesses of this kind for which its champions have to work hard to find explanations. Often these are plausible enough, but it needs more than plausibility for us to accept the spiritists' explanations as to why the spirits favour long white robes, darkened seance rooms, and sitters who sing and indulge in other noisy manifestations. These things tend to discourage our belief. When they are said to be the expressed wishes of the spirits, they tend to discourage our belief in the spirits.

4.1 ENCOUNTERS WITH EXTRATERRESTRIALS

People have been claiming to encounter their gods throughout recorded history; they have been claiming to encounter spirits of the dead for almost as long. But only recently have they begun to claim encounters with beings from elsewhere in the universe.

Not surprisingly, therefore, it is the least widespread and the least studied of our three categories. There are still many cultures on our planet which are unaware that the human race has entered the 'Space Age'. True, you don't have to know that Space Beings exist in order to be visited by them, but if you don't know that such beings exist you may mistake them for something else. This was graphically demonstrated by a study which French researcher Bertrand Méheust conducted among the villagers of Gabon, who when shown pictures of a typical 'UFO landing' interpreted the aliens as mineral prospectors or American spacemen.[171]

Nevertheless, though the epoch of extraterrestrial encounters more or less commenced with the Age of the Flying Saucer — that is, subsequent to 1947 — the number of people claiming such encounters is already very substantial, and the associated literature testifies to their abundance as well as to their impact. Though the majority of us are probably unaware even of its existence, extraterrestrial contact now constitutes a subculture as significant as that of visions of the Virgin Mary, and there has been time not only for the fabrication of stereotypes but also for them to develop in complexity and sophistication. Furthermore, a number of retrospective cases have been reported, where witnesses now reveal experiences they claim they had prior to the present period, which at the time, like the Gabon villagers, they were unable to recognize, but which they now realize must have been extraterrestrial encounters.

UFOs have received no scientific investigation worthy of the name apart from a few sociological studies directed at 'UFO cults' rather than at the phenomenon *per se*. However, the subject has attracted the dedicated interest of many hundreds of serious researchers, as well as the less critical enthusiasm of many thousands more. At its best, ufology has achieved a respectably high standard of both documentation and interpretation.

Widespread ignorance of the subject has led to a variety of sceptical attitudes. For some, ufology is little more than space-age religion, for others it is an updated version of the age-old flight from reality; for some it is do-it-yourself science fiction, for others a pseudo-science more exciting and less demanding than the genuine article. Each of these attitudes can be partially justified by certain manifestations on the part of those who involve themselves with the phenomenon, but each is totally inadequate to account for the phenomenon itself.

In this study, however, it is not with the phenomenon itself that we are concerned, only with alleged encounters with alien beings. For the witness, his experience is part and parcel of the UFO phenomenon. We may or may not come to agree with him, but since he makes that claim, we must be aware of the UFO phenomenon, and what it means to him, before we attempt to evaluate what he tells us. Even if the 'extraterrestrial encounter phenomenon', should turn out to have no essential place in the 'UFO phenomenon', we must still be aware of the cultural context involved; for this it is which enables the encounter witness to give his experience a label and a meaning, and which may, in addition, provide him, or whoever is responsible for staging his encounter, with the necessary script and props.

Contact experiences, flying saucers and UFOs

Whatever interpretation we put upon the synchronicity, it is patently significant that the current wave of contact experiences coincided with the first tentative explorations of the cosmos by the inhabitants of Earth. What encourages a sociological explanation is that such previous contacts as have been reported *also* coincided with an era of intense interest in extraterrestrial matters. We shall study this finding, clearly of the greatest significance for our study, before we turn our attention to today's ET encounter experiences.

Equally significant is the fact that contact claims escalated, after a natural time-lag, following the 1947 sighting by American pilot Kenneth Arnold of a number of fast-moving objects which he was unable to identify with any terrestrial aircraft.[64] Ironically, when the first contact claims were made, it was the serious UFO investigators who refused to give them a serious hearing.[259] Since then, the question of the connection has remained ambiguous. On the one hand, it seems obvious that if people are encountering entities who come to earth in their spacecraft, those spacecraft may well be the objects which the ufologists are so woefully failing to identify. On the other hand, the incredibility of most contactee accounts does seem incompatible with any attempt to formulate a scientific evaluation of the UFO phenomenon.

Moreover, while it is possible that both the contactees' entities and the ufologists' UFOs are of extraterrestrial origin, it is no less possible that *neither* of them are! There is no hard evidence to support the extraterrestrial hypothesis for UFOs, and, as we shall shortly see, there are many reasons for doubting that the beings who purport to be alien visitors are what they claim to be.

What *is* clear is that over the past forty years there have appeared among us many thousands of people who claim to have had encounters with beings not of this Earth. If true, this is arguably the most important thing that has happened in the history of mankind. At the very least, if so many people have been afflicted with the same delusion, this is a social phenomenon which warrants study.

Because the advent of the 'age of the contactee' coincided so closely with the start of the 'space age' it is easy to see the first as a cultural artefact resulting from the second. When Jung titled his landmark study of Flying Saucers 'a modern myth of things seen in the sky'[126] he saw the new phenomenon as a direct psychological consequence of man's new preoccupation with space. That this is a substantial part of the truth cannot be questioned; what *can* be questioned is the nature of that cause-and-effect. For there is considerable plausibility in what the alien visitors themselves say, that it is *because* of our Space Age that they have started to take an interest (or a *renewed* interest, or a *closer* interest) in Earth.

ETs and humanity

Virtually no theologians, and only a handful of psychical researchers, have considered the cosmic contactee as worthy of serious attention. Behavioural scientists have taken an interest in the cult aspects of the UFO phenomenon, but few have considered the human implications in any broad sense. (With a few honourable exceptions[100,226,235]).

If any such person is reading these pages, I hope that what you read here will encourage you to take a closer look at the sort of thing that is happening to a remarkably large number of people in our world today. To pick out almost at random just one such person from the many hundreds, consider Judie Woolcott:

Judie is a 48-year-old mother of five who runs a cake catering business in Wisconsin. She is also a leading member of the Fox Valley UFO Discussion and Support Group, whose dozen members have been meeting twice a month for eleven years. They possess a library, they subscribe to a newsclipping service, they put out a local access cablevision programme.

Judie saw her first UFO in St Petersburg, Florida, in 1958. She has photographed one, and once had a 30 cm hologram of a UFO in her kitchen, which she interpreted as a 'thank you' sign in appreciation of her sympathetic interest. 'I'm trying to tell people about the space brothers and what they are trying to do for man,' she told an interviewer in 1985, 'and they are trying to turn around and do something for me. It's as if they are guardian angels.'

She sees UFOs fairly frequently: 'I saw nine last week in Canada, high-flyers, mother-craft high up in the atmosphere.' They travel, she explains, on 'free electromagnetic energy'. How does she know this? 'Some things you just know.'

In 1986, in the course of hypnotherapy sessions, she and fellow member Bonnie Meyer discovered that they have been abducted six times together, and each of them once separately. Judie also learned that in the course of one of her abductions implants were inserted behind her ears. The operation was extremely painful, and sometimes she hears 'static' in her ears, or buzzing sounds that persist for hours. She believes that her abductors use the implants to force-feed information into her brain for future use. 'I'm not supposed to understand yet. We are being taught to help the people of Earth. We are being taught to be teachers. When the time is right, the information is there. I don't have the faintest idea what it is.'

Judie is a Catholic, and compares her association with UFOs to a religious experience. 'There's a certain feeling with seeing a UFO. A warm, tender feeling. I don't want it to sound like we worship UFOs, but there is a feeling that goes with seeing a craft . . . I attend church every Sunday. The more you study UFOs, the more religious you get, the more contact with God and nature you get.'[271]

The discovery that they had been abducted was an alarming event. 'I said, "Oh, my God, we really were aboard a spacecraft". It's one thing to say it, but it's another to find out that it's true.' Her attitude to the space aliens, none the less, reflects the general consensus among contactees that their encounters are purposeful and benevolent. This view is shared by many ufologists: Italy's Roberto Pinotti, for example, suggests that the ETs plan an induced or programmed mutation of our species[196] while Spain's Pedro Quinones insists that UFOs are neither physical spacecraft on the one hand nor subjective hallucination on the other, but devices fashioned from the ideas of the witness, operating on an esoteric plane to guide us into the higher level of understanding which is the next step in human development.[202]

Whether as programmers of our species and teachers of higher development, or simply as guardian angels, it is evident that the ET entities have found a role to play in the lives of thousands of our fellow humans. Or should we rather say that thousands of our fellow humans have found a role for the entities to play? Perhaps their reports of their experiences will enable us to decide whether our Earth is indeed being watched over and visited by Cosmic Guardians.

4.2 ENCOUNTERS WITH MARTIANS

Those who seek to establish a respectable lineage for the UFO phenomenon have been able to locate no lack of historical instances of people failing to identify flying objects from classical and biblical times to the present day.[52, 269] Whether these are in any way related to the contemporary phenomenon is less certain. In any case, few of these early reports contain anything which could be construed as an encounter with extraterrestrial beings.

Serious claims for such encounters do not occur before the eighteenth century, and even then they are sporadic and ambiguous. The Swedish mystic Emanuel Swedenborg wrote: 'It has been granted me to converse not only with the spirits and angels who are near the earth, but also with those that are near other earths, with some for a day, with some for a week, and with some for months.'[248]

Though he admits he saw them 'not with my bodily eyes, but with the eyes of the spirit', this did not make them any the less real for Swedenborg; it may, however, diminish his claim in others' eyes. He described the inhabitants of each planet in our solar system as well as in others, and also of the moon, but so improbably that, whether or not they encouraged belief in his teachings, it is doubtful if they encouraged belief in extraterrestrial life.

The German physician Joseph Ennemoser, writing in 1843, tells us he had a clairvoyant subject who, under hypnosis, gave descriptions of life on Mars which more or less agreed with those of Swedenborg, though her descriptions of Martians are very different from his. The interest for us is that she should describe them at all.[56]

Scientific discussion of the possibility of extraterrestrial life grew more frequent as the nineteenth century advanced, and this was reflected in popular literature. The science fiction of the period included many stories of earthpeople's voyages in space or spacepeople's visits to Earth. Fantasy fiction such as Verne's *De la terre à la lune* (1865) and H. G. Wells' *War of the Worlds* (1896) along with speculative articles by respected scientists like the French astronomer Flammarion, directed public interest toward the stars. It is against this background that we must picture the first claims of extraterrestrial encounters.

From India to the Planet Mars

The case of Catherine Elise Muller (1861–1929), better known by her pseudonym of 'Hélène Smith', is revealing not only by its wealth of detail but also because it was subjected to prolonged study by the eminent Swiss psychologist Théodore Flournoy.

Hélène was a non-professional spirit medium whose evident psychic gifts were brought to Flournoy's attention by one of her sitters. This led to a friendship which enabled him to give us a detailed and intimate account of the workings of her mind. He found that her psychic experiences took the form of prolonged and circumstantial sagas in which she displayed remarkable mental faculties. What was it, he wondered, which stimulated Hélène to have these imaginary adventures? Why should they take the form of complex sagas? And why should the most striking of them involve visits to Mars?

He learned that Hélène was one of those who believe they were 'born for better things':

> It was a case of a protest of idealism against grey reality, an inaccessible refuge whither, on the wings of dream, the individual flies, hoping to escape the thousand and one discouragements of the prosaic every-day . . . everything we know about her character, both as a child and as a young woman, shows us that the emotional note which dominated her was that of an instinctive internal revolt against the humdrum surroundings in which fate had caused her to be born.[77]

It even reached the point where Hélène seriously questioned her parents whether she was really and truly their child. Couldn't the nurse have brought home another child one day from their afternoon walk?

Flournoy learnt that, when Hélène's younger sister died, their mother had had a mysterious vision of an angel. There seemed to be some kind of hereditary disposition towards psychic experiences. Throughout her childhood Hélène was subject to hallucinations, visions and premonitions. At the same time she was physically healthy, even robust; she was popular despite her retiring temperament; she was bright and intelligent, and had a responsible office job. Nor did she regard her psychic powers and subsequent mediumship as in any way pathological, a view which Flournoy shared.

When family friends, knowing of her psychic powers, introduced her to spiritism, she took to it readily, and quickly became the central figure of a private circle. Characteristically her earliest 'controls' were romantic figures like Victor Hugo and Cagliostro. Flournoy saw these as 'try-outs' for the more complex sagas which followed.

It seems to have been a chance remark by one of the sitters that triggered Hélène's Martian adventures. A M. Lemaître, after reading Flammarion's prediction that 'Martian humankind and Earth humankind may one day enter into communication one with the other', expressed a hope that this would come about. When Hélène started to recount her Martian adventures, one of her first remarks was 'Lemaître, here is what you wanted so much!'

Hélène could be described as a 'multi-medium', for beside her formal séances she had all kinds of other psychic experiences, some while sleeping, some when awake, each of them liable to produce some new revelation or recollection of life on Mars — the houses, the gardens, the customs. It was anything but an ordered account, which led Flournoy to the conclusion that *there was a part of Hélène which was 'living' her Martian experience every moment of the day and night* — a conclusion which I emphasize for its profound implications for our analysis of the encounter process later in this study.

It seems that whenever Hélène passed, as it were, into the 'psychic mode', she switched from her Earth existence to her Martian existence. For example, one night in September 1896 she was wakened from sleep by a high wind, and was alarmed for some flowers she had set out on the window sill. After rescuing them, instead of going back to sleep, she sat on her bed looking out — except that now her bed was a bench beside a Martian lake, whose pinkish-blue waters were spanned by a bridge whose edges were transparent . . . and so on. She watched the scene for nearly half an hour, during which time she was convinced that she was awake, not sleeping.

Although Hélène supplied much detailed information about Mars, this was always incidental to the on-going relationship she kept up with her Martian friends. It was in this way that her knowledge of the Martian language revealed itself in scattered fragments, not as a coherent exposition. However, the scraps which emerged in this piecemeal manner were nevertheless part of a consistent and organized structure, with a coherent syntax and the kind of patterns we would expect a language to display. Flournoy was able to show that Hélène's 'Martian' was in fact a pseudo-language based on French, but this makes her achievement if anything more remarkable; for it means that she had created, rapidly and with no conscious effort, a new language which she assimilated so perfectly that ever afterwards she could use it as consistently and faultlessly as her own.

Remarkable as Hélène's account is, there is clearly no question of her having a real encounter with extraterrestrials. If her case is important to our study, it is for purposes of comparison. We shall find it helpful to keep in mind, when considering other encounter claims, the most extraordinary creative abilities displayed by the subconscious mind of Hélène Smith.

Messages from Mars

In 1895 a Mrs Smead, wife of an American clergyman, began to receive some extraordinary psychic messages. She had had many kinds of previous psychic experience, some spontaneous, such as seeing apparitions, others deliberate, such as spirit communication via the planchette (a device to facilitate automatic writing), which she had practised since childhood. But these latest messages were different from anything she had previously experienced.

The alleged communicators were her three deceased children, and her husband's brother, likewise no longer living. Almost from the start their messages contained references to the planets, and daughter Maude, asked where she was now, replied 'Some spirits are on the Earth and some are on other worlds.' Five weeks later, her brother reported that Maude and their uncle had gone to Mars, while another sister spoke of Jupiter as 'the babies' heaven' to which those who die in infancy are taken because they are 'better than grown-up people'.

Maude was able to describe her new home on Mars in some detail, though still on a very simple level. She supplied a map which confirmed that the 'canals of Mars' were indeed, as American astronomer Percival Lowell had proposed, artifically constructed by the Martians. This was the theme of much debate at the time, and indeed articles on the subject had appeared that very year in *The Atlantic Monthly*: the Smeads however claimed not to have seen them.

For some reason the sittings were abandoned for five years. Remarkably, when they were resumed, so were the messages from Mars, as though there had been no interruption. Further details were provided, and a rudimentary language quoted from, though never in anything like the detail of Hélène's. In the view of the eminent researcher James Hyslop, who was invited by the Smeads to assess the communications, they originated with a secondary personality of Mrs Smead:

> We find in such cases evidence that we need not attribute fraud to the normal consciousness, and we discover automatic processes of *mentation* that may be equally acquitted of fraudulent intent; while we are also free from the obligation to accept the phenomena at their assumed value. Their most extraordinary characteristic is the extent to which they imitate the organising intelligence of a normal mind, and the perfection of their impersonation of spirits, always betraying their limitations, however, just at the point where we have the right to expect veridical testimony to their claims. [116]

That Mrs Smead in the United States and Hélène Smith in Switzerland should independently produce communications so similar in theme is particularly interesting for our study. Clearly, in each case the choice of theme reflects public interest in the subject; but that is only part of the explanation. We must look also for some element in each of these ladies which responded to that public interest — another aspect of the encounter experience which we shall consider in greater detail later in this study.

The star-dweller on the Zurich train
In 1899 the Swiss psychologist Carl Jung had as a patient a Miss S. W. (whom I propose to baptize 'Sophie' rather than use his inhuman initials).

Sophie was a 15½-year-old Protestant girl whose family history contained many relatives who had experienced hallucinations and other visionary experiences, somnambulism, prophetic utterances, hysterical episodes and nervous heart-attacks. Her father died while she was still an adolescent, her mother was erratic and eccentric. Not surprisingly, Sophie's childhood was unhappy and disturbed. But though moody and often absent-minded and abstracted, she displayed no outwardly hysterical symptoms.

Like Hélène Smith, Sophie found a distraction from her unsatisfying home-life in spiritism; she too turned out to be an excellent medium. Even when not in trance she received visits from 'spirits' — 'shining white figures who detached themselves from the foggy brightness . . . wrapped in white veil-like robes . . .' — of whose reality, she told Jung, she was totally convinced:

> I do not know if what the spirits say and teach me is true, nor do I know if they really are the people they call themselves; but that my spirits exist is beyond question. I see them before me, I can touch them. I speak to them about everything I wish, as naturally as I'm talking to you. They *must* be real. [124]

Like Hélène, Sophie did not consider these experiences a sign of illness. She enjoyed the journeys to spirit worlds located in 'that space between the stars which people think is empty' which she made in trance, and she was able to bring back details about life on Mars. Her account was even less detailed than that provided by the Smead children, but she had one experience that neither Mrs Smead nor Hélène enjoyed:

> She once returned from a railway journey in an extremely agitated state. We thought at first that something unpleasant must have happened to her; but finally she pulled herself together and explained that 'a star-dweller had sat opposite her in the train'. From the description she gave of this being I recognised an elderly merchant I happened to know, who had a rather unsympathetic face.

Subsequently Sophie abandoned spiritism and got a job which she performed with skill and enthusiasm, while her character quietened down. Jung's diagnosis of the episode was that it reflected the breaking-through of her new adult personality, a process which externalized itself in this symbolic form. Here again, the interaction between personal motivation and the cultural context is graphically demonstrated.

Mireille and the electric fields

In 1895 — the same year that Mrs Smead had her first Martian messages — the French researcher Colonel de Rochas was asked to help a family friend. 'Mireille', a lady aged 45, had been known to him since childhood. Knowing that he used hypnosis to relieve suffering, she hoped he could help her with a troublesome ailment.

Mireille proved to be a good and willing subject, and in return for his (successful) therapy, was willing to co-operate with his experiments in hypnosis. It was in one such session that she described how she seemed to be rising through space, which she told him was brightly luminous, and peopled with 'phantoms'. Among these she noted a childhood friend Victor, who had been dead for ten years.

In subsequent sessions she revealed that she had paid further visits to Mars and other planets, though she was not able to provide much information beyond vague references to the canals which also figure in the Smith, Smead and Sophie communications. Then one day, instead of recounting her own experiences, she seemed to be taken over by Victor himself. He told de Rochas that he had nearly 'lost' Mireille, owing to the electric fields she had to penetrate in order to reach Mars.

From this time on, Victor used Mireille as his channel of communication on several occasions. The change in personality was very striking. Thus, de Rochas would normally hold Mireille's hand while she was in trance; but as soon as Victor took over, the hand was withdrawn. Though Mireille didn't smoke, Victor did; what puzzled him was why he was wearing female clothing.

Even Victor was not able to give much specific information about extraterrestrial life, though his affirmation that where he now lived it was the *arms* which are the organ of affection is original, at least. But what Victor failed to offer in the way of checkable facts, he made up for in the intelligent comments he made on his present state:

> One day I revealed to Victor my doubts as to the reality of his existence outside the imagination of Mireille. Happily, Victor replied, your doubts as to whether I exist don't prevent me existing! . . . You are mistaken if you think there is a profound difference between the world of the living and that of the dead, or any hiatus separating them. The spirit life continues beyond the tomb with no more transition than if, in the life of flesh, the inhabitants of a house being at first gathered in a ground-floor room dimly lit by narrow windows, a few should separate from the others and go upstairs to where the rooms are illuminated by daylight. [214]

Victor spoke eloquently in favour of his own existence:

> It's now several months since we started talking together about serious matters. You have seen that you can't find any error in what I say, and that if there's something I don't know, I freely admit it. If I was one of your earthly acquaintances, you wouldn't hesitate, I hope, to call me your friend and trust me; yet it wouldn't be my *body* you put your trust in, would it? So why not treat me in the same way, even though I have no body that you can see? I am sure you have earthly friends whose existence you never question, even though you know them only by the letters you exchange with them.

However, de Rochas retained his doubts. For him, as for Hyslop in the Smead case, Victor was no more than a secondary personality of Mireille.

This does not, of course, make the case any the less remarkable, or any the less instructive for the purpose of our study. Like each of the other cases we have looked at, it demonstrates the remarkable creative powers of the subconscious mind, and how effectively those powers may be harnessed to the needs of the individual. We shall now have to consider whether a similar process may be at work in our more recent encounter cases.

4.3 CONTACT ENCOUNTERS

In our own time, a time dominated by the concept of the exploration of space, a great many people are claiming to have had encounters with extraterrestrial beings (ETs), who have generally travelled to Earth in their spacecraft. These encounters take many forms, of which the most frequently reported are:

★ seemingly casual encounters with ETs near their spacecraft. (In some cases the existence of the spacecraft is not established, merely presumed);

★ seemingly casual encounters leading to temporary abduction of the witness on board the spacecraft, apparently for the purpose of physical examination or biological experiment, which may include copulation with an ET;

★ deliberate encounters between ETs and witnesses who have been selected for specific qualities, and who may be entrusted with a mission by the ETs;

★ communication with ETs by telepathy or via a medium in a psychic trance.

Any of the foregoing may lead to:

★ journeys on board the spacecraft, sometimes brief as though the ETs are displaying their powers, sometimes prolonged to include visits to the ETs' home planet;

★ ongoing relationships in the form of more or less continuous communication and occasional visits by the ETs.

In seeking to evaluate these claims, it is essential that we recognize that:

★ ET encounters are a widespread phenomenon involving many hundreds of alleged witnesses from many countries and cultures.

★ ET encounters occur to individuals of all social and cultural classes, from the highly educated to the illiterate, but so far as we know never to individuals who are unaware of the concept of ET life and possible visits.

★ ET encounters conform fairly closely to a limited number of basic scenarios, for example as regards the appearance of the ETs and their spacecraft, their behaviour and what they say, and in their accounts of life on their home planets; but there are significant variations, at least some of which relate more to the witness than to the ETs, as when a witness is subjected to an experience manifestly related to his personal circumstances.

★ ET encounters are known to us only by the personal testimony of the witness; there is virtually no supporting evidence, whether in the form of physical traces or artefacts, or from secondary testimony by uninvolved observers.

In short, a great many people, most of whom we have no reason to distrust, are telling us they have had extremely improbable, though often plausible, encounters, for whose actual occurrence they can produce no evidence, with seemingly extraterrestrial beings whose existence is not known to us by any other means and whose account of themselves is generally unsatisfactory.

Divested of its ET trappings, the ET encounter is seen to be essentially the same kind of paradoxical experience as encounters with divinities or spirits of the dead. So, while we must not dismiss the ET aspect as irrelevant, we may hope that by studying what the three kinds of experience have in common, we may be helped to understand the underlying nature of the ET encounter and resolve the paradoxes with which it confronts us.

A broad distinction is generally drawn between 'contact' cases, in which the witness is seemingly approached by the ETs in his own right, and 'abduction' cases in which he is apparently picked at random because he happens to be in the right/wrong place at the right/wrong time.

We shall find that this distinction may be less valid than it appears, but for the time being it is a convenient way of subdividing the bulk of testimony that confronts us. Even so, that bulk is probably far greater than is suspected by one who has studied the subject only casually or hardly at all. I have literally hundreds of books and journal articles describing these encounters, often in the witness' own words. It is essential that we bear in mind that the ET encounter is not a sporadic rarity but something that is happening on a scale which many would think alarming.

Nor is it only the quantity of these experiences which is significant, it is also their impact. As a result of claimed ET encounters many lives are being changed, not only those of the witnesses themselves but also of those who gather round them in messianic and millenarist cults. The social implications are profound and far-reaching.

The fact that ET encounters are likely to be less familiar to readers than encounters with divinities or spirits has presented me with a particular difficulty. What I propose to do is to be fairly generous with my case histories, because unless you are aware of the quantity, the variety and the nature of the ET encounter experience, this study will be worthless. However, I do encourage you to skim through the material fairly rapidly, especially if you are already familiar with it. I shall indicate the salient features which are likely to be helpful for our subsequent analysis.

Finally, we must beware of thinking that because the nature of the ET encounter is bizarre, with its sci-fi trappings and fantasy elements, the witnesses are less to be respected than those who encounter divinities or spirits. We may seem to be a long way from Teresa d'Avila and her mystical encounters, but the distance may be more apparent than real.

Eugenio Siragusa

ET encounters, like any other kind, tend to run to a pattern, but no single case is entirely representative. Siragusa's experience is better for our purposes than most because:

★ It is very well documented.

★ The core experience conforms closely to the stereotype.

★ It is relatively rich in incident.

★ The encounter was followed by more developments than is often the case.

★ The witness has sought, or been subjected to, considerable publicity, providing us with unusually prolific material for assessing his character.

It may be objected that Siragusa has been widely condemned as a fraud and charlatan. The same is true, however, of many other ET witnesses, and I think that the particular virulence with which Siragusa has been assailed stems more from his personal conduct than from the nature of his original experience.

Ostensibly the case began on 23 March 1952, the day of Siragusa's 33rd birthday. He was then living in the Sicilian coastal town of Catania, married to Rosario Mirabella, and with two sons Liberto (born 1944) and Franco Marzio (born 1949). He worked in the customs office.

Around 6 a.m. that morning he was waiting for the bus to take him to work:

Suddenly I saw, suspended in the sky and moving at a very great speed, a luminous disc, the colour of mercury. As it came closer it grew brighter. At the same time, within the light I began to make out an object shaped like a toy top or a priest's hat. The object hovered over my head. I confess I was terrified. I wanted to run away, but I couldn't; it was as though I was petrified.

What could this object be? A phantasm? An experimental machine? A wave of thoughts was flooding my mind when a luminous ray, shaped like a nail, was directed towards me by the unknown object and penetrated my whole being. At once an unspeakable happiness filled me, dispersing all my fear.

After a moment the luminous ray faded, as if reabsorbed by the strange object. Then the object itself — which later I knew to be a flying saucer — described a great arc in the sky and disappeared towards the horizon. As I recovered from my emotion, I realised immediately and intensely that something extraordinary had happened to me; a sort of redimensioning of my personality, of my whole being.[200]

Even this opening incident, notably less dramatic than what was to follow, presents similarities with other types of encounter. The overall similarity to a mystical experience is evident — and of course Siragusa lived in a solidly Catholic culture. We see that he at once put onto a higher plane what might seem merely to have been a curious sighting of an unknown flying object. This had marked psychological effects:

The traumatism was terrible. Physically I felt awful. And as if that wasn't enough, the geometry of the houses and the objects passing in front of them nauseated me, disgusted me aesthetically. Everything looked archaic.

That's a curiously sophisticated reaction for a customs officer, and we may suspect a degree of hindsight. But evidently it is on a psychological level that we must evaluate the experience, not omitting the surely more-than-coincidental circumstance that it was his birthday. If we accept Siragusa's assertion that the ETs deliberately brought about the event, we must suppose that they chose the anniversary on purpose.

Whether or not it was psychological in essence, the event had a physical dimension, about which we would like to know more. Not knowing how far away or how large the object was, it is difficult to assess how frightened it would be natural for him to be, and only in the light of that could we evaluate a panic which seems disproportionate if he really thought he was seeing no more than some kind of experimental machine.

Understandably, when his bus came he didn't take it, but returned home. From that day on both his family and his colleagues were aware of a transformation in him, noting that he 'distanced himself little by little towards inaccessible places and concepts'. This, he later revealed, was because he was now in continual telepathic contact with the ETs:

This voice began to instruct me in geology and cosmogony. It initiated me into the mysteries of the Creator. It formed in my mind visions of the past and of my previous lives. It reminded me that, 12,000 years earlier, I had been a student on the island of Poseidon, in Atlantis. It made me relive that marvellous era when Wisdom and Love were the pillars of civilisation.

He learned that he had lived several times previously on Earth, always as a key figure of a 'messenger' type:

- ★ on Atlantis as a scholar named Barath;

- ★ in Ancient Egypt, when he was Hermes Trismegistus;

- ★ in Biblical times, when he was John the Evangelist;

- ★ during the Renaissance, when he was Giordano Bruno;

- ★ in the age of the Enlightenment, when he was Cagliostro;

- ★ in the crisis of the twentieth century, when he was Grigori Rasputin.

He has even been able to meet his Bruno-period mother, for she has also been reincarnated to the present day, as an Italian housewife named Fraulisa Savolina.

Thanks to the teachings of his Cosmic Brothers, who work for the Higher Cosmic Intelligence, Siragusa was able to piece together a detailed system of knowledge and belief. Thus he confirms that mankind did not evolve on Earth, but came from the planet Lucifer when it was destroyed by a nuclear chain reaction set off by ignorant scientists who thereby upset the balance of the entire solar system. The Brothers are concerned that the descendants of those scientists may be about to repeat their error. That is why there are now some six million ETs mingling with humankind, taking steps to prevent another catastrophe.

It was made clear to Siragusa that he was not simply an initiate, but an 'operator', of whom there are less than fifty on Earth. As such he has a duty to bring enlightenment to the rest of humanity. To this end, he founded a Centre of Cosmic Studies and brotherhood, which was eventually to be housed in a space-age college on the slopes of Mount Etna. For the time being it was housed in a villa.

Siragusa's teachings are characterized by a notably Christian aspect.The entire project is subordinate to the desire and will of the Heavenly Father, and looks forward to a Second Coming. Not surprisingly, it is in Catholic countries — Spain, Switzerland, France, French Canada and Latin America — that he has had the greatest impact. But perhaps because some of his views diverge from established doctrine, or perhaps on account of his personal conduct, Siragusa has not received official approval from the Church.

One day (30 April 1962) I suddenly felt I had to go up on Mount Etna. As soon as it was night, I left Catania. I had the feeling that it wasn't me who was driving, but that my Fiat was controlled by a superior force. Following a winding way, I approached Mount Manfré at 1370 m altitude. I stopped the car and continued on foot by a path which led to the lip of the extinct volcano. About halfway up the slope, I saw the silhouette of two individuals whose costume, like that of spacemen, shone in the full moon. They were tall and athletically built, with blond shoulder-length hair. At wrist and ankle they wore shining bracelets, apparently gold; on their chests they wore luminous belts with strange boxes. At the sight of them, the blood froze in my veins and I felt drenched in a cold sweat. For ten years I had been waiting eagerly for this experience, but the isolated site, the darkness of night and the suddenness of the encounter didn't exactly stimulate my courage.

One of the ETs directed a ray of green light towards me from an object in his hand; at once I felt penetrated with a strange sensation of calm and serenity. My heart, which had seemed ready to explode, now beat regularly and steadily. I waited, watching the pair of them, as if stupefied. By the moon's light I could make out their delicate features and piercing, arresting gaze. One said to me, in Italian, 'Peace be with you, my son. We were waiting for you. Engrave in your mind all we tell you.'

The voice didn't sound human, it seemed metallic, as if coming from a recording. They gave me a message, and I did my best to memorise it so that I could type it out the moment I got home. They raised their hands as if to bless me, saying 'Peace be with you,' and went off towards their disc which was beside one of the craters.

The message, which embodied a plan to achieve world peace by means of nuclear disarmament, was duly despatched to all the world leaders. The only reply came from one of de Gaulle's staff. This failure to change the course of world history does not seem to have discouraged the ETs, who despite having millions of agents on Earth were for several years to persist in employing Siragusa's aid in this rather unpromising course of action.

The improbabilities scarcely need to be pointed out. Even given the choice of Siragusa in the first place, why arrange so inconvenient a rendezvous as the slopes of a volcano at night? Why entrust so important a message to Siragusa's memory? Why suppose that the world's leaders will redirect their policies on nothing more than a Sicilian customs officer's say-so? And so on.

All he saw of their spacecraft on this occasion was a disc parked by a crater. On a later occasion, they made up for this by taking him on a flight for more than two hours, ample time in which to visit Black Moon, their artificially floating base near the moon. On the moon itself he saw, in suspended animation, the bodies of six million ETs currently on mission on Earth.

During the early years of his contact Siragusa enjoyed the support of his family; for instance, they confirmed that between April and September 1962 they had seen UFOs over their home on several occasions. When the Cuban missile crisis occurred, Siragusa achieved considerable press notoriety by assuring the world that war would not follow, because his Cosmic Brothers had personally intervened by calling on President Kennedy, and presumably on Khrushchev also. Neither government, however, has confirmed that these meetings occurred.

Siragusa continued working for the customs until 1972, when he took early retirement at the age of 52, to devote himself full time to his mission. He left his wife and family, who henceforth took no further part in his activities. He formed a commune which became the headquarters of a cult which, though he insisted it was for the mission as a whole, centred round his charismatic but increasingly autocratic personality. An important activity was the study of geophysiobiopsychotherapy, which as the name suggests is a holistic form of healing.

In the autumn of 1978, Siragusa gave a supper party at which he predicted that he would shortly be betrayed by two of those present. He had for some time been aware that the forces of evil, through their earthly agencies the CIA and KGB, were seeking to sabotage his mission. Among his research assistants were a young Canadian couple, Kelly Hooker and his attractive young wife Leslie Meadowcraft. In November 1978 they brought court charges against him of fraud, sexual violence and mental conditioning. To Siragusa it was evident that they were agents of the evil forces.

The two months he spent in prison, awaiting the verdict, were easily turned by his supporters into a martyrdom and that 'last supper' was not the only parallel drawn with the mission of Jesus of Nazareth. In addition, UFOs were seen above the prison, and two strange entities visited the prison itself.

The verdict of acquittal, when it came, was also turned to advantage. There was no evidence of fraud; the rape charge could not be proved as, even though we may doubt Siragusa's claim that on the instructions of the ETs he had foresworn sex for ten years, Leslie Meadowcraft was not the only nubile cult member to reveal that he had persuaded her to accept his sexual attentions in order to bring to birth the 'prophet of the new age', weakening his claim however, as one of the girls pointed out, by withdrawing before ejaculating. The third charge, that he had 'brainwashed' members of the cult, was even less easy to prove; the Hooker couple had certainly entered the community voluntarily, and it is doubtful if anything more than their gullibility was needed to ensure their adherence.

But though the acquittal won considerable sympathy for Siragusa, who does seem to have been more than usually harassed by the authorities, he closed down the Centre shortly before the trial, claiming that his mission had come to an end. He left Italy for 'exile' in France; and though as recently as 1981 he was still comparing himself to John the Baptist, like him an 'announcer' of greater things to come, his missionary activities seem to have come to an end.

At the time of his encounter, the leading Italian newspaper *Domenica del Corriere* probed into Siragusa's life, talking to family, neighbours, work colleagues. All spoke highly of him, and confirmed that he was not likely to have indulged in conscious fraud. He was certainly a person of charm and charisma, expressed in his writings and statements, and manifested in the loyalty of his supporters.

At the same time, the contradictions, inconsistencies and sheer improbabilities of his claims are self-evident. Nobody could accept them

'I saw them with the eyes of my body as clearly as I see you,' Jeanne d'Arc told her judges, 'and when they went away I cried, and wished they had taken me with them' (illustration by Kaulbach for Schiller's drama *The Maid of Orleans*).

Mélanie and Maximin, while looking after their sheep near La Salette in south-eastern France, see the Virgin weeping; she speaks to them, then flies away. 19 September 1846 (from Louis Carlier, *Histoire de l'apparition de la Mère de Dieu sur la montagne de la Salette*, 1912).

For many, the physical reality of divine beings is an accepted fact. Chilean priests despatch letters written to the Virgin by burning them before the altar; the smoke carries the messages to Heaven (from *L'Illustration*, 1864).

Citizens of Napoli attack a statue of their patron saint, San Gennaro, because he has allowed Vesuvius to erupt and endanger their homes (from *The Graphic*, 1972).

The Catholic Church will not recognize a Saint without hearing the reasons *against* canonisation, presented by the *advocatus diaboli* (G. Amato in *Illustrated London News*, 1909).

Left A Yakut shaman, from northern Russia, conjures his god to cure a sick person; part-priest, part-doctor, the shaman acts as a professional intermediary between his people and the deity who has the power to heal (anonymous engraving circa 1800).

Folklore thrives in war conditions: during World War One, 'The Comrade in White' was one of many otherworldly beings who aided the Allied cause (A. Pearce in **The chariots of God**, 1915).

Above and right Between the 14th and 18th centuries, thousands of people —
most of them women — told fantastic tales of leaving their homes via the chimney
on a broomstick to attend orgiastic sabbats where they danced and copulated
with Satan and his minions ('The Departure for the Sabbat', etching by Teniers,
17th century; 'A Sabbat in the Basque Region of Labourd', 1609, depicted by
Martin van Maele for Michelet's *La Sorcière*, 1911).

Gassner, the priest-healer from Ratisbon, Germany, whose practices inspired Mesmer and thus led to the discovery of hypnotism, believed that spiritual power enabled him to drive out possessing demons (contemporary engraving by Chodowiecki, circa 1775).

Geraldine Cummins (1890-1969) took an open-minded view of her automatic writing, was by no means convinced that the spiritist explanation was the correct one.

Helène Smith, the Swiss medium who created a Martian language, depicted herself in company with her Guardian Angel in 1912 (from an oil painting reproduced in Deonna, *De la Planète Mars en Terre Sainte*, 1932).

Above and right The efforts of spirits of the dead to materialize are seldom wholly convincing. On 15 May 1873 'Katie King' materialized in the home of William Crookes thanks to the efforts of medium Florence Cook, and was photographed in magnesium light by F. W. Hayes. On 6 January 1933, in her own home, Helen Duncan produced a materialization of 'Peggy', seemingly from ectoplasm exuded from her nose. Katie's fondness for loose white drapes, so convenient for rapid costume-changes, and Peggy's choice of a material strongly resembling the kind of butter-muslin most easily concealed in body orifices, do not encourage belief.

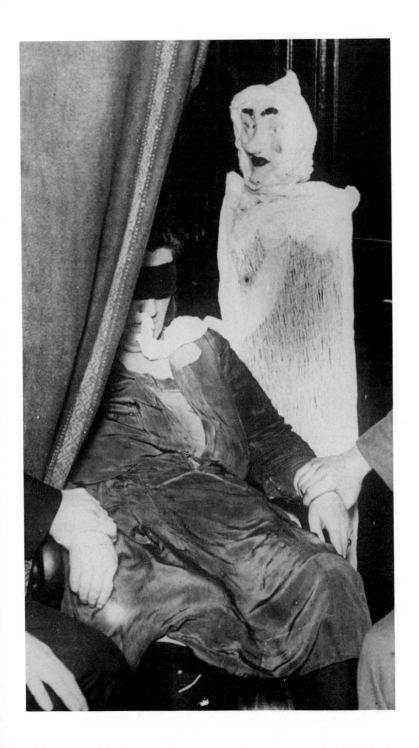

George Adamski stands beside a somewhat idealized painting of his Venusian contact.

WE MET THE
SPACE PEOPLE
THE STORY OF THE MITCHELL SISTERS
BY HELEN and BETTY MITCHELL

$1.00   SAUCERIAN PUBLICATIONS, CLARKSBURG, W.VA.

Even when glamorized for a book cover, Helen and Betty Mitchell hardly match the space-hero good looks of their extraterrestrial companions. It is too cynical to suspect a wish-fulfilling fantasy?

American contactee Howard Menger, with his Venusian wife Marla.

Police officer Herbert Schirmer is about to be taken aboard a UFO at Ashland, Nebraska, 3 December 1967 (from *Saga's UFO Report*, 1971).

Abduction fantasy by Hal Crawford, who better than any other artist has depicted the archetypal quality of ET contact (from *Argosy Special UFO Annual*, 1977).

God as spaceman: spaceman as God — the ultimate encounter (from *Angeles ayer, extraterrestres hoy*, published by La Asociación Adonai para la Fraternidad Cósmica Desojo).

The aftermath of encounter: five years after his visionary meeting with the Virgin, Delphine (kneeling at right) meets at the scene every afternoon with family and friends to pray to the Virgin and sing her praises (author's photo).

who had not abandoned all critical standards or who was not psychologically predisposed to see them as surface obstacles to belief, to be disregarded in favour of some 'deeper truth'.

Even this brief summary of the Siragusa case fails to do justice to the wealth of significant detail which is to be found in it. I have, for instance, spared you samples of the messages which were evidently such an inspiration to the members of his community. Three full-length books have been devoted to him and his teachings, together with many smaller publications.

For our present purposes, however, it is more helpful to pick out a few salient features. Among those which I suggest are particularly significant are these:

★ The experience was *wholly subjective*; neither at the bus stop nor at any subsequent incident were there any witnesses to anything (if we except his family's alleged confirmation that there were UFOs over their home).

★ The *mystical-religious interpretation* which from the start the witness put upon his experience, which expressed itself in a dissatisfaction with earthly things, such as the buildings and other objects which he suddenly found aesthetically displeasing.

★ The sense the witness had of having been *chosen for a mission* by powerful but benevolent ETs, to the extent that his present life was only the latest in a succession, during most of which he had been a prominent world-figure, with the implication that he was once again a prominent figure in this life; the total effect being, evidently, to enhance his self-respect and give him a sense of identity which working for the customs office probably did not provide.

★ The overall *transformation of life-style* brought about by the experience, and whereby his life was clearly enriched. If the ultimate consequences were socially regrettable, this can be blamed as much on society as on himself.

In evaluating the Siragusa case, we do not necessarily have to render an all-or-nothing verdict. We may, for instance, entertain the possibility that on his 33rd birthday he had a 'genuine' 'experience' (whatever interpretation we choose to put on either of those words), and it was only subsequently that, confused by what had happened to him, not receiving any useful guidance from others and forced to make his own way based on his own interpretation, he was gradually drawn into more devious ways.

If something of the sort occurred, then it graphically demonstrates that our study of the encounter phenomenon is something more than academic game-playing. If it can help us to understand what is happening to people like Eugenio Siragusa, it can help us to guide such people when they badly need guidance.

That assertion begs two questions. First, that 'something of the sort occurred'. We are a long way from being sure that it did. On the other hand, we have seen that there are aspects of Siragusa's experience which are not so very different from other experiences we have noted, and as a working hypothesis I think it not unreasonable to continue extending to him the benefit of our doubt at least until we have made our analysis of the encounter experience in its entirety.

Second, are there 'other people like Siragusa'? Is his experience a one-off event, or are there many others in the same predicament? To answer that, we must look at some more cases.

Pierre Monnet

Pierre Monnet, in 1951, was a young man of 19, living in Orange, in south-eastern France. His fiancée lived in a village a few kilometres away, and he used to visit her by bicycle. One July night he left her at 1.30 a.m., and was on his way home when he and his bicycle were suddenly teleported to a quarry some 5 km the far side of Orange. He dismounted at the entrance to the quarry, made his way into it 'as if directed by an irresistible force', and there saw a domed disc, some 15–20 metres in diameter, hovering over the ground, giving off a blue-white light which lit up the surroundings. The closer he got, the less aware he became of the sounds of everyday life, though there was traffic passing on the road he had just left.[180]

Four 'human beings' wearing close-fitting clothes were standing near the object:

> They were so beautiful that for the moment, despite the fact that they had no obvious female breasts, I was confused as to what sex they were. Long blonde-white but neatly combed hair fell to their shoulders; their look was of a clearness, a frankness and a gentleness which I have never seen in a fellow being. They smiled and radiated tranquillity, gentleness and goodness; a profound peace seemed to characterise them.

The ETs communicated a long message to him, which they said would be imprinted on his memory, so that he was later able to transcribe it perfectly. They also — though he wasn't aware of this at the time — took him on board their spaceship to perform an operation of 'regeneration' which would enable him to live to 120 (he is still alive as I write this, but then he's younger than me in any case).

He remembers turning away from them without saying goodbye, and remounting his bike. Then he must have been teleported again, for the next thing he knew, he was arriving at the outskirts of Orange at the same time he had left his girlfriend's village, 1.30 a.m.

One of the ETs' instructions was to 'keep in contact', but they weren't very helpful about how he was to do this. He told nobody about his experience until 1962, and when he did he encountered only scepticism. In 1974 he for the first time read of flying saucers, though this seems contradicted by his claims to have seen a disc while doing his military service in Indo-China as well as subsequently in France, and by his statement that he had been interested in the possibility of ET life since the age of 4!

In 1974 he had a further contact. He was paying for petrol at a service station when he recognized two men, putting petrol in a Renault, as either his original ETs or their look-alikes:

> As in 1951, I gazed at them with a sort of admiration and interior joy. As in 1951, I was in ecstasy before these two men. I felt myself light, and in a state of exceptional well-being. As in 1951, they radiated tranquillity, power, peace, love and goodness to others.

They gave him a penetrating look, transmitted a telepathic message, and left.

His 'third contact' took the form of a 'telepathic journey' travelling alone in one of their spacecraft, in the course of which he was given a visionary tour of space, which, however, only lasted about six earth minutes.

Apart from these 'outward' experiences, Monnet received telepathic messages intermittently from 1956 onwards. Often he would wake in the night with the sense of having received a lengthy text which he felt compelled to get out of bed and write down at once. Though he calls the process 'automatic writing' he did not feel he had been taken over by another personality; he was simply transcribing a message which had been communicated to him.

Monnet was keen to understand his experience, and was well aware of the contradictory elements in his story. Besides forming a UFO research group of his own, he co-operated with serious UFO investigators who were interested in his case, and made a very favourable impression.

Once again, my brief synopsis does scant justice to this rich and revealing case. We note again certain recurrent features:

★ All the experiences were *subjective*.

★ The witness felt that a *mission* had been entrusted to him by benevolent beings, who made him the recipient of teaching messages for mankind.

★ The experiences involved *unreal* incidents such as teleportation, and the night-time communication of messages which he felt compelled to transcribe immediately.

George Adamski

The case of American contactee George Adamski, who claimed to have met beings from other planets in 1952, is much the best-known, thanks to his own published accounts, the first to come to the notice of the general public. Though probably few believed his story, the fact that it was published at all opened people's minds to the possibility that what had hitherto been fantasy could become fact. *Flying Saucers Have Landed*[4] takes its place along with the writings of Verne and Wells as a landmark in the development of man's ideas about the universe.

The difference, of course, is that whereas Verne's *De la terre à la lune* and Wells' *War of the Worlds* made no pretence to be anything but fiction, Adamski insisted that his experience had actually occurred. To this day, controversy rages about his claims. Though most serious critics dismiss him as a charlatan, even twenty years after his death in 1965 he retains a fervent if diminishing number of loyal believers.

George Adamski was born in Poland in 1891 or 1893, but came with his parents to the United States when he was 2. He was educated by 'private tutors', and became an American citizen in 1915 while serving in the army. He married, but though his wife Mary lived to 1954 she rarely figures in his story. He is known to have had various jobs, but no settled career.

From about 1926 he was a teacher of 'philosophy' — a vaguely occult mix of religion and metaphysics. From 1930 he was based at Laguna Beach, California, where as 'Professor Adamski' he was the leading figure in the 'Royal Order of Tibet' which had its own 'monastery'. Ray Stanford, an American ufologist of mystical tendencies, claims Adamski told him:

> During the Prohibition I had the Sacred Order of Tibet. It was a front. You know, we were supposed to have the religious ceremonies: we make the wine for them and the authorities can't interfere with our religion. Hell, I made enough wine for half of southern California. In fact, boys, I was the biggest bootlegger around. Then Roosevelt came along and knocked out the Prohibition. If it hadn't been for that man Roosevelt, I wouldn't have to get into all this saucer crap.[237]

Adamski also confided to Stanford that he had begun his contactee career with the fiction work *Pioneers of Space*.[1] His supporters have argued that it was the other way about, and that he first told his experiences in fiction form, on the grounds that nobody would believe him. (Dutch contactee Stefan Denaerde later made a similar claim.[44])

During the 1940s Adamski set up some kind of self-supporting commune at Valley Center, and in 1944 he bought a 20-acre property on Mt Palomar, on which a friend Alice Wells built the Palomar Gardens Café. Here he spent much of his time, lending a hand with running the café, where uncertainty about his status enabled his detractors to stigmatize him as a 'hired help'. After flying saucers became news in 1947 he began incorporating them into his teachings. In October 1949 he told a Rotary Club audience that he had seen a saucer himself in 1946, and in August 1947 had seen 184 of them in a single mass sighting, the largest number of UFOs ever reported at one time. In addition he had photographed one, in the course of his astronomical work, but had not realized its significance at the time.

His claims brought him some media attention, and he became more and more of a public figure. The FBI began keeping files on him from at least as early as June 1950, noting his adverse comments on the U.S. Government and favourable references to Russia.

On 20 November 1952 he went with a group of friends into the nearby desert, where he claimed to have heard that flying saucers were landing. He stopped the cars at Desert Center, a deserted area, saying he 'knew' the ETs wanted to contact him. A large spacecraft was seen by the party, though not by other people in the area. When the appearance of some terrestrial aircraft caused it to leave, Adamski asked his friends to drive him to a more isolated spot and leave him there, saying 'That ship has come looking for me'.

Shortly after being left on his own, he was joined by an ET. This was Orthon, a Venusian, whose small 'scout ship', which had brought him from the larger 'mother ship' seen earlier, was hovering nearby. Adamski and Orthon talked for about an hour, first with signs and then by telepathy, succeeding in exchanging a considerable amount of information. Orthon would not let Adamski take any photographs, but left behind a message in the form of symbolic marks on a shoeprint in the sand. Fortunately, one of Adamski's companions had had the foresight to bring with him some plaster so that a cast could be made of the print.

All six persons, some months later, signed an affidavit that they had seen the craft. Alice Wells, proprietor of the café, was able to make a sketch of Orthon whom she had observed through binoculars, confirming Adamski's description of a young man with shoulder-length golden hair, wearing a one-piece costume like a track suit, and very good-looking.

A few weeks later Orthon flew over Adamski's home and dropped a film containing some of Adamski's photographs. Their publication brought further media attention — and also another visit from the FBI. They were interested when he told them of a Mr Hunrath who would send him a machine which could bring down both flying saucers and terrestrial aircraft. Little is known about this incident, but from now on Adamski was associated with all kinds of parasite people, such as 'Dr' George Hunt Williamson, one of the witnesses to the Desert Center sighting, who went on to write a number of somewhat improbable books advancing such claims as that the entire flying saucer phenomenon was a political plot engineered by Russian Communists in the pay of Jewish financiers.[266] Such associations do not enhance Adamski's credibility.

World fame came to Adamski almost by chance when in 1953 English publisher Waveney Girvan offered to include his account as an appendix to some historical UFO material by occultist Desmond Leslie. Since no American publisher would take the story, Adamski agreed. His account (ghost-written by Clara John) made Leslie's book an instant bestseller, reprinted five times between September and the end of the year. Adamski claimed that 100,000 copies were sold during his lifetime. Translations and subsequent reprints will had added vastly to that number.

In subsequent books[2,3] he described further meetings with the

'Brothers' as well as journeys in their spacecraft. In 1953, for instance, he visited Mars and Saturn. The details he provided of these travels, some demonstrably false, others surprisingly perceptive, increased the controversial character of his story, but did nothing but enhance his fame with the general public. His claim to have been chosen by the ETs as their earthly ambassador made a particularly strong appeal to the Germans, the Swiss and the Danes. But as a world-known figure he travelled widely, and if he was often assailed by hostile critics, wherever he went he also had dedicated disciples enthusiastically supporting his urging that mankind should 'get acquainted' with the friendly ETs. One of them was his friend Alice Wells, who at the time of his death wrote:

> I wonder how many realise that he was a member of the Interplanetary Council. This is a group of men of high Cosmic Consciousness Awareness that evaluate the conditions of our system and keep their representatives informed of the changes. [13]

She revealed that because of Adamski's loyalty to the cause, he would be granted a new body by the Council. He would not be reborn as a baby, for 'when an individualised intelligence is as aware of Cosmic Consciousness as his was, this is not necessary. There is nothing fantastic about this when the Laws of the Cosmos are understood.'

Adamski himself worked hard to make the rest of us understand the laws of the cosmos. Beside his popular accounts he wrote and lectured on 'philosophical' matters. His teachings remained pretty much those of his old 'Royal Order of Tibet' days, for, of course, it was on account of those teachings, which showed him to be on the right path of understanding, that the ETs had picked him out. For many people he was himself more than human. Admirer Laura Mundo reported, 'I have had one person tell me they saw a silver aura around his head denoting very *high* involvement, and another one watching him on TV said the face of Christ became superimposed over his for a brief moment and his suit changed to robes.' [13] Desmond Leslie believed Adamski was reincarnated from another planet for karmic reasons, in order to instruct our ignorant planet. He revealed that 'his navel was not like a human navel at all. It was a huge solar disk with deeply cut rays extending out about six inches all around it, from waist to groin. What this signifies I have no idea — unless it is truly a sign of "Child of the Sun".' [13]

Other scenarios were proposed. One-time disciple Carol Honey thought his original contacts had been genuine, but that later he had been misled by psychic forces *impersonating* spacemen. Publisher Gray Barker agreed that the initial experiences were genuine, but that the later incidents were fabricated to keep the game going. [13] Dr Leon Davidson thought Adamski was nothing but a stooge for the CIA, who had rigged the whole business as a test of public reaction. [38] Ufologist David Stupple sees him as a misguided utopian, who faked the whole thing in order to bolster his sincerely held philosophical beliefs. [66]

The Adamski case is so rich, and bears on so many facets of human experience, that it is easy to get lost in its intricacies, as I discovered when preparing this woefully inadequate summary. There are so many unresolved questions whose answers would give us a surer footing from which to evaluate his experience. Few would accept that all his claims were true. The question is how many of them, if any, were true? Charlatan or dupe? One who fooled others or was himself fooled? There are grounds for either belief, and for many others beside.

It is significant that his case should have been enriched by such picturesque folklore elements as the belief that he would be reborn in order to fulfil his mission, a stock element in hero myth. His burial in Arlington Military Cemetery, Washington DC, was seen as proof that he had been closely involved with the US Government (predictably there were conflicting suggestions as to the nature of that involvement). His meeting with Queen Juliana of the Netherlands, and rumours of a secret meeting with Pope John XXIII, gave further cause for speculation. [273]

All this can be seen as confirmation that there was substance to the original experience, or as irrelevant accretion, or as characteristic of the snowball effect whereby certain encounter experiences lead the witness into ever more complex behaviour. But perhaps our comparative study will help to clarify our thinking about Adamski, for many features of his experience match those of other encounter witnesses, and not only in the ET category:

★ The *specific events* are at best dubious. Though there are sworn witnesses to some of them, we have good grounds for hesitating to accept the testimony of a witness such as Williamson, with his paranoid fear of world conspiracy, or Wells who believed Adamski would be karmically reborn. Such physical evidence as is available, notably the photographs, tends by its dubious character to weaken rather than strengthen Adamski's claims.

★ Adamski claimed to have been picked out by the ETs because he was uniquely suited to be their representative and carry out a *mission* to mankind.

★ Although his encounter followed on from his previous career as 'philosopher', it marked a *transition* from private teacher with a handful of disciples to world figure with a world audience, a transition which could hardly have been made without some such dramatic event.

★ As the result of his experience a *cult* was created with strong spiritual/religious overtones.

Orfeo Angelucci

Orfeo Angelucci was a 40-year-old employee in a Los Angeles aircraft works when he had his first encounter with ET entities, in May 1952. Working the night-shift, he had earlier felt sick, though he had blamed this on an old illness. He just managed to stick it out to the end of the shift at around 1 a.m. Driving home, his 'eyesight was glazed and the sounds of traffic were oddly muffled and far-away'; then he saw a 'faintly red-glowing oval-shaped object' ahead of him. Referring to himself in the third person, Angelucci recorded:

> The object now seemed to come closer, and for the first time 'approachable'. Orfeo's symptoms increased in intensity. The object was now so close it seemed to be master, commanding, almost breathing. There was yet not a sound from it, but as it went to the right Orfeo was impelled to do likewise . . . He was in a way dissociated from the world, and felt associated with only this object, and its ethereal origin. [8]

About 2 km down a side road, Orfeo felt impelled to stop. The red UFO vanished and its place taken by two small fluorescent green discs, from which he was greeted by 'a most delightful masculine voice'. After reminding him of some earlier sightings of flying saucers, the voice realized that Orfeo was thirsty, and at once a bottle (or a crystal goblet in another version) appeared containing 'the most satisfying nectar he had ever tasted'.

Two entities now appeared from the globes, 'a man and a woman near a possible ultimate of perfection . . . These exquisite personages conveyed kindness, understanding, experience, moderation, complete joy of the five senses. Life in full. All this and not a word spoken.'

Once telepathic communication had been established, Orfeo learnt that three Earthpeople had been chosen as their first contacts — one in Rome, one in India, and himself the first. Through him they wanted to help the world: 'With deep compassion and understanding we have watched your world going through its growing pains. We ask that you look upon us simply as older brothers.' They explained that there were limits to what they could do for Earth, because they had to operate within 'planetary and cosmic laws as implacable as the natural laws of Earth'. But they were worried by 'the creeping menace of Communism that is threatening the world'.

This was only the first of several meetings, each of which occurred without warning except physical sensations which he came to recognize. He was given to going on solitary walks at night, and his encounters often occurred at such times. During one such walk he came across a flying saucer on the ground, which he felt impelled to enter. He was then given a vision of the Earth, amounting to a kind of spiritual rebirth. He learned that:

> in allegorical language Christ is indeed the Son of god. The star that burned over Bethlehem is a cosmic fact . . . Jesus is Lord of the Flame, an infinite entity of the sun . . . Above the strains of the Lord's Prayer, played as though by thousands of violins, the voice said 'Beloved friend of Earth, we baptise

you now in the true light of the worlds eternal'. In that sublime moment I knew the mystery of life!'

Because he had been entrusted with a mission, Angelucci published an account of his meeting. The Brothers warned him that he would be ridiculed, and they were right. Nevertheless he became one of the best-known of the contactees, and was the instigation for one of the most insightful studies of the UFO phenomenon, written by C. G. Jung.[126] A different kind of tribute to Angelucci came from the well-known radio personality Long John Nebel, who interviewed many UFO contactees on his show: 'As far as I'm concerned, although I don't buy any of these bits, this man's was, and is, the most imaginative, the most beautiful, and the most fascinating of them all.'[185]

In January 1953 Angelucci had a further and even stranger experience, but one which is not easy to narrate in terms which do not imply a particular interpretation. For Angelucci himself, it was quite simply that he spent a week away from Earth with his ET contacts. On returning to Earth he found himself back at work, tools in his hands. The date on a newspaper was the only indication that he had been gone for a week. Workmates and family alike had noticed nothing unusual in his behaviour. As he learnt later, this was because one of the cosmic Brothers had controlled his body while he was visiting Lucifer.

Indeed, his visit was really a return, for this planet, located between Mars and Jupiter, had formerly been his home. The personal ambition of its prince had led to secession from the 'etheric hosts' of the cosmos, and then to the destruction of the planet itself, thus giving rise to our legend of Lucifer, Son of the Morning, and his war in Heaven.

So what Angelucci was taken to see was the new civilization that had developed on a planetoid fragment of the original planet. Though grossly materialistic compared with the time-frame inhabited by the Brothers, life on Lucifer is in many respects superior to ours on Earth — the food and drink are marvellous, the furnishings are of crystal, colours are soft shifting pastel shades, no vehicles pollute the grass, trees and flowers which 'sparkle with living colours that seemed almost to glow with a light of their own', the fantastically beautiful buildings are constructed of 'a kind of crystal-plastic substance that quivered with continuously changing colour hues', and all is accompanied by 'waves of soft exquisite music'.

As for the inhabitants, all without exception are 'statuesque and majestically beautiful', notably Lyra, with her long golden hair, large expressive blue eyes and wearing a long Grecian gown. Telepathic communication betrays the fact that Lyra arouses lustful sentiments in Angelucci, but he is made to feel ashamed of them, and their relationship culminates in a more spiritual union:

I turned and looked into Lyra's wonderful eyes shining with sympathy, compassion and purest love. My own heart swiftly responded. Then suddenly, miraculously we were as one being, enfolded in an embrace of the spirit untouched by sensuality or carnality.[9]

Once again I am conscious that this skimped account does less than justice to Angelucci's extraordinarily rich and passionately (if illiterately) described experience. I can only hope I have indicated its essential quality. Although his experience shares many common features with those of Siragusa, Monnet and Adamski, like them it has also marked individual features of its own.

★ Angelucci's ET encounter, for all its space-age format, is essentially a *spiritual* experience, giving him a quite explicit 'new baptism' as a rite of passage to a new phase of spiritual development. In this respect his experience differs from many encounters with divinities only in the fact that the Brothers play the role of the divinity.

★ Like each of our other contactees, he had the sense of having been *chosen for a mission*.

★ Like the others, he had always felt an 'insatiable hunger for knowledge' and a dissatisfaction with his circumstances which seem to provide a *preparation* for the experience.

★ The sense of being on a *different level of reality* is strongly marked, both in his initial encounter and in the subsequent week-long visit to Lucifer. This is emphasized by the occurrence of myth-like incidents, such as the provision of a drink by the ETs as a prelude to their association — a standard element in mythic narrative.

★ *Personal preoccupations* intrude, notably the Brothers' concern about the menace of communism which they share with the Virgin of Fatima.

★ Angelucci shares with the others a tendency, following the encounter, to see ETs in all kinds of everyday situations. Monnet saw two at a gas station, Siragusa identified the entities who visited his prison as ETs, Adamski sitting in a cafe identified another customer as an ET to his companions. Paranoia? A pathetic attmept to offer proof of the reality of their experiences? Genuine delusion? It seems in any case to parallel another shared feature, the tendency to interpret trivial incidents as having a deeper significance; when Angelucci had a minor accident at work, the resulting scar was for him 'a constant reminder of the proximity of unseen visitors'.

Though it is too early for us to start drawing conclusions, I think we can fairly say, on the basis of these four cases, that one thing has become manifestly clear: ET encounters are *not* merely stereotypes in which each witness duplicates the experience of others. Whatever common features exist are individualized according to the witness' nature and circumstances. Each, in short, is *a personalized experience occurring within a shared cultural framework.*

George King

'Prepare yourself! You are to become the voice of Interplanetary Parliament.' That was the simple and precise Command I received one sunny Saturday morning in May 1954. The crisp tones of the voice which uttered the words, coming as it did from apparently empty space in my little flat in London, brought me to a state of shocked immobility. There was no mistaking the meaning of the message or its importance. Nor was there anything eerie about it, for sunshine and eeriness do not seem to go together. [132]

George King's detractors are apt to refer to him as a London cab-driver, as though experiences suitable for Spanish mystics, and even for French shepherdesses, are not appropriate to an Englishman with so humdrum an occupation. One question which we must ask, however, is whether it isn't precisely this aspect of the ET encounter experience which is the clearest clue to its essential nature?

As it happens, King was far from being *merely* a cab-driver. His mother (who would later become a contactee in her own right) ran a healing sanctuary, and King himself had been a student of occultism for ten years before his cosmic summons at the age of 35, and the relevance of his studies to his experience was revealed eight days later:

On the following Sunday evening I was somewhat startled by the entrance of another man into my rooms. As is the general practice before attempting meditation, I always carefully lock the door. This had not deterred my visitor who, I discovered later from his method of exit, had obviously walked straight through the door. I recognised him immediately as an Indian swami of world renown. I am not permitted to divulge his name nor much of what passed, but any lingering doubts were soon dispelled.

King emphasizes that the swami was actually, physically present:

Even the chair had creaked slightly as he sat down. I had often read about feats performed by Masters of the East, who could project themselves for thousands of miles in a flash, and appear as life-like as if they had just alighted from an aeroplane. But this was the first time I had ever witnessed such a feat performed by someone whom I knew to be very much alive.

The swami confirmed that King had been chosen:

You are only one of many called upon to prepare yourself for the coming conflict between the materialistic scientist, who has arrived at his conclusions by the cold application of mathematics, and the occult scientist who has arrived at his conclusions through the recognition that God is all.

King soon realized that nothing less than the well-being of Planet Earth was in jeopardy. His original communicator, now identified as 'Aetherius', a denizen of Saturn, was one of a Cosmic Brotherhood who were concerned to protect Earth, and for that reason were appointing 'specialized individuals' like King as their representatives:

> We can help you in your meteorological difficulties, thereby cutting down the death rate caused by aircraft crashing when they fly through certain clouds . . . We can help you irrigate and cultivate your deserts, so that they can again become as fertile as when the Great Pyramids were built . . . We can help you in your primitive educational system, so that every pupil is given that experience demanded by his karma . . . We can help you in your hospitals, so that cancer, tuberculosis and venereal diseases are things of the past . . .

Bearing such good news, King gave his first lecture at London's Caxton Hall in 1956, and founded the Aetherius Society the following year with ET guidance, notably from a Martian named 'Mars Sector Six', a Chinese saint named Goo-Ling, and Jesus Christ, now revealed to have been a Venusian. (Asked by Fred Archer, editor of *Psychic News*, how he knew it was Jesus, King said it was because of his radiations. Asked how he knew they were Jesus' radiations, King said he 'just knew'.)

In 1959 King was directed to move to Hollywood, California. From his headquarters there King has published a stream of books and pamphlets containing the teachings he has received on our behalf. In addition he has been summoned by Cosmic Intelligence to attend conferences on board their spacecraft, and has witnessed the formal transition to a higher state of an Earthly adept who had worked out his necessary karma on our planet and was ready to move on to higher things. [133] On another occasion he met a great Master, with whom he communicated by telepathy:

> He looked about 30, but I learned later that he was at least three times that age. His long brown silken hair hung down to his broad shoulders. For a moment I caught his eyes and saw in them the depths of Wisdom I have never seen in any terrestrial eyes.

In 1958 his mother, Mary King, was awakened in the middle of the night in her Devon cottage. Going to the window she saw a flying saucer and four figures whom she knew at once were higher beings from another planet. They gave her a reassuring message by telepathy. Later, her doorbell rang:

> When I opened the door there stood before me what I thought for a moment was a man but as I looked again at his face I knew he was no Earth-man!

I asked Him to come in and as he did so my living room was filled with the perfume of a thousand flowers. I knew beyond doubt that here was another Great One from Outer Space, come to converse with me. [136]

Though it had been snowing, her visitor left no tracks when he left, from which King inferred that he either levitated or dematerialized or was taken up by some spacecraft hovering overhead.

Like Siragusa's ET contacts, King's were alarmed by the 1962 Cuba crisis, and the Aetherius Society were called on to help prevent it. It is not clear to which of these two powers the world owes its deliverance. Conceivably they were acting together. Since then several other operations have been carried out, notably the Primary Initiation of the Earth which came about on 8 July 1964 without most of us noticing, though King declares: 'The Cosmic happening was so stupendous that it dwarfs any other happening in the history of the world.' The entire success of the operation, writes Revd Abrahamson, one of his followers, 'must be credited to the man who, though his shoulders have borne an inhuman burden, has never failed any aspect of the Cosmic Plan entrusted to his care'. [135]

In many respects King is the most impressive of the contactees. His claims are the most grandiose, but they are based on a plausible belief-system, and the incidents hang together to form a homogeneous story which commands our admiration even if, for sheer lack of solid evidence, it does not compel our belief. Though it often reads like science fiction, it contains many elements which we have noted in other cases, though with variations particular to himself:

★ His *early studies* in occultism certainly paved the way for his encounter experience.

★ He was chosen to carry out a *mission* for which he was uniquely fitted.

★ His experience embodied his *beliefs* — for instance, his witnessing of the reception of the adept.

★ Like other contactees, he encountered an *entity* of striking physical appearance as well as superhuman wisdom.

The King case emphasizes another essential characteristic of contactee cases, which is that it virtually never happens that more than one contactee encounters the same entity. By contrast with encounters with divinities, where several witnesses might claim to encounter a being that each identifies as the Virgin Mary though describing its appearance in very different terms, each ET witness encounters a slightly different entity, from a different place of origin, and is given a slightly different assignment, receives slightly different messages, and so on.

Moreover, each witness responds differently to the experience, bringing to it the interests and preoccupations peculiar to him — Adamski his 'philosophy', King his occultism, Monnet his interest in space, and so on. It is no less important for us to take these apparent differences into account than to note the features they have in common.

Because we cannot be sure which features of these cases are the ones which will guide us towards their explanation, I have thought it worthwhile to try your patience a little further by adding notes on a further selection of contactee cases. Although many of these stories have been given book-length treatment comparable to those I have already summarized, I shall be even more ruthless in concentrating on those features of them which seem to me to be significant.

Howard Menger
Menger's ET contacts began when he was 10 years old, playing in the woods near his New Jersey home:

> There, sitting on a rock by the brook, was the most exquisite woman my young eyes had ever beheld! The warm sunlight caught the highlights of her long golden hair . . . the curves of her lovely body were delicately contoured — revealing through the translucent material. Even though very young, the feeling I received was unmistakeable — a tremendous surge of warmth, love and physical attraction. She spoke my name and I trembled with joy: 'I have come a long way', and she paused smilingly, 'to see you, Howard.'[175]

She and her people had been observing him for a long time and knew he had a purpose on Earth. 'We are contacting our own . . . As you grow older, you will grow to know your purpose.'

During his schooldays he felt different from the others, isolated. He and his brother both saw flying saucers, one of which landed one day in a field where they were playing. Further experiences while he was doing his army service confirmed that the ETs were still keeping him under surveillance, but formal contact was not renewed until 1946, when he again met the lady he had met in 1932. She had not aged at all during those years, but then, as she informed him, she was more than 500 years old, so a further 14 could make little difference.

Now Menger was given more details of his mission, and instructed as to his conduct, such as that he should become a vegetarian. He performed many duties to help the ETs who came to Earth on their missions. For instance, he cut the hair of the males, who wore long hair when this was unfashionable in crew-cut America, and bought clothes for the females, though they giggled when he produced bras, and refused to wear such things!

He was allowed to photograph the spacecraft, though his ET friends warned him that the pictures would turn out fuzzy, and this proved to be the case. But at least he was able to produce them as evidence to his wife, who had been perturbed about his getting up and driving away into the night.

His account of the flights in space to which he was treated include this pleasant exchange:

> 'Was that the moon?' I asked.
> 'Yes, we just passed it,' he replied in a matter-of-fact manner.

He was taught the music of Saturn while visiting there, with the result that when he returned to Earth, though hitherto he had been an indifferent pianist, he was able to amaze his friends by playing them his space music. Indeed, he now learned that he was in fact of Saturnian origin, having been a teacher there. Moreover, during that earlier lifetime, while on a visit to Venus, he had met and fallen intensely and overpoweringly in love with a Venusian girl called Marla, but it was fated they should not stay together, for he had his mission on Earth to fulfil. Now, however, he learnt that Marla too was on an Earth mission, and what's more, living in his own state of New Jersey. Their earthly marriage in 1958 allowed their interrupted romance to blossom at last.[174]

Many years later Menger made a curious final appearance on Long John Nebel's radio show, on which he had formerly been a frequent guest. As Nebel tells it:

> Howard said nothing, and un-said most of what he had originally claimed. Where he had once sworn that he had seen flying saucers, he now felt that he had some vague impression that he might have on some half-remembered occasion possibly viewed some airborne object — maybe. Where he had once insisted that he had teleported himself, he now speculated that strange things did happen to people and if it hadn't actually occurred to him, well, that's the way the story crumbles. Where he had formerly stated that he had been to the moon, he now suggested that his had most likely been a mental impression of the other side of his consciousness. In other words, Howard Menger backed up, and backed up, until he fell into a pit of utter confusion and finally sank forever into the waters of obscurity.[185]

This is one of the rare instances — indeed, I don't know of another — of a contactee failing to stick to his story. How we should interpret it we can't say without subjecting him to a psychological examination. But it is surely a significant element in his story.

That apart, it runs fairly true to type, even if its details make somewhat heavier demands on our credulity than most. We note once more the sense of having been singled out for an important mission, thanks to his special qualities, and the childhood feeling of being different from other children. The wise and beautiful being conforms to accepted stereotypes, with the true-to-myth feature of looking only a fraction of her 500-plus years. Few contactees, however, have been able to carry their encounter experience to the extent of marrying one of their entities.

Daniel Fry
The jacket of Dr Fry's first book describes him as an 'internationally-

known scientist, researcher and electronics engineer who is recognised by many as the best-informed scientist in the world on the subject of space and space travel'. His PhD was awarded by 'St Andrew's College', London, actually a collegiate church to which anyone may apply for a doctorate who submits a 10,000 word thesis and a modest fee. [139] Dr Fry's thesis was an elaboration of his realization that 'natural laws are curved, not linear', [84] a statement which sounds meaningless to me.

I mention these squalid details less to undermine Fry's credibility than because they illustrate one of the problems which beset the encounter witness whose experience does not sufficiently conform to what is acceptable within his cultural milieu: how to achieve respectability? (We shall consider this aspect of the matter in more detail in Chapter 6.3.) Who the 'many' are who have so high an opinion of Fry's scientific standing is matter for further conjecture, but perhaps it stems from the fact that, being a qualified engineer, he was able to ask rather more intelligent questions than most of those who have been privileged to travel in an ET spacecraft.

> On the evening of July 4, 1950, I had the experience of seeing, touching and riding in an unmanned, remotely controlled space capsule which landed near the White Sands Proving Grounds, New Mexico. I soon learned that this amazing vehicle had obviously been created by a technology considerably more advanced than any known to exist upon this earth. [83]

The first words spoken to him as he approached the spacecraft were 'Better not touch the hull, pal, it's still hot!' This was, however, a disembodied voice, that of A-lan, a spaceman, emanating from a mother craft 1500 km above. Fry was invited to enter the craft, and taken on a half-hour flight to New York and back, at an approximate speed of 13,000 km/h. During the flight he was given details about the spacecraft and the history of those who flew them — descendants of the people who once lived on Earth in Atlantis and Lemuria, first emigrating to Mars but now independent of the planets, living permanently in their spacecraft.

A-lan also explained to Fry that his encounter was not accident:

> When you say that you happen to be here by the merest accident, you underestimate our ability to select the ones to whom we wish to speak. The brains of many earth men transmit readily, but you are one of those rare individuals whose brain also receives well. We have carefully investigated the minds of many of your top scientists. In every case we found that their minds had hardened into a mould based on their present conceptions.

Fry never met A-lan physically or even visually, but they conversed on several subsequent occasions, providing Fry with much information which formed the basis of his teachings. He became a well-known figure on the lecture circuit, and founded an International Cultural Center one of whose functions is to provide training courses enabling spacemen to adjust to the conditions of life on Earth.

Fry, like our other contactees, had a conviction of having been chosen, with the specific responsibility of carrying out a mission he was uniquely qualified to execute. In most other respects his story is less rich in detail, on account of the purely auditory nature of the encounters themselves.

The special interest of the case is that, just as Adamski's encounter confirmed and escalated his role of teacher of philosophy, so Fry's turned him from an undistinguished engineer to the prophet of a new scientific understanding. Had he been at all eminent beforehand, he would already have had his doctorate. His obtaining one by these somewhat dubious means can be seen as an attempt to add authority to an encounter which, while it led to his becoming a celebrity, can hardly have enhanced his scientific status.

Truman Bethurum

Truman Bethurum was aged 54 when he had his initial encounter experience on 27 July 1952, while working for a construction company in California's Mojave Desert. In the course of a private trip he came across a landed spacecraft, which he described as a 'scow (a flat-bottomed boat), 100m in diameter, hovering low over the desert floor'. Its crew of small uniformed humanoids took him to meet their captain:

> That is where my eyes bulged again. I stood before their captain, a beautiful woman. My eyes were glued to the woman, and I paid no attention for the moment to the interior of the saucer. She was a trifle shorter than any of the men I had seen [i.e. less than 1.5 m]. Her smooth skin was a beautiful olive and roses, and her brown-eyed flashing smile seemed to make her complexion more glowing. So this queen of women was the lady captain![17]

Fortunately Aura Rhanes spoke English, for people from the planet Clarion are able automatically to speak the language of any planet they land on. (Regretfully, it must be said that when tested in French they proved less fluent, giving the impression of someone making skilful use of a dictionary.) In the course of their eleven meetings she gave him much information about her home planet, located the far side of the Sun, which is why it is not known to earth astronomers. She had also visited other parts of the solar system, including Mars where — contrary to the findings of our own space probes — she described how 'every home has a beautiful lawn where flowers and shrubs abound; each is a country estate and has five acres of ground'. Life on Clarion too is idyllic — no politics, no taxes, no wars, no delinquency.

At first his wife refused to believe Bethurum's story, but when his two grown-up daughters by an earlier marriage accepted it, and it had been endorsed by 'Professor Adamski and other scientists', she began to believe him, and eventually became a loyal supporter during the public appearances he made when, as a consequence of revealing his story, he had become a well-known figure.

Exceptionally, Bethurum was *not* chosen by the ETs:

> I said, Some people wonder why a common workman like me should be chosen by you to be the recipient of your nocturnal visits instead of some scientist or public official who is well known.
>
> She nodded as it she could understand why some people would wonder about that. Well, it's this way. We looked around this planet Earth for a place to safely land. You happened to be close when we came down.

Nor, apart from the information Aura gave him, was there any mission, any message, any instructions. True, in a later book, Bethurum describes a follow-up visit in 1955 from Aura Rhanes, when she asked him to found a 'Sanctuary of Thought' which would be a place where people would come together to plan to improve the world. But we may reasonably suppose that the naïve Bethurum got the idea not so much from the ETs as by noting the conduct of his fellow contactees.

Bethurum's case is sufficiently different from the others that it is not surprising that UFO historian David Jacobs should write:

> All but the most desperate contactee advocates have considered Bethurum's book to be a hoax . . . a relic of the 1950s, a time when contactees were 'media events'. Its main importance is an example of how individuals have tried to exploit the UFO phenomenon for their own gain. [245]

From the ufological point of view, this is fair comment; such stories are evidently valueless in that respect. But the question of 'gain' is perhaps more complex than Jacobs suggests. No doubt Bethururm did gain, but it is hard not to believe that the first person he fooled was himself. Even if, as well may be, his story has no basis whatever in fact, there are other explanations beside hoax.

What encourages us to pursue those other explanations is the man's naivety. He kept a private scrapbook in which he lovingly collected not only items concerning himself but also others which might lend support to his story, along with his personal comments. We must ask if a calculating hoaxer would produce an item like this:

THIRD VISIT TO MORMON MESA Aug 18 1952

We sat and talked and visited, too
And I admired her build and complexion.
My mind was full of things to ask,
And above all I wanted to feel,
And see, if all I imagined
In this gorgeous creature, was real.
You know, I knew she could read my mind,
And she said, 'Go ahead and see what you find'.
She also added, 'Please have restraint
You might guess something that really ain't'.
Her flesh was real and plenty firm,

> Her shape was like an expensive urn.
> She was just over four feet tall,
> And certainly entrancing, all in all.
> She was beautifully draped, like the modistes will,
> And, I'll say, to know her is my number one thrill.[19]

Granted, we are further now from Teresa d'Avila than we have ever been; even if we allow ourselves to be seduced — as many were — by Bethurum's naive sincerity, we are not going to believe one word of his story. But we still have no yardstick whereby we can separate contactees into 'genuine' and 'fake', and until we can establish some such criteria, we must provisionally extend the benefit of the doubt even to poor old Truman Bethurum and cute little Aura Rhanes from the far side of the Sun.

Helen and Betty Mitchell

ET entities do not seem to be respectors of women's rights: female contactees are very much in the minority. Though this may seem to offer a bleak future for womankind when Earth truly enters the Space Age, this sex-differential may be a revealing clue to the essential nature of the encounter experience.

These two sisters were approached in a St Louis coffee shop in 1957 by two men who identified themselves as Space Brothers from Mars. Later they met an ET from Venus also. They were told that the space people had been watching them on and off since birth:

> We were strangely shocked when they told us of incidents in our childhood that no one could have possibly known excepting the family. They told us that we had been selected as contacts by the people of space to serve as channels through which they could give certain information to Earth . . . the space people were here to guide Earth along the lines of Brotherhood and Science. We were very much amazed at their words, and we noted particularly the kindness and warmth that shone in their eyes. With a single glance from them we seemed to sense the vast wisdom and brotherhood which they must have lived among.[177]

The sisters were supplied with communication devices to facilitate future contact. One day Helen was driven by car to Illinois where she was taken via a small spacecraft to the mother ship hovering high overhead. From here she could see into her own home and phone Betty to say where she was. After a prayer in 'the universal tongue', she enjoyed a superb meal and a display of dancing followed by a game resembling shuffleboard except that you don't have the bother of moving the pieces — your mind does it by telekinesis.

They were given much information, some of which confirmed Angelucci's account of the decline and fall of Lucifer. Helen learnt enough of the interplanetary language to speak some of it at a meeting of the

Kansas City Saucer Club. They passed on warnings that mankind is destined to repeat the catastrophe of Atlantis unless we change our ways. We are also to keep an eye out for fallen angels who are moving among us with evil intent.

The Mitchell sisters have not been heard of since 1964. They were promised a trip to Mars. Perhaps they went, and liked it enough to stay.

Their case is unusual not only because they were female but also because there were two of them. In other cases involving more than one person, one is very much the dominant witness. Thus Howard Menger was the primary contactee, his Venusian wife Marla playing only a secondary role. The Mitchell sisters, by contrast, seem to have shared their experience more equally, though there are indications that Helen played a major role.

Buck Nelson

In more than one sense, Buck Nelson represents the contactee phenomenon at grass roots level. When, following his 1954 experience, he spoke at lectures, he always appeared in his farm clothes. In his account, privately published in Missouri in 1956 and simply entitled *My Trip to Mars, the Moon and Saturn*, he explained: 'I always wear bib overalls no matter where I am. They are what I am used to, and I see no reason to change now. The space men tell me it is best that way, also, because people can recognise me easier that way.'

On 30 July 1954 60-year-old Buck photographed two flying saucers over his Ozark mountain home. The photo is one of the least convincing ever taken of a UFO, being two luminous white patches hovering over a rural scene, but the public accepted the picture as well as his account of a ray 'brighter and hotter than the sun' which instantaneously cured the lumbago and neuritis from which he had suffered for 15 years. Six months later, the flying saucer returned and, hovering overhead, told him via a kind of public address system that they were considering landing in his back pasture and wanted to know if they would be welcome.

Further visits followed, and in April he was taken on a trip to space. He was even permitted to bring his little dog along — so that America's Teddy, not Russia's Laika, can claim to be the first animal in space. Together they visited Mars, which is very colourful; the Moon, where they had a meal in the ruler's house in a crater; Venus, where the cars have no wheels or fenders but otherwise look 'a good bit like our new ones'; on his return Buck stated that 'folks on Mars, the Moon and Venus look like us here on Earth, but are much better looking in general'.

Why, you may well ask, am I inflicting this nonsense on you in the course of what is supposed to be a serious study? The answer is that many people *did* take Buck's account seriously: the author of the preface to the privately published account of his journey, a Mrs Fanny Lowery, wrote in 1956:

The experience of Mr Nelson can fairly stagger the mind of even those of

us who have studied the laws of ontology. However, if you think of him as
a person whose work is similar to that of John the Baptist, foretelling the
coming of a great teacher, then it isn't too hard to take.

What is significant about Buck's story, and sufficient reason why we
should take note of it, is that it provides a measure of what people are
ready and seemingly able to believe. Is the American public any more
or less gullible than ordinary people the world over? There is no reason
to think so. The apparitions of the Virgin Mary at Vallensanges which
we looked at in Part Two, and any number of the seance-room absurdities
which I might have included in Part Three, testify to that credulity which
Ernest Renan said was the only thing which enabled him to conceive the
meaning of infinity.

It would seem that our task is clear: to find the dividing line which
will set Buck's manifest nonsense apart from the genuine experiences. But
it may not be that simple. *We must face the alternative possibility that
the concept of 'genuine' is meaningless in the context of the encounter
experience, and that the 'nonsense' we may discover is irrelevant.*

'Dino Kraspedon'

The actual incidents of Brazilian contactee Kraspedon's encounter
experience are not sufficiently remarkable for us to bother with them here,
though his account[140] is well worth reading. He had long scholarly
conversations with entities from Io and Ganymede, satellites of Jupiter.
What is interesting about his case is the light it throws on the character
of the encounter witness.

Kraspedon, though living in abject poverty, was well educated, and
able to pose questions in Hebrew, Latin and Greek, besides his native
Portuguese. That this is traceable to the time he spent in a seminary for
priests tells us, perhaps significantly, that he is the kind of person who
sets out to become a priest but changes his mind. After his experience
he described himself as more an atheist than anything, but it must be
significant that his ET visitor came to him disguised as a priest, and not
only that, a *Protestant* priest, in overwhelmingly Catholic Brazil.

In 1965 he revealed his true identity, Aladino Felix, and predicted various
disasters including the assassinations of Robert Kennedy and Martin
Luther King, and violent activities by Brazilian terrorists.[26] In 1968 he
was himself arrested as a terrorist, and though one account says that he
had earlier admiited that his book was 'nothing more than sheer invention',
after his arrest he stated 'My friends from space will come here and free
me and avenge my arrest. You can look for tragic consequences to
humanity when the flying saucers invade this planet.'[128]

His five-year prison sentence was reduced to eight months on condition
that he transferred to a house of custody for treatment. Clearly, his entire
case must be judged in the light of this indication of mental instability.
What is interesting is that, despite that fact, it is so true to type.

Woodrow Derenberger

The spate of UFO-related encounters which occurred in the United States in the 1950s caused at the time considerable public and media interest: Adamski, Menger, Bethurum, Nelson, were all in demand for lectures or radio and TV appearances. Even after that interest had faded, witnesses continued to report such experiences, but now they found their audiences in UFO-related cult groups. If fame and fortune had ever been the primary incentive to have an ET encounter (which I personally feel was rarely the case) this was certainly no longer so.

This enhances the credibility of such latter-day accounts as that of travelling salesman Woodrow Derenberger who, driving a van full of electrical equipment in West Virginia one cold and rainy November evening in 1966, was halted by a spaceship blocking his road. From the spaceship an entity emerged, and contact of the standard kind was established between the witness and Indrid Cold, who was visiting Earth on behalf of the Guiding Council of Inter-Galactic Circle, who are concerned that Earth is the only inhabited world that is not a member of the Circle.[46]

Cold took Derenberger on more than one space journey, and he found much the same idyllic conditions as have been reported by other space travellers, though he reports a greater amount of nudity, particularly on Venus and Lanulos, a refreshing change from the Grecian robes which seem to be standard wear on most other worlds. The Lanulos life-style is evidently beneficial, for he met a couple who had emigrated from Acapulco who, though in their 80s, looked to be in their 50s.

I have included Derenberger's case in order to quote from the preface to his book by John Keel, a veteran ufologist whose permissive attitude in the matter of what constitutes fact and what fiction requires continual vigilance on the reader's part, but whose insights and perceptions have been seminal in encouraging paradigm-replacement in ET and UFO research. Of Derenberger he writes:

> I half-expected to find a wild-eyed kook spouting pseudo-science and sophomoric philosophies. Instead, his sincerity was obvious. He did not try to give a 'contactee' sales talk, but merely to present the 'facts' as he knew them. I have had considerable experience with UFO witnesses and 'contactee' claimants and have developed a set of rather tricky questions which I use to cross-check their stories. I was somewhat amazed when Mr Derenberger was able to relate certain details common to many 'contactee' stories, even those details that have never been published and are unknown even to the hard core UFO buffs.
>
> I cannot endorse his story, but I do feel I know the man well enough to say that he seems to be telling the truth as he knows it. He sincerely believes that these things happened to him. By taking a public position on all this, Woody has suffered a great deal. Speaking out has cost him dearly, and he has made no money from it, indeed his insistence has led him to the brink of bankruptcy.

Stefan Denaerde

'Stefan Denaerde' is the pseudonym of a prominent Dutch industrialist whose name if revealed would at once be recognized, so to preserve his anonymity no details are released except that he lives in Den Haag in a tree-lined road facing a park, with his wife, son and daughter, owns a sailing-boat of the *tjalk* type, and is 1.93 m tall; there is also a full-length photo of him in his book.[44]

If that book reads like science-fiction, this is a tribute to his literary skill, for his Iargan contactees specifically instructed him to write his account in that form. He met them in 1967, while sailing. The ETs, whose spacecraft was submerged beneath the waters of the Oosterschelde, were having some difficulties; Denaerde was able to help. In return they treated him, sitting for two days in their submerged spaceship while his family waited, to a detailed briefing about their planet Iarga.

This formed the substance of his book which was originally presented to the Dutch-reading world as a sci-fi novel. Only in its English-language edition, published thirteen years later, was the fiction revealed to be fact.

How much fact there is in it is open to question, but a recent development is intriguing. Denaerde claims that his original briefing was subsequently supplemented by telepathic communications at 4 p.m. each afternoon. Well, it seems that it is at just this time of day that NATO in Den Haag has been bothered by mysterious incoming radio frequency electronic signals.

It is of course the ambiguous status of the Denaerde book which is intriguing. Should we accept his explanation? Should we prefer to think he is lying, conning his American publisher knowing that whereas his Dutch compatriots would never swallow his story, the more gullible Americans would *prefer* fact to fiction? Once again, the question turns on our evaluation of the witness himself.

Elizabeth Klarer

The case of Elizabeth Klarer is the most extravagant to be found within these pages. Against that we must set the fact that Mrs Klarer herself has impressed everyone she has met. She is clearly an intelligent and cultivated person, and her account of her encounter experience[138] is far superior to the general run.

Elizabeth Klarer comes from an upper-class British background, but has lived most of her life in South Africa. She saw her first flying saucer, in the company of her sister, in 1917 when she was a child of 7; it was in the process of diverting the course of an asteroid which would otherwise have hit our planet. In 1937, still long before flying saucers were public knowledge, she had a strange sighting while flying with her husband. They reported it to the military authorities, who were puzzled, but 'my woman's intuition told me this was an alien ship from the far reaches of outer space'.

While serving in wartime Britain, she was given an assignment by the British Government:

> Our planet is under close surveillance by an alien but highly advanced civilisation from outer space. And you, my dear, seem to be dedicated to this. You know what to look for, you are not afraid, and I can think of no one more qualified. Besides, you have intuition and imagination, which is very important in this advanced research . . . You have been thoroughly vetted. We know the full history of your family and its ancient lineage. This extraordinary ability you are so liberally endowed with can be of tremendous value to us.

It was not only the British Government who had been vetting her; the space beings likewise had recognized her unique abilities. So it came about that when, after the war, she returned to South Africa, she had a further sighting of a UFO over her Natal home, and eventually met its occupants. Akon, a scientist from Meton, a planet in the Alpha Centauri constellation, was seeking an Earthwoman as a mate for experimental purposes.

But their relationship rapidly became something more than clinical experiment: 'I surrendered in ecstasy to the magic of his love making, our bodies merging in magnetic union as the divine essence of our spirits became one . . . and I found the true meaning of love in mating with a man from another planet.' As a result she conceived and, after surviving an attempt by the Russians to kidnap her by forcing her into *their* spacecraft, she flew — together with her motor car — to Akon's home planet. There she gave birth to her son Ayling.

Like any other ETs' home planet, Meton is idyllic. There is no pollution, everyone is vegetarian, and there are horses for horse-lovers like Elizabeth Klarer to ride. There is, however, one drawback: Meton has a different vibratory rate from ours on Earth. So, though her lover was able to keep her for four wonderful months while she gave birth, she could not stay with him permanently. So back to Africa came the spaceship, to lower her MG and herself onto the road; a final farewell wave to lover and son, and then she was driving home to scones and honey.

In presenting Buck Nelson's story, the question emerged, whether the American public is especially gullible. By way of answer, it is notable that Elizabeth Klarer's case is hardly known in the United States but has been enthusiastically welcomed in Germany, where the first edition of her book was published and where she has been the guest of honour at national conferences. Researcher Cynthia Hind is by no means the only ufologist to have been impressed, despite the improbability of her story, by the personality of the witness.[110]

We, for our part, must recognize that the improbability is only one of degree. Many features of the Klarer case match those of the classic pattern — her early involvement, the sense of having been chosen for a mission; these remain the core of her experience as they are the core of others, and we must not let ourselves be blinded by the particular circumstances. *This does not mean that the individual differences which distinguish one case from another are unimportant; on the contrary, they are an essential element in the experience. But to understand the experience we must start with what each has in common with others.* Thus our starting-point, in trying to understand what happened to Elizabeth Klarer, is her sense of having been chosen for a mission for which she was uniquely fitted. We can deal with her inter-terrestrial child later.

4.4 ABDUCTION ENCOUNTERS

ET entities are benevolent, kindly, caring; they exude a feeling of warmth, often of love; they frequently take a personal interest in the witness, recognizing his individual merits; they ply him with interesting information and sometimes with delightful drinks, take him on exciting journeys in space and visits to other worlds: this we have seen to be true, to a greater or lesser degree, of each of our contact cases.

But they are not the only kind of case in which ET entities are encountered. We now turn our attention to the so-called *abduction cases*, which appear to form a whole new category with its own set of characteristic features. One question we shall have to resolve is, just how different are abduction encounters from contact encounters? and we must also resolve the puzzling fact that the contact cases, by and large, pre-date the abduction cases. Any explanation of the cases as such must also explain why we had first the one kind of case and then the other.

One of the first cases to contain a hint that ET encounters might take a more sinister form occurred in 1957, when a Brazilian farmer, Antonio Villas-Boas, told how he had been taken on board a spacecraft and confronted with a beautiful spacewoman, with whom he was, more or less reluctantly, compelled to have sexual intercourse.[245]

Those who accept his story rationalize it by supposing that the ETs were conducting some form of biological experiment, and wished the spacewoman to be impregnated by an Earthman in the interests of medical research. This is a plausible enough explanation, and indeed it is the *only* explanation which begins to make sense of this case and of the dozens, maybe hundreds of abduction cases which have since been reported.

But though we may say that it makes sense of a sort, it doesn't make very good sense; and we may well ask, if so inadequate an explanation is the best we can propose, might we not be better off with none at all? Suppose, instead, we take as our starting-point this very fact, that these cases *don't* make sense?

In considering our abduction cases, we should have in mind these alternative methods of approach. We shall find that while some features support the thesis that a massive project of ET intervention in earthly affairs may be taking place, there are others which suggest that the explanation may be found closer at hand. Which is not to say that there is a simple answer in terms of current knowledge. The abduction encounter sets us a remarkable and extraordinary problem; we shall not resolve that problem with an unremarkable and ordinary answer. The abduction encounter is something new in human experience; so, too, must be the explanation we find.

The Hill case

Because this classic case raises virtually every question of the abduction encounter experience, and because almost every incident in it may contain a clue which will help us understand what happened, it seems worthwhile studying it in some detail. If you are already familiar with the case, I suggest you skim it, pausing only to note the specific points which seem significant for the purpose of our study.

Barney and Betty Hill lived at Portsmouth, New Hampshire. Barney was a 39-year-old coloured man who worked as a Post Office sorter, a job rather below his intellectual capacity. He was also active in the campaign for civil rights for coloured people. His wife Betty, 41, was a child welfare worker. Both had been married previously; they were popular and had many friends. Their inter-racial marriage, though sometimes inconvenient, was happy and caused them no obvious tension.

On the night of 19–20 September 1961 they were driving home after a short spur-of-the-moment vacation in Canada. They were driving through the night because their funds were running low. They stopped for a snack at a roadside restaurant, leaving a little after 10 p.m. to drive down US Route 3.

The nearest thing we have to a witness statement is a letter written by Betty five days later to Donald Keyhoe, a prominent flying saucer investigator, whose book she had found when, wanting to know more about their experience, she had visited her library to get more information about flying saucers:

> My husband and I have become immensely interested in this topic, as we recently had quite a frightening experience, which does seem to differ from others of which we are aware. About midnight on September 20th we were driving in a National Forest area in the White Mountains. This is a desolate, uninhabited area. We noticed a bright object in the sky which seemed to be moving rapidly. We stopped our car and got out to observe it more closely with our binoculars. Suddenly it reversed its flight path and appeared to be flying in a very erratic pattern. We continued driving and then stopping to watch it. As it approached our car, we stopped again. As it hovered in the air in front of us, it appeared to be pancake in shape, ringed with windows in the front throughout which we could see bright blue-white lights. My husband was standing in the road, watching closely. He saw wings on each side and red lights on the wing tips.
>
> As it glided closer he was able to see inside this object, but not too closely. He did see several figures scurrying about as though they were making some hurried type of preparation. One figure was observing us from the windows. At this point my husband became shocked and got back in the car in a hysterical condition, laughing and repeating that they were going to capture

us. As we started to move, we heard several buzzing or beeping sounds which seemed to be striking the trunk of our car.[85]

At this stage, there was no more to the case than a fairly dramatic UFO sighting — alarming enough to the witnesses, but nothing more. Then, in the course of questioning by investigators from Keyhoe's organization, NICAP, the 'missing time' puzzle emerged. Barney reported:

They were mentally reconstructing the trip. One of them said, 'What took you so long to get home? You went this distance and it took you these hours: where were you?' I thought I was really going to crack up . . . I realised for the first time that at the rate of speed I always travel, we should have arrived home at least two hours earlier than we did.

So, one 'folklore' element — that *as soon as* the Hills got home they realized there had been 'something odd' about the time they'd taken on the journey — turns out to be not so. Similarly with the allegation that they unaccountably turned onto a side road, the implication being that the ETs somehow brainwashed them into leaving the main road for one which ran in quite a wrong direction. In fact, the map shows that Route 175 — the one they took — runs almost parallel to Route 3. Travelling at night it would be easy to take the other, which in any case is a perfectly viable alternative route.

These trivia are noteworthy, not because they show that anyone was deliberately falsifying, but because they illustrate the mythmaking process at work. To understand the *meaning* of what happened, we must first establish what *did* (and didn't) happen.

Ten days after the incident, Betty started to experience a series of disturbing dreams, in which their sighting, instead of ending when they get back into the car, continues with a series of dramatic events. As they drive, they see a group of men standing in the middle of the road. Barney slows down and the motor dies. The men surround the car, open the car doors, take Barney and Betty by the arms and lead them along a path through the woods to where the spaceship is parked. They are taken inside, and led to separate rooms where they are stripped and subjected to what seems to be a medical examination. The entities are not unfriendly, and the experience is not especially unpleasant. The leader apologizes to Betty for frightening her.

Then she is reunited with Barney, they are led back through the woods to their car. Betty by now is talking with the leader, saying *she is happy about meeting him and begging him to return.*

Intriguing though they were, Betty's dreams were seen by the investigators as part of the case only because they confirmed the impression made on her by their sighting. The investigators in their turn were impressed, and Walter Webb, an astronomer who served as advisor for NICAP, judged that the Hills 'were telling the truth, and the incident occurred exactly as reported except for some minor uncertainties and technicalities . . . I was impressed by their intelligence, apparent honesty, and obvious desire to get at the facts and to underplay the more sensational aspects of the sighting.' Significantly he added:

> Mr Hill believes he saw something he doesn't want to remember. He claimed he was not close enough to see any facial characteristics on the figures, although at another time he referred to one of them grinning . . . It is my view that the observer's blackout is not of any great significance. I think the whole experience was so improbable and fantastic to witness — along with the very real fear of being captured added to imagined fears — that his mind finally refused to believe what his eyes were perceiving and a mental block resulted.

In the course of the ensuing year, Barney's 'block' assumed a growing importance. His health deteriorated and with it his mental state; he was exhausted and depressed. Seeking for a cause, it is not surprising that the Hills should wonder if their UFO sighting could be responsible? They put this to their doctor, who suggested that hypnosis might indicate how the sighting might have affected them. The Hills welcomed the suggestion, and Betty, perhaps with the benefit of hindsight, explained why:

> The moment they suggested hypnosis, I thought of my dreams, and this was the first time I began to wonder if they were *more* than just dreams. I thought, if I have hypnosis, I'll know one way or the other, because I thought, well, maybe my dreams are something that really happened.

In December 1963 Barney and Betty commenced a series of hypnotic sessions which were to last seven months. Dr Benjamin Simon was an open-minded practitioner of experience and repute who enabled the troubled couple to explore their experience in a climate of sympathetic understanding.

The sessions had a specific purpose, to see what relevance the alleged UFO sighting might have to Barney's physical and psychological state; they were not intended to provided a detailed account of Barney and Betty's psychological state, beliefs, attitudes, etc. Consequently there are many questions whose answers would help our inquiry, but about which we can only speculate. One point worth making, though, is that the sessions were being carried out entirely at the Hills' own instigation, and what must have been very considerable expense for a couple in their modest circumstances. Evidently there was an exceedingly strong motivation on their part.

Each of the two was hypnotized separately, with the other out of the room. Neither heard the recording either of his/her own session or the other's until the series of sessions was completed. When they finally heard the tapes, they found that each, independently, had told a story which matched in detail Betty's troubling dreams; but with this difference, that now the events were recounted as direct experiences, each describing them as seen from his/her viewpoint.

For many, the ostensible explanation is the logical one. The Hills had had an alarming experience and so had repressed the memory of it, but it had nevertheless caused unconscious anxiety and conflict. Betty's dreams had revealed this, and now hypnosis had enabled them to bring their worries into the light.

What reasons do we have to look for an alternative explanation?

★ As always, there is not a scrap of supporting evidence. Nobody else saw the UFO, nobody saw the Hills themselves at any stage of their journey, nobody saw them arrive home so as to be able to confirm the 'missing time'. Their testimony is our only reason to suppose that anything occurred at all.

★ Many of the incidents are illogical or inconsistent. The accounts are detailed; but are they as detailed as they should be if they were truly based on something that had really happened? Sometimes, for example, it is suggested the ETs communicated with the witnesses by direct voice, sometimes by telepathy. Surely this is something they might be expected to remember correctly? Such inconsistencies remind us that the story they told is far from being a neat, watertight narrative. [60]

★ The whole case rests on the allegation that the Hills were extremely upset by their experience. But in her account, Betty tells us that as they returned to their car after leaving the spaceship, she told the leader how glad she was to have had the experience and that she hoped he'd return, and she explained her later silence by saying she wished to please the leader. It is surely surprising that a dream which is supposed to reveal repressed anxiety should express such positive feelings?

★ A further assumption is that the Hills attributed Barney's sickness to anxiety over their experience — which at this point, don't let's forget, they believed to be only a sighting, not an encounter. Yet we know that Barney was ill *before* the incident: he did not develop an ulcer in 1962, rather, the ulcer he already had grew worse. Ulcers are notoriously the result of psychological stress; the fact that he possessed the ulcer *before* the incident implies a likelihood that he was *already* suffering from stress. So their UFO experience, while it may have *contributed* to his sickness, did not *cause* it.

★ It is noteworthy that Betty had a history of psychic experiences. The family history includes poltergeist phenomena; as a teenager she had experienced traumatic precognitive dreams; and she reported to psychologist Berthold Schwarz, 'all my close family members have witnessed UFO sightings; my parents, my sisters and brothers, my nieces and nephews'.[226] While this may have no bearing on their experience, it could imply a readiness to look for a paranormal explanation when something unusual occurs.

★ As Dr Simon himself pointed out, revelations in the hypnotic state are not necessarily to be taken at face value: 'The charisma of hypnosis has tended to foster the belief that hypnosis is the magical and royal road to *truth*. In one sense this is so, but it must be understood that hypnosis is a pathway to the truth as it is felt and understood by the patient . . . this may or may not be consonant with the ultimate nonpersonal truth.'[85]

Those who accept the Hills' story as founded on fact, that is, nothing less than an abduction by physical ETs, assume that they had the adventure they described, and that this caused, first Betty's dreams, and subsequently their hypnotic revelations. But an alternative scenario is possible: that *some* incident caused the dreams, *which in turn* led to their hypnotic 'revelations'.

What is the likelihood that Betty's dreams offer a veridical account of a factual experience? This is not what most dreams do: they are generally either total fantasy, or a fantastic reworking of material drawn from a variety of sources — the dreamer's daily life, his reading and televiewing, his wishes and fears. So, even if the events were real, it is not likely that Betty's dreams would have reported them exactly. Consequently, the close agreement between the 'dream-account' and the 'hypnosis-account' strongly suggests that the latter was based on the former, rather than on the original incident.

What is the likelihood that the 'hypnosis-account' offers a veridical account of their experience? The general consensus is that under hypnosis witnesses tell the truth as they see it, as far as they can, but readily supplement it with invention. So the Hills' hypnosis-account could equally well be what really *did* happen, or what Betty dreamed happened, *whichever was the version the two of them believed to be the truth*.

This does not of course rule out completely the possibility that an actual abduction occurred, but it certainly diminishes it. We are faced with difficulties, whichever of the two options we choose:

★ If we accept the abduction story at face value, we have to believe that, exceptionally, Betty had a *factual* dream replay of a real-life experience, and that the *same* experience was subsequently narrated by both witnesses under hypnosis.

★ If we consider the abduction story to be fantasy, we have to accept that an extremely complex psychological process occurred, whereby both witnesses shared a common fantasy based on Betty's dreams, which themselves had been triggered by some appropriate incident.

Though I know of no exact precedent in the literature, some such version as this second option is what Dr Simon himself was inclined to favour. Though he discreetly refrained from committing himself, he stuck his neck out far enough to say:

> I was ultimately left with the conclusion that the most tenable explanation was that the series of dreams experienced by Mrs Hill, as the aftermath of some type of experience with an Unidentified Flying Object or some similar phenomenon, assumed the quality of a fantasised experience.

However we try to explain the Hill case, we have to accept that something very remarkable occurred. But then any encounter experience — on whatever level of reality it occurs — is a remarkable event and will require of us a remarkable explanation.

Consistency or conformity?

Most subsequent abduction accounts have been virtual repeats of the Hills' story. This was notably true of the most dramatic case in Britain, the Aveley abduction, where in October 1974 a young couple named Avis were taken aboard a spacecraft, together with their car and their sleeping children, to have some kind of physical examination. Here too there was a mixture of the plausible and the improbable; here too the 'real' facts of the matter were ascertained through hypnosis, suggested by a 'missing time' phenomenon similar to the Hills'. [245]

Where the Avis case differs from the Hills' is in the effect on the witnesses. The consequences of the English case seem to have been almost entirely beneficial, leading to a change in life-style, new interests, a concern for ecology and a conversion to vegetarianism, and so on. This has an obvious bearing on our estimate of what happened. If a broadly similar experience can have such different effects on different people, it implies that the explanation may be found by studying the people rather than the event.

In any case, the abduction event itself tends to conform to a stereotype with minor individual variations. This raises the question that we have already posed in regard to other kinds of encounter experience: do encounters resemble one another because some external agency is inflicting more or less the same experience on a number of people, or because they are created by the witnesses who model them on an appropriate stereotype?

Either way, where so many cases conform to a basic pattern, it must clearly be a very successful pattern and one which achieves its purpose whatever that may be. What we have to ask, then, is what was that purpose: does it relate to the ETs or to the witnesses? In the notes which follow, therefore, our chief interest will be in the kind of people who have such experiences, and what effect the experiences had on them.

The Schirmer case

Police patrolman Herbert Schirmer, aged 22, was alone in his patrol car cruising the streets of Ashland, Nebraska, at 2.30 a.m. in December 1967, when he came across an unidentified aircraft hovering low over a crossroads. It took off rapidly into the sky. When he reported it a few minutes later (his logbook entry reads: 'Saw a FLYING SAUCER at the junction of highways 6 and 63. Believe it or not!'), he found that 20 minutes more time had elapsed than seemed explicable. Later, under hypnosis, he revealed that he had been taken out of his vehicle by humanoids who had compelled him aboard their spacecraft.

Once there, however, they did no more than talk to him about their presence and their purpose; there was no 'examination'. As is normal with abduction cases, there is no suggestion that Schirmer was specially chosen, though there may be some significance in the entities' first words to him, 'Are you the Watchman of this town?'

Cases like this, of which many have been reported, seem to have very little in common with contact encounters beyond the fact that ETs are involved. Not only was the witness not specially selected, but there seems to have been no previous preparation, and though information was given him it was not in the form of a high-flown message to mankind — no lofty spiritual values, no philosophy. So, while in other cases we may look to some disposition on the witness' part as likely to lead us to an explanation, that is not a factor which seems to play a part here. Rather, everything points to the fact that something objective occurred — except that "everything" means only the witness' own and unsupported testimony. [245]

The Kentucky abduction encounter

Three ladies from near Stanford, Kentucky, were driving home after a late dinner in January 1976, when they all saw a huge disc-shaped object in the sky which they described in classic UFO terms. This was followed by a strange loss of control while driving, and luminous phenomena which, when they got home, seemed to have affected their eyes and skin. They also noted that their journey seemed to have taken 1½ hours longer than would be expected.

Investigation by a UFO group led to hypnosis. During the sessions, each of the three reported having been taken away from her friends to undergo something like a physical examination, but it wasn't the same kind of examination in each case, and other circumstances were different. Nor was there any specific indication that the examination took place on board a spaceship at all. Anxiety was displayed by the witnesses during the sessions, and there was some suggestion of mystical and out-of-the-body experiences. There were long-term personality changes in at least one of the witnesses, who subsequently dressed more colourfully and became more outgoing in her social attitudes.

If we find it hard to explain how the two Hills, living in husband-and-wife intimacy, could share an encounter experience, it is even more of a problem to say how three ladies, who were friends and nothing more, could share what, despite the divergences, we must recognize as essentially the same experience. By far the easiest course is to go along with psychologist Leo Sprinkle, who examined them: 'Although it is not possible to claim absolutely that a physical examination and abduction has taken place, I believe that the tentative hypothesis of abduction and examination is the best hypothesis.'[245]

The Godfrey abduction encounter
At Todmorden, Yorkshire, in November 1980, 33-year-old policeman Alan Godfrey was alone in his car, checking on a reported incident, when he saw a remarkable domed object over the road. He failed in his attempt to make a radio report (this is not necessarily significant, as radio reception is erratic in the area) so made sketches. Then abruptly the object vanished, without his seeing it leave. He returned to town, picking up a colleague whom he told about the sighting; they returned to the location but found no trace of the object.

He reported the incident officially, and some reports from colleagues suggested UFO activity in the area that night. His own memories were confused, and when investigators proposed hypnosis he readily agreed. Under hypnosis he described a typical abduction-and-examination scenario, though he had put up considerably more physical resistance than most. His reliving of his experience was marked by extreme anxiety.[203]

Although the incident seems to have come to the witness out of the blue, it may be relevant to note that he had some strange childhood episodes involving lights in his bedroom, and that he had recently been involved in a police investigation with some bizarre aspects. While there is no obvious connection between either of these circumstances and his encounter, we cannot afford to ignore any possible clue.

Even after watching the videotapes of his hypnosis sessions, Godfrey keeps an open mind as to whether his abduction experience physically occurred. He told ufologist Jenny Randles:

> I never consciously claimed to be abducted. What I said under hypnosis is a mystery to me. I'll accept the fact that it might be something I've read, dreamt or seen . . . If I really believed what I said under hypnosis I probably would not be able to cope. So I have to convince myself that it was a hallucination.

The Andreasson abduction encounter
The Andreasson case is one of the most thoroughly investigated of all abduction cases; it is also the richest in detail. While no doubt it was because of its richness of detail that it was investigated so thoroughly, it could well be that other cases, subjected to such investigation, would reveal more than they do. So we must not be tempted to think that the Andreasson affair is necessarily exceptional in itself, only that it has been exceptionally investigated.

On the evening of 25 January 1967, 30-year-old Betty Andreasson was at home in South Ashburnham, Masschusetts, with her parents and her seven children. Her husband was in hospital following a car accident.

About 6.35 p.m. the house lights failed and a reddish glow was seen outside the house. Her father went to look, and saw some creatures 'like Hallowe'en freaks . . . a funny kind of head-dress imitating a moon man. It was funny the way they jumped one after another — just like grasshoppers. When they saw me looking at them, they stopped — the one in front looked at me and I felt kind of queer.'[79]

Betty, but none of the others, saw the entities enter the house, passing through the door without opening it. They put the rest of the family under a kind of suspended animation, communicating only with Betty, and with her only telepathically. To reassure Betty that her family were in no danger, 11-year-old Becky was temporarily released from her inanimate state. Before being entranced again she saw the entities briefly, and so was able to some extent to corroborate her mother's account.

Betty assumed she had been visited by angels, but in 1975, reading a newspaper article in which ufologist Allen Hynek appealed for cases, she wondered if perhaps hers had been a UFO experience, and wrote to him. After some delay, investigation began in 1977, and it was decided to see if hypnosis would yield results.

Indeed it did. Betty now revealed that she had been persuaded to leave the house and her inanimate family, and to accompany the entities to their spaceship, parked on a nearby hill. In this she seems to have been taken to a larger ship, where she was subjected to a complex series of physical tests. She was very nervous, they did their best to reassure her.

After the tests she was taken via a tunnel to another world, seemingly underground, but with vistas and views of cities. She had a traumatic encounter with a huge bird which she subsequently identified as a phoenix. Eventually, at around 10.40 p.m., she returned home, the family were restored to life, and everyone went to bed, mostly unaware what had happened.

The investigators learned that this was by no means the first encounter Betty had had with her ET visitors. In 1944, when she was 7, while playing alone, she had been approached by a small ball of light which circled her head five or six times, then seemed to sting her. At the time she had thought it was a bee, but later she came to think it might have been the implant of a monitoring device.

In 1949, when she was 12, she saw an entity resembling those of her 1967 visit emerge from a hole in the ground. He directed a small ball of light at her, like the one that stung her at age 7; it hit her in the same place as the earlier one. The next thing she knew, she was lying in the leaves feeling sleepy, and heard — telepathically — a voice saying 'she's got another year'. The voices also told her they were preparing things for her to see, that will help people in the future.

In 1950, when she was 13, she was transported — she couldn't say how — to a room where physical operations of some kind were performed on her. Then she was treated to some visionary experiences, beyond her power to describe. She was told 'This is for you to remember so mankind will understand. You shall enter the Great Door and see the glory of the One.' The 'One' was evidently a supreme being, who gave her spiritual counsel from which the only idea she could express in words was 'those that do not have love have nothing; love is the answer.'

In 1961, when she was 24, she met another ET, who was pleased because she had now accepted Christianity on her own. He told her that many things would be revealed to her, and that she had been watched since her beginning.

In 1967, when she was 30 she received a further message, confirming that she had been chosen to show the world, but telling her that 'the time is not yet' but that secrets were being locked within her mind.

If we can take this remarkable series of encounters at face value, there seems little question what is happening: Betty has been groomed since childhood by the ETs as a suitable instrument to eventually pass on spiritual guidance to the rest of mankind. But some features of her story discourage us from such face-value acceptance:

★ On the purely physical level, the 'suspended animation' of her family is hard to accept. Much has been made of Becky's temporary resuscitation, as confirming her mother's story; well, it's better than no confirmation at all, but the testimony of an 11-year-old in what was evidently a highly charged emotional climate is not to be given unquestioning credence.

★ Betty was a 'born again' Christian; she is reported as poring over her Bible continuously, and she subscribed to the literal interpretation of the Bible as the word of God. Such fundamentalist beliefs, even if they did not actually lead her to a religious experience of this sort, would certainly be liable to direct the way in which she interpreted it.

★ It may be more than coincidence that her husband was not at home at the time of her experience, and that shortly afterwards they divorced and she remarried. (She believed that her entities directed her towards her second husband, who had himself had an abduction experience.)

★ The content of the messages, in so far as Betty was able to put it into words, does not seem to offer anything more profound than unexceptionable precepts which we humans have already thought out for ourselves, even if we have not yet found a way of living up to them. A phrase like 'Love is the answer' is, as a statement, quite simply meaningless. So is the injunction that mankind must 'study nature', or the promise that knowledge will be given to those who are 'pure in heart' and 'seek with earnestness'.

★ Betty's story is full of incidents which suggest dream. Thus at one point Quazgaa, her guide, asks her to look over at the spaceship, and he has made the bottom like glass so that she can see right through it.

★ Although we are told that she got in touch with UFO investigators as the result of a newspaper article in 1975, on another occasion we learn that between her 1967 experience and her 1975 letter to Hynek she studied books and articles about UFOs. All this, by the time of her hypnosis sessions, was therefore available for her to feed back as cryptomnesic hidden memory, or to serve as raw material from which her altered-state mind could construct a fantasy scenario.

This extraordinarily revealing case presents us with a witness whose encounter represents overall a classic abduction experience, but introduces many features of the contact experience. While most abductees seem to have been chosen because they were where they were, Betty had been marked since childhood; and her visionary experiences were custom-made for her, no doubt with her spiritual development in mind.

Betty Andreasson is far from being the only abductee who seems to have been chosen for her individual qualities. Indeed, the very fact that such experiences have been reported by the score if not by the hundred gives the basic problem an intriguing additional dimension.

From contact to abduction

Since the 1960s, the great majority of ET encounters have been of the abduction rather than the contact pattern, and if we knew why there has been this swing from one pattern to the other, it would help us to understand the phenomena themselves.

The simplest way of accounting for it is to suppose that the visiting ETs had reached a point in their study of Earthpeople where they found it necessary to conduct physical examinations of specimen humans. In support of this interpretation some very ingenious scenarios have been offered, in many of which our human race is regarded as being at the level of livestock on a farm, placed on this planet by some more advanced species and periodically inspected to keep track of our progress. The best-known formulation of this is Charles Fort's 'We are Property'.[78]

The working out of such a hypothesis has generally been left to sci-fi writers, and few ufologists take it seriously. However, Jean Giraud and his GABRIEL group, seeking a theory which would provide a global explanation for the UFO phenomenon, proposed a scenario wherein beings from another world, discovering that the human race (which they may even have brought into existence) shows primitive signs of intelligence, and being unable to make direct contact because they are so totally different from us, despatch humanoid robots (= ETs) to monitor our development. The abduction phenomenon would fit such a hypothesis quite well, but Giraud and his colleagues admit that it is no more than speculation.[91]

Those who devise such entertaining speculations are working from the premise that abductions do in fact take place and are pretty much as described. There are others, though, for whom such a premise is less easy to accept than its contrary, that abductions do *not* occur but are a fantasy of some kind.

Support for this view has come from the work of Alvin Lawson and his colleagues in the 'imaginary abductee' experiment.[148] This came about as a consequence of a UFO investigation, the Brian Scott case, in which investigator John DeHerrera was puzzled by the ambiguous indications of a witness who refused to admit that any abduction had occurred, yet under hypnosis fabricated an *imaginary* abduction of extraordinary verisimilitude.[42]

The experiment consisted of hypnotizing volunteer subjects — who have no particular interest in the UFO phenomenon — then suggesting to them that they are involved in a UFO-abduction situation.' They are led through its successive phases by means of guided questions, so there is no claim that the subjects fabricate the entire story. But what the experiment showed was that the bare bones of the questions, involving a minimal suggestion, were sufficient to inspire the subjects to create an elaborate, detailed and dramatic story — which was of course entirely fiction.

Moreover, the way in which the 'imaginary abductees' developed their story, the details they supplied, were strikingly similar to the claims of the 'true' abductees.

There have been a number of critical comments on this experiment, but the central finding is unequivocal: it seems to be beyond coincidence, and can hardly be ascribed to cryptomnesia — though one or two subjects might be drawing on hidden memories of abduction stories they had forgotten they'd read, it is asking too much to suggest this could be true of an entire batch.

Any conclusions we draw from this experiment must be tentative, since neither Lawson nor anyone else has pushed the research further or even replicated the original findings. But — and this is important — it is safe to say that *while the experiments do not prove that the 'true' abductees are making up their stories, they do suggest that anyone who subconsciously wishes to do so is able to find within himself the necessary resources.*

The Lawson experiments did indicate one major area of difference between the 'imaginary' and the 'true' abductees: the emotional effect, and sometimes the physiological effect, on the witness. The volunteers were not in a strongly emotive state, they had no psychological after-effects such as amnesia, dreams, nightmares or psychic experiences; 'true' abductees are liable to have all these things, including physiological effects.

This is often interpreted by critics of the experiment as a demonstration of the reality of the 'true' experiences. But it demonstrates nothing of the kind. What it demonstrates is that the 'true' abductees are in a truly emotional state. But we can now say, significantly, that it is at least as likely that a witness has an abduction experience because he is in an emotional state as that his emotional state is the consequence of an abduction experience.

It is clear that, whatever its nature, the abduction witness has a genuinely emotional experience; no one who sees the videotapes of Yorkshire policeman Alan Godfrey's recall of his experience under hypnosis could be in any doubt of that. But while it shows that he had something to be emotional about, we must not jump to the conclusion that the abduction experience was the cause. As we shall see when we go into this question more fully in our concluding analysis, it may have been part of the cure.

Hallucination or reality?

A psychologist who has made a special study of alleged abductees, Dr Aphrodite Clamar, says: 'The question persists: is the UFO experience genuine, or are those who claim to have been abducted the victims of hysteria or their own delusions? After spending more than fifty hours with a dozen subjects under hypnosis, I still cannot answer that question. I am persuaded that all of the subjects do believe that something strange and unknown did occur' — but conviction can, as we saw with the witches who were so sure they had attended a sabbat, be founded on hallucination. 'It is the curious similarity of their experiences that gives pause.'[112]

It is largely his finding that one witness after another, who could not have been aware of one another's experiences, came up with substantially the same story with the same bizarre details, that has convinced investigator Budd Hopkins that abductions are physical and literal fact:

> For me, the conclusion is inescapable: They [the ETs] are already here . . .
> Though I do not *want* to believe this, and feel decidedly unnerved by it, I
> believe it is true: extraterrestrials have been observing us in our innocence
> for many years.[112]

Apart from the similarity of the stories, he believes we have more tangible evidence. For instance, he finds that a great many of his subjects have inconspicuous scars, usually on their legs, and that these are often associated with some rather mysterious incident in childhood. The implication is that they relate to the kind of surveillance we saw in the Betty Andreasson case, and may indicate the implant of a monitoring device, or be the result of a blood test or some such.

Hopkins has more than once been able to successfully predict that a witness will find a scar on his body that he didn't know he had, and this certainly points to the reality of the phenomenon. But difficulties remain.

If ETs are putting implants in substantial numbers of children, surely by now *some* doctor *somewhere*, examining a child, would have come across one? Again, our earthly surgeons can make incisions which leave virtually no scar: surely these advanced beings could be expected to have found a way of carrying out their tests without leaving tell-tale traces?

What alternative explanations are on offer? There is always coincidence, of course. Have you ever examined your body to check whether you, too, have such a scar you have forgotten or never even noticed you had? Or perhaps they are some kind of stigmata effect? Or perhaps it was finding such scars that prompted their owners to fantasize an explanation of how they came by them? Lame explanations, I'm the first to admit; but even if we dismiss natural causes and look to the paranormal, we are still not committed to the ET-abduction hypothesis.

The scar phenomenon is not the only curious recurrent feature of abduction cases, but it is perhaps the most striking evidence for their reality. If so, it is clearly too soon to abandon the search for alternative explanations.

Evaluating the abduction experience

Abduction experiences confront us with a paradox, and with very little that might help us to resolve that paradox. They offer very little objective evidence, and that little ambiguous; they offer us only a *story*, told in all good faith, no doubt, but none the less subjective and unsubstantiated. And as every psychologist and every schoolteacher knows, and as Lawson has shown to be no less true in this specific context, everyone can tell a story.

Nevertheless, those who like Hopkins feel that the weight of the evidence is in favour of real experience have persuasive grounds for their belief:

★ Abduction experiences are spontaneously reported by witnesses who are not ostensibly seeking material advantage.

★ They involve a genuine emotional response. Lie-detector tests confirm that the stress is real enough.

★ In multiple abductions the accounts tally close enough to persuade us that the witnesses shared the same experience.

★ Recurrent features, reported by witnesses who could not be aware of others' testimony, suggest that the same external process is happening to many people.

★ Independent tests[86,131] have shown that abduction witnesses have no obvious pathological background or discernible predisposition to paranormal experience.

★ Abductees often report a change in life-style and outlook. The Gansbergs, who carried out follow-up investigations of several

American abduction witnesses, reported that in almost every case the witness felt his life had benefited: and we saw that this was true of the Aveley case. [87] Such real benefits suggest a real cause.

This is a formidable challenge. However, the objections are hardly less forceful:

★ The stories are implausible. The ET visitors are improbable in themselves — it defies reason that so many spacecraft should successfully avoid detection while visiting our planet, particularly since no two ET crews seem to be the same, implying a vast number of points of origin. Their behaviour towards the witness is illogical, no matter how much allowance we make for the possibility that ET logic may be different from ours.

★ There is a total lack of hard evidence. When witnesses try to retain souvenirs, they are always prevented. There are no convincing photographs of spaceships, not to mention the entities.

★ No abduction has ever been witnessed by an outsider. The closest we come to it is the 1975 Travis Walton case, in which six companions of a forestry worker signed an affidavit to say they saw the witness walk towards a spaceship. None saw him actually go aboard the craft where he claimed he spent the ensuing week. That sounds sufficiently impressive, but the manner of investigation has been criticized and the findings remain ambiguous. [245]

★ Though psychological tests suggest that abduction witnesses are normal people who are telling the truth as they know it, they also indicate that they suffer from 'a mild paranoia — hypersensitivity, wariness etc' [86] Hardly enough to build a case on, admittedly, but a reminder that we rarely have psychological data on witnesses *before* their experience. We do often have anecdotal testimony, however, and this often points to some kind of predisposition. Both Betty Hill whose story we have noted, and Charles Hickson, one of the witnesses in the classic 1973 Pascagoula abduction, [108] testified to anomalous experiences previous to their abduction.

★ Not only do we know little about witnesses' psychological state, we are often not well informed about the outward circumstances of their lives, though these could well have a bearing on their attitudes and behaviour. John Rimmer [211] noted that out of eleven abduction witnesses whose personal circumstances are known, eight were widowed, divorced or having sexual or marital difficulties at the time. He suggests that this would make them particularly vulnerable to suggestion.

★ American sociologist Ron Westrum has noted a 'contagion effect' whereby a rash of abduction reports occurs immediately after the publicizing of a story like that of Barney and Betty Hill. [86] This is a complex sociological phenomenon which can be interpreted in different ways, but one of the possibilities is that the abduction experience has become as much part of American folklore as the phantom hitchhiker. That virtually every abduction encounter occurs in the Americas may simply relate to the social acceptability of being an abductee, but there could be a deeper explanation.

★ In many abduction cases, e.g. the Schirmer and Hill cases, it is alleged that the ETs have programmed their captives not to consciously remember their experience, and to this is attributed the fact that most abduction experiences are revealed only via hypnosis. It may be so, but the implication, that the ET abductors, for all their technological superiority, are unaware of the process of hypnosis as a method of information retrieval is hardly probable. Could there be another reason?

What happens to someone when he is hypnotized is still not fully understood, but it is well enough established that hypnosis, along with other altered states, facilitates many kinds of psychological and psychic processes which are inhibited in the normal state. If whatever happened to the witness occurred on some other level of reality than the here-and-now, this could be a good reason why he would need to be in one of these altered states in order to retrieve it. Hypnosis is currently the most amenable to control of such states, hence its use for this purpose, but I think it likely that other states would serve equally well if they were as much at our bid and call. (We shall be considering the implications of this in section 5.2.)

In fact, the necessity for hypnotic recall, rather than bearing out the veridical nature of the experience, seems the strongest possible indication that whatever is happening, is doing so on some other level of reality than the here-and-now.

★ The existence of a folklore tradition of kidnapping by fairies and other otherworldly entities[63,102,260] shows that the *idea* of abduction is widespread and deeply rooted. While this is not an objection to the abduction claims *per se*, it reminds us that it is a mistake to think of the abduction experience as a novel phenomenon born of the Space Age. It has served as the basis for fantasy experiences in the past (unless, that is, you accept the tradition of fairy kidnapping as fact) and it may be doing so again.

Setting these two sets of factors side by side, it is evident that neither adds up to a clear case for or against the reality of the abduction experience. Nor is it likely to until more solid evidence is offered us.

4.5 ENCOUNTERS WITH COSMIC GUARDIANS

The nearest thing to tangible evidence left after an ET encounter is the messages.

We have seen that messages are a feature of all kinds of encounter experience. Man's first encounters with God were to receive instructions, present-day encounters with the Virgin Mary are doom-laden with warnings for humankind. Millions of pages must have been covered with messages dictated by the dead. And to judge by my bookshelves, it won't be long before as many more are filled with messages from Cosmic Guardians.

ET messages differ from many of the others in that they are not usually associated with a rigid belief system. Not that this has prevented many people finding a place for them among their own beliefs. Fundamentalist Christians are particularly prone to this sort of thing:

> The devil's angels are certainly no respectors of God, and have indeed appeared to man. *They are calling themselves visitors from space today* . . . The appearance of UFO in our skies means the devil is intensifying his satanic campaign against good and against God.[28]

I don't know whether Stuart Campbell is basing this assertion on his personal experience, but he produces no other evidence that ETs are diabolical by nature. Nor does American evangelist Billy Graham who, though less dogmatically, favours the contrary view:

> Some Christian writers have speculated that UFOs could very well be a part of God's angelic host who preside over the physical affairs of universal creation . . . UFOs are astonishingly angel-like in some of their reported appearances.[97]

It is significant that most such attempts to fit ET encounters into existing belief systems are made by commentators rather than by the witnesses themselves. They, for their part, are ready to take their encounters at face value: their entities are simply people from other worlds, existing on the same plane as the rest of us, otherworldly in the literal sense of the word, rather than heavenly or nextworldly.

We have already seen, when considering other categories of encounter, that this need not be so great a difference in practice as it might seem to be in principle. Many, perhaps most witnesses have tended to treat their entities as though they were human beings like themselves. After all, that is what many of them — Jesus, Mary, the Saints, the dead — are supposed to have formerly been.

Though ET encounters have been occurring (unless you accept the ancient-astronaut thesis) for only a relatively short time compared with our other categories, that has been time enough for them to form their own myth (by which I mean a consensus 'story', like the Virgin Mary story and the spiritist story, implying neither that it is true nor that it isn't).

The ET myth exists in several versions, some of which contradict others (as is no less the case with the Virgin Mary myth and the spiritist myth). The principal ingredients are the *entities* the witness encounters; the *worlds* from which those entities come; and the *messages* those entities have left those worlds to bring us.

The entities

Central to most encounter experiences is the notion of ET entity as 'Cosmic Guardian', 'Space Brother' and so forth. They exist in a variety of versions and are known under a number of labels, the differences between labels reflecting the differences in the way they are conceived. For many, the notion of 'guardian' or 'brother' is altogether too benevolent, while for others it is hardly adequate to describe the intensity of love and depth of compassion the beings radiate.

Common to all, however, is a recognition that these beings are superior to ourselves. Here is just one example, from contactee Kelvin Rowe's account:

> I, as many others of this planet Earth, have met, associated with, benefited by and enjoyed the presence of these highly superior beings from other worlds whose development is inconceivable to people of Earth. We have found them to be shining examples of what we of Earth should be, what we can be, and shall become despite man's solely materialistic minds and egotistical, dominating, destructive nature.[217]

The other worlds

Often witnesses tell us not only of cosmic entities but of entire cosmologies. George King, who is kept informed of events in the universe by virtue of his privileged position as the terrestrial representative of Interplanetary Parliament, offers us a coherent and plausible scenario which, had there been any evidence for it apart from the statements issued by King himself, might have attracted a wider following than the 1,000-strong membership (1980 figures,[220]) of his Aetherius Society.

We have seen that some ET encounters were first presented as science fiction, and the snippets I have quoted from witnesses' accounts of life on other worlds show either that the sci-fi authors are remarkably good prophets, or that all other worlds resemble one another, whether they are fact or fiction.

The messages

Sadly, it is largely true that when you have heard one message from Outer Space, you have heard them all. Here is one that will serve as a sample of the rest, chosen almost at random. I must point out, though, that it is characteristic only so far as its content goes; the typical message is verbose, repetitive, confused and confusing, generous with the platitudes but miserly with practical advice, often illiterate, frequently ignorant of scientific fact, prone to reflect the personal preoccupations of the witness, and above all stupefyingly long. No brief excerpt can convey the impact of the thing itself.

In this instance, some time in the 1960s, the proprietor of a rustic inn in the Ardennes and his friend the narrator had gone out in the snowy field to investigate some strange lights, only to find an ET spacecraft parked in the field. The voice that came to them from inside it told them, among other things:

> We are not the first extraterrestrials to come from a distant galaxy to visit you. Beings like us are among you in all parts of your planet, for our total knowledge of the body enables us to reproduce an individual in multiple starting from his genetic code, and has given us the power to mingle with you in order to know the nature of your development and with a view to eventually establishing scientific contacts.
>
> Alas! Without realising it, you have committed the error of taking the path whch leads inexorably to destruction without the chance of retreat, and the present age is the final phase of that path.
>
> You have not polluted your planet with impunity; radio-active dust impregnates its atmosphere after each insane atomic test explosion. And the least war, be it nuclear, chemical or bacteriological, would lead to the biological end of your generation.
>
> Life will continue for millions of years on Earth, but the way things are going, it is highly unlikely that man will be among the surviving species.
>
> What we say to you now, we have said many times before. We know that nobody will believe you if you dare to report this declaration, just as those we have warned in the past have not been believed. [160]

Almost we seem to hear the Virgin warning us that she cannot hold back the hand of her angry son much longer . . . and here, just as with the visions of Mary, we have to ask: why go on giving these futile warnings (which in this instance the speaker himself acknowledges to be futile!) to unknown persons in out-of-the-way spots?

It is no exaggeration to say that I could find scores of such messages from the material on my shelves: our Earth is on a collision course with catastrophe, thanks to your greed and my materialism. Sometimes there is hope — if we act promptly; sometimes there is no hope, we are doomed to inevitable destruction; sometimes — but very rarely — the ETs offer to help us.

In the latter category are the messages given to Marion Dorothy Martin

('Mrs Keech') who in 1949–50 was warned that a catastrophe involving the destruction of the world was imminent, but that those who believed the ETs would be rescued in time. She managed to persuade a handful of others: Charles Laughead ('Dr Armstrong') of Michigan State University gave up his university post and devoted himself entirely to spreading the warning, issuing press releases about the forthcoming event and the possibility of safety by evacuation for some. Others gave up less prestigious employment, left their home, broke family ties, and joined Mrs Keech in waiting hopefully for rescue.

Among them, though incognito, were sociologists who had seized the opportunity to observe the cult from within. The resulting study [74] gives unique insight into the motivation of believers who allow themselves to be persuaded by the ET myth.

As it turned out, the expected flying saucers never arrived to take the group members to safety on some other world. However, since the announced catastrophe never took place either, this did not matter too much — except in what it did to the lives of those concerned.

ETs among us
The claim is frequently made that the space beings have representatives living here on Earth, and recently claims of people to actually *be* such ETs have proliferated. The 1 May 1979 issue of the *National Enquirer* reported that 'top-ranking American scientists' agree that there may be such 'Star People' living among us. The *Enquirer* is not widely regarded as a primary source of information on matters scientific, nor are we informed by what ranking procedure these unnamed scientists qualify as 'top'; but be that as it may, it is certain that a considerable number of people — mostly citizens of the United States — have persuaded themselves that they are ETs, sometimes born of ET parents, sometimes inhabiting Earthperson's bodies (a young lady in Wyoming told me in utter seriousness that she is an ET who has swopped bodies with an Earthgirl so that she can carry out her mission on Earth).

The popular American author Brad Steiger has worked hard to promote this concept. Many years ago, Steiger wrote books with titles like *Flying Saucers are Hostile*, but since then he has learnt that they are not, their intentions are honourable. This he discovered about the time that he met his wife Francie who, interestingly enough, is a Star Person herself. In a book they wrote together [240] Francie and Brad list more than a score of signs which tell you if you are one of 'them': you have compelling eyes; you had unseen companions as a child; you often have flying dreams in which you move freely through the air; you are hypersensitive to electricity and electromagnetic fields; though you express love for your parents, you feel that your mother and father are not your 'real' parents; you sense that your true ancestors came from another world, another dimension, another level of consciousness, and you yearn for your real home beyond the stars.

Clearly, the 'Star People' myth is very close to the ET encounter myth, and indeed to encounters of all kinds:

★ The individual is set apart from the rest of mankind, and given a sense of identity, even of importance.

★ The individual who is bothered because he feels somehow 'different' from other people is provided with a plausible and even flattering rationale.

★ Sanction for this situation, and recognition of the individual's status, come from superior beings in an authority position, to whom the individual can relate and who act as referee for his claims.

We shall see that these aspects will be of the greatest relevance when we assess the cultural and psychological aspects of the encounter experience as a whole.

4.6 COMMENTS ON PART FOUR

Each encounter case can, and *should*, be seen on the one hand as an individual experience, and on the other as part of a universal phenomenon. But whichever way we look at them, there are questions to be asked.

If the same thing is happening to each of our witnesses, why do we find so many differences between their accounts? There should be a general consensus as to the identity of the ETs, their purpose, their *modus operandi*, etc. Though in the broadest terms we do find this, it is evident, for instance, that no two ET spacecraft crews are identical, or for that matter their spacecraft. Which suggests that each encounter is a one-off event.

Yet if each is a one-off event, why do we find so many common features — the physical examinations, the scars, the messages, the appearance of the entities, and all kinds of specific details?

This paradox is at once the challenge we have to resolve and the key which will help us to resolve it.

ET encounters as a global phenomenon

The cases I have referred to here are just a handful from hundreds, maybe thousands. The sheer quantity of these happenings makes them important, whether they turn out to be 'real' — that is, if Earth is truly being visited from other worlds — or 'unreal' — that is, if our witnesses are only imagining the visits.

At first sight the number of events seems like an argument in favour of reality. For why — unless he was reporting something that really happened — would a Brazilian truck-driver claim to have an experience which closely replicates one reported by an American schoolteacher?

That matters aren't that simple is indicated by the closest parallel we have for such a global phenomenon — the witchcraft mania. There, too, a great number of people, strangers to one another, claimed to have what was basically the same kind of experience. Although there is still a great divergence of opinion among scholars on many aspects of the subject, there is a general consensus of agreement that, to put it crudely, witchcraft events occurred only because the idea of witchcraft existed; or to put it another way, if the idea of witchcraft had not existed, there would have been no witchcraft events.

This does not mean that witchcraft was an idea without foundation;

certainly there must have been a 'something' round which the idea of witchcraft could form like a pearl round a grain of sand.

Nor does it mean that without the idea of witchcraft, *no* event would have occurred. No doubt some event would have occurred, but it would not have been a witchcraft event, but something else.

But the witchcraft phenomenon, as we know it, was a social artefact — a process whereby an idea, because it happened to be the 'right' idea in that social context and at that time, inspired certain events, which, by their very occurrence, seemed to turn the idea into reality.

To say that what is happening today in the case of ET encounters is the same as what was happening then in the case of witchcraft is pure hypothesis; but it is a hypothesis we must consider, because it is the only way of accounting for the phenomenon which has any precedent in human experience.

ET encounters as individual experience

Not everyone in the Middle Ages had a witchcraft experience; it was something that happened to some people and not to others. And it wasn't like the Black Death, striking indiscriminately; it was something that chose its victims — or which the victims themselves chose.

It is easy to forget that there must have been reasons for this discrimination — because we have no means, now, of getting at the individual witness and finding out what was motivating him, we tend to concentrate our attention on the broader, social aspects of the phenomenon. But to the individual involved in witchcraft, the personal aspect must have far outweighed the other; and so it is with our ET encounters today. Far and away the most important question we can ask about them is, why do some people have them and not others?

The *idea* of ET encounters, how that idea grew and why it caught on — and the *discrimination* of ET encounters, why they happen to some and not to others: these are the two most intriguing questions posed by this kind of encounter, and two promising lines of inquiry for us to follow in the analysis upon which we now embark.

5.1   THE PROCESS OF ENCOUNTER

Thousands of people now living, to say nothing of people in times past, claim to have had experiences more or less like those we have looked at in the preceding phase of our study. This is to say, a significant proportion of the human race has claimed encounters with otherworldly beings; and many more, without having had such experiences themselves, believe that those experiences were genuine. In 1980, Lourdes alone received 4,350,000 visitors from 115 countries, most of whom, we may presume, accepted the assertion of young Bernadette that she had met the Virgin Mary.

Yet, as we have seen, the grounds for that assertion, and for all such assertions, are ambiguous at best. What can we do to resolve this ambiguity? What is really happening when a witness has such an experience?

First, though, let us be in no doubt that a genuine experience of some kind occurs in the vast majority of cases. Conscious deception and deliberate fraud certainly occur, but sufficiently rarely that for our purposes they are of interest only because they give us a useful 'control' whereby to judge witness motivation and public response. Second, we cannot seriously entertain such nebulous explanations as 'mass delusion', 'mass hysteria' or 'mass hallucination' unless we can offer evidence that such processes actually exist and that they may be operating in encounter cases.

What then are our options?

★ We can believe that *all the accounts are true as reported*. However, we have clear evidence that some witnesses are mistaken, for example witches who are tucked up in bed when they claim to be meeting the devil, or 'psychics' who meet beings we know to be imaginary because they have been deliberately concocted by researchers. In addition, we find inconsistency and contradiction between encounters, meaning that if some are true, others must be false.

★ We can accept that *some of the accounts are true and others are not*. Not one of the pilgrims who accept Bernadette's claim also believes that the other alleged visionaries of Lourdes had genuine encounters. Yet it is hard to see on what criteria those others should be rejected. Similarly, spiritists believe that sometimes they make genuine contact with spirits of the dead but on other occasions encounter mischievous impersonating spirits. Yet the notion of such spirits is pure speculation: there is no independent evidence for their existence; they are no more than a useful *a posteriori* device for explaining how spurious encounters occur. If we are to exercise discrimination, we must establish clear-cut yardsticks for distinguishing the true from the false.

★ We can assert that *none of the alleged encounters occurred as claimed*. To prove a negative proposition is notoriously difficult; probably the most we could accomplish would be to show that an alternative explanation exists, and that it has a greater probability than the ostensible explanation. Two things would add to this probability: first, if we could show it to explain a wide variety of experiences which at present require a diversity of one-off explanations; and second, if it accounted for both the 'true' and the 'spurious' claims.

This is where we may hope that the comparative approach will pay off. For example, the Andreasson abduction case is extremely impressive as it stands. There seems little doubt that the witness had a remarkable experience which transformed her life. Though there are some uncomfortable questions — why didn't the neighbours notice the UFO sitting for so long in her back yard or rising in the sky to take her to wherever she was taken to? — they do not justify us in dismissing her story as mere fabrication.

However, when we range her experience alongside others, questions of a different kind suggest themselves. Why are her ET visitors totally independent from the ET visitors encountered by other witnesses — especially since they themselves state that she is just one of thousands they have contacted? Where are those others? Certainly not among the numerous other encounter claimants, whose accounts make it clear that they have not been abducted or contacted by Betty Andreasson's particular visitors.

It rather looks as though what happened to Betty was something like this: she had an experience (we'll get around to how and why she had it later) which she was sincerely convinced was a visit from otherworldly beings (we'll also sort out why her experience took this particular form) and which did indeed have several features in common with other visits from otherworldly beings as reported by other witnesses. However, her account contains dubious features which make others question whether what *seemed* to happen *really* happened: rather, it seems she had a *personal* experience, dressed up to look like other cases (no doubt to convince her that it was the real thing), but in fact unique to herself.

It may in fact be something like a girl's dress: if my daughter is offered a dress, the first thing she will want to be sure of is whether it conforms to the current fashion, and only then will she consult her personal tastes. So, it seems, encounter experiences are required to conform, overall, to an accepted format or pattern, and only when that has been observed are they adapted to the individual's needs.

If so, it seems that the most important thing encounter cases have in common is, paradoxically, what they *don't* have in common: that despite ostensible similarities each is a one-off experience created with the individual witness in mind. If this conclusion is correct, we know what we must start by looking for: a process which will enable someone to have an experience which, though others can see it's not what it seems to be, is sufficiently convincing to make the witness himself believe he has had a genuine encounter with an otherworldy entity.

5.2 HALLUCINATIONS AND ALTERED STATES

It is likely that most people who seek to account for encounter experiences, as opposed to accepting them at face value, do so in terms of *hallucination*.

By hallucination is generally understood *the apparent perception of an object when no such object is present*. (It is possible to elaborate on this set of words, and many have done so, but the basic proposition remains the same.) Strictly speaking, then, the issue is clear: either the Virgin Mary was objectively present when she appeared to Delphine, or Delphine was hallucinating. However, 'hallucination' is not a definition, merely a label which denotes a process in general terms — and, what is more, describes it negatively. The phrase 'when no object is present' applies only to the level of physical reality we think of as 'real' in everyday usage; it leaves the door open for hypotheses such as that the Virgin may have been *subjectively* present. Montmorand, a French psychologist uncharacteristically sympathetic to the mystics' claims, takes advantage of this door to state categorically: 'If supernatural beings ever manifest, since they are discarnate or purely spiritual in essence, they cannot do so except by means of provoked hallucinations.'[182]

'Hallucination' is, in short, a *relative* description. It leaves theologians and others who hold that other levels of reality exist free to believe that some encounters, at least, occur on these levels. So a visionary like Delphine may be temporarily transposed onto some other level for the purpose of having her experience.

From the standpoint of that level, I dare say, she would not be hallucinating but having a real experience. However, we are making our study from the terrestrial standpoint, and on the terrestrial level Delphine is hallucinating.

It is this confusion which has made theologians reluctant to see obviously valuable experiences reduced (as it seemed to them) to morbid psychological processes. Once it is seen that what is involved is shifting the point of view, rather than reduction, and that there is far more to hallucination than a morbid psychological process, it should be possible for theologians and psychologists to keep company a while longer along the path.

If it could be demonstrated that other levels of reality exist, we could suppose that encounters take place on two levels in the same way that the wine used in the Catholic Mass, which from a terrestrial standpoint is fermented grape juice, becomes under appropriate conditions, according to Catholic doctrine, the blood of Jesus. As things stand, however, the existence of this other level is no more than an article of faith associated with a particular belief system, and while we must certainly regard it as a possibility, science gives us no right to assume it and indeed requires us to see how far we can manage without it.

Hallucination as malfunction

One reason why theologians and other 'believers' have been reluctant to classify mystical encounters as hallucinations is because they associate hallucination with mental malfunction.

Hallucinations occur so frequently in pathological states that we can understand why the two should be associated; nevertheless an intelligent commentator should know better. When a person hallucinates he is doubtless in a *special* state, but not necessarily a *pathological* one. There are other altered states, favourable to hallucination, beside those induced by sickness, drugs or intoxication.

Similarly, there is no reason for theologians to suppose that a different process is involved in their 'true' and their 'spurious' mystical experiences. The eminent and generally perceptive French scholar Lhermitte falls into this trap when confronted with a case like the following:

A good and pious man, for many years occupied in public administration, was accustomed each day to make prolonged devotions to the Holy Virgin. One day, without warning, he thought he heard the Virgin murmur into his ear these actual words: 'Be blessed; pray and I will favour you.' Such utterances so surprised him that at first he couldn't bring himself to believe them; but they were soon repeated, and so frequently that eventually he came to suppose himself favoured, however unworthily, by the Virgin. Unfortunately, matters didn't stop there. Haunted by his voices, and despite his modesty inferring that he was one of those for whom Heaven reserved exceptional and mysterious favours, he began to detect divine intervention in the most trival acts of his everyday life; and in the final stage he became the object of the devil's attention. Satan was close by him, he continually heard his voice and replied to it; at times he saw him, in the shape in which he is generally represented or as a serpent. It is noteworthy that, despite the intensity of the hallucinations of every kind with which this unfortunate man was plagued, his outward conduct was such as to cause no criticism.[157]

Lhermitte believes that the devil was responsible for the whole business. If that's what he chooses to believe, so be it; we shall not argue with him on those grounds, nor shall we disagree with his diagnosis that the witness was hallucinating. What we *shall* question, though, is his assumption that because it was the devil who was responsible, and because therefore a different kind of experience was taking place, it follows that a different kind of *process* was involved.

In the same way that a fake Vermeer is just as 'real' as the genuine article, in the sense that both alike consist of paint on canvas, so a spurious encounter is just as 'real' as a genuine one, in the sense that both alike involve the process of hallucination.

To sum up: hallucination is not necessarily a malfunction consequent upon a pathological condition; it is simply a label for a mental process, and carries no implication of its origin.

Hallucination and the ecstatic state

Commentators on mystical experience identify a state termed *ecstasy*: this is how Dean Inge defines it:

> Ecstasy may be defined as an abnormal state of consciousness, in which the reaction of the mind to external stimuli is either inhibited or altered in character. In its more restricted sense, as used in mystical theology, it is almost equivalent to 'trance'. During ecstasy, the visionary is impervious to messages from without, and can even feel no pain . . . It is generally, but not always, associated with religion, since the experience is most easily explained by supposing that the soul has been brought into communication with higher powers.[117]

Whether or not we are willing to accept the terms 'soul' and 'higher powers', this is a useful account of a state which may well be that in which our encounters occur. Inge is not afraid to use words like 'abnormal' or the comparison with 'trance' to indicate that a person in ecstasy is in a different state from the everyday, a state in which, he adds,

> the dominant interest and aspirations of the inner life are heightened and intensified, and the enhanced force of auto-suggestion seems to project itself outside the personality, and to acquire the mysterious strength and authority of an inspiration from without.

Inge is a Church of England theologian whereas Lhermitte is a Catholic, which is why Inge is willing to accept the subjective character of the state. He does not on that account consider the experience of ecstasy any the less valuable. He confirms that in classifying the ecstatic state (in which we may suppose that visionary experiences occur) as subjective (which makes those experiences, by definition, hallucinatory) we are not making a value-judgement, we are simply finding a place for it in the scheme of knowledge we have about the way the mind works.

Laski, whose approach to these matters is none the less respectful because she is not a Christian, suggests that 'ecstatic experiences are manifestations (probably exaggerated manifestations) of processes facilitating improved mental organisation'.[144] She sees them as valuable, purposeful processes, into which the individual enters unconsciously in order, as it were, to put his spiritual house in order. The encounter experience would thus be part of a therapeutic process, self-administered to meet a self-diagnosed need.

Obviously, Lhermitte and his fellow theologians wouldn't go along with that all the way; yet they might not quarrel with Laski's claim that 'not even those who most fervently believe in a divine source for religious experience maintain that personal interpretations of such experiences have any validity save for the person who proffers them'.

So having shed the notion that hallucination is synonymous with malfunction, we are moving towards a view of hallucination as capable of performing a positive function.

What is happening in a hallucination

We can form pictures in our minds either unconsciously, as in our dreams, or consciously, as when we try to recall a scene. Either way, it is basically a physical process. The brain we use for the job is a physical instrument, and image-making is one of its functions. Interfere with the brain, and we interfere with its image-making capability:

> An Israeli lawyer was wounded in the 1970 missile crisis, and a piece of shrapnel had entered his brain and destroyed a portion of the *locus coeruleus*, long suspected to be the source or trigger or switch of the dreaming process. Medical researchers at Haifa discovered that over a five-night period he showed no dream activity, and over the subsequent five nights only five minutes a night, less than any subject ever documented. [147]

Such findings remind us that there is a level at which even imaginary images possess physical reality, and reinforce the view that to describe an experience as a hallucination in no way implies that it doesn't exist.

Hallucinations seem to occur when the brain is in a special state, but there are a disconcertingly large number of these states:

★ Basically physiological:
   fatigue, mental or physical
   undernourishment, voluntary or otherwise
   physical pain
   drugs or intoxicants
   physical illness
   just-waking or just-falling-asleep.

★ Basically sensory:
   sensory deprivation
   sensory overload
   meditation and similar sensory-input-limiting disciplines.

★ Basically psychological:
   emotional stress such as crowd excitement
   emotional stress such as private fear or phobia
   emotional stress such as hope or expectation
   social isolation
   approach of death
   religious ecstasy.

As my use of the qualification 'basically' suggests, I recognize that the categories are not exclusive — that the psychological states are accompanied by chemical changes in the body, while the physical conditions are likely to induce psychological responses.

So long a list — and it would be easy to prolong it — makes it hard to discern any common element; but this difficulty is in itself helpful, since it tells us that it will have to be a very basic function of our minds which can produce a hallucination in so many different circumstances.

But is that in fact what is happening? We assume that in certain states our brain is *triggered* to produce hallucinations; but could it not be the other way round: that what happens in these states is that we are *enabled* to produce them? In other words, should we look, not for an *event-inducing* factor, but for a *restriction-removing* one?

There is, for example, a hypothesis that we are dreaming all the time, and that what we call the 'dream state' is simply the time when we are *aware* of dreaming or of having dreamt.[58] If this is so, we may conjecture that the states listed above are those in which this continuous dreaming process is brought to our conscious attention in forms other than our sleeping dreams.

We may suppose that each of the states listed affects our body chemistry in some way, and that it is to this modification of body chemistry that we must look for the physical basis of the encounter experience. This is certainly borne out both by clinical experiment and by real-life accounts. Kroll and Bachrach offer a vivid example, comparing the recorded diet of the seventh-century English hermit Guthlac of Croyland with the United States Recommended Dietary Allowance:

> We can postulate that Guthlac suffered from night blindness, scurvy, and probably central nervous system involvement secondary to protein and vitamin B deficiency, resulting in such experiences as: 'While Guthlac was keeping his accustomed vigil in the dead of night, all of a sudden he saw the entire small cell filled with horrible hordes of foul spirits . . . they came up through holes in the floor and down through the thatched roof. They were horrible to the sight, in terrifying shape.'[141]

While we may accept that Guthlac's hallucinations resulted from (that is, were triggered or enabled by) his poor diet, it does not follow that everyone who suffers from malnutrition will undergo the same kind of experience, or indeed undergo any kind of hallucinatory experience at all. We are certainly not in a position to relate a particular kind of physiological state to a particular kind of hallucination. Clearly, even if we blame Guthlac's diet for the fact that he hallucinated, we cannot hold it responsible for the foul spirits, which were evidently the consequence of his religious vocation, whether we see them as real demons sent to plague him, or as projections of his own private hang-ups.

The composite elements of the hallucination process are clearly presented by a French doctor, Pascal Brotteaux, in his 1934 book on the contemporary encounters with the Virgin in Belgium. He starts off by taking as self-evident the proposition which Lhermitte and other theologians are so reluctant to accept:

> Careful analysis of the nature of religious apparitions, whether or not we are believers, obliges us to acknowledge that in every case *the visionary is hallucinating*. To maintain the contrary is to fall into gross materialism, which is untenable because if it were so, everyone present would see this material body and the accompanying phenomena.
>
> Differences of opinion are restricted, therefore, to the *cause* of the hallucination. For the Catholic, it is the Virgin who causes the children to hallucinate; for a few others, it is the demon; for the spiritists, it is the spirits. For the rest of us, on the other hand, the visions are provoked by purely natural causes. [23]

Brotteaux proposes that to have an encounter experience the witness must have the appropriate kind of *disposition*, and further, must be in an appropriate *state*; whereupon the necessary *trigger* will provide the immediate impulse. Discreetly, he recognizes that this leaves open the possibility of an external trigger, though personally he considers this merely a theoretical possibility, and inclines towards a natural explanation.

Though his proposal relates only to the *process* of the encounter, and though he was concerned with only one particular cultural context, Brotteaux' model still seems to me eminently viable even after a further half-century of research, and will serve us well as the starting-point for our own model. Ours, however, must be capable of a broader application if it is to answer for the extraterrestrials who in Brotteaux' day rarely emerged from the pages of the science fiction stories, and must go deeper into the question of *why* and not merely *how* these experiences come about.

A model for the encounter process
The witness (1) who is either a special kind of person (1a) or a normal person in a special kind of state (1b) is in appropriate circumstances (2) compelled or enabled to undergo a process (3) wherein some agency, internal or external (4), for reasons related to the witness' personal circumstances (5), interferes with his normal experience of reality and either imposes upon it, or interpolates into it (with no passage of time) or substitutes for it (with passage of time though not necessarily at the normal rate) an alternative experience (6) which embodies various factors personal and cultural (7) which lead him to believe he has undergone an encounter with an otherworldly being.

[The figures relate to sections of the discussion which follows.]

1   Special persons and special states

I suspect that most of us, off the record, would say we have a fairly good idea of the kind of person most likely to have an encounter experience. I suspect also it would be the kind of person we would — still discreetly off the record — describe vaguely as 'psychic'. The encounter experience would be a lot easier to understand if it could be shown that it happens only to a particular kind of person. Unfortunately, all the research carried out to date, such as witness studies by Keul and Phillips[131] and the Fund for UFO Research,[86] fail to show that encounter subjects are significantly different from the rest of us by any of the accepted yardsticks of psychology.

Perhaps different yardsticks would give different results; but the fact that no criterion has yet been observed shows that if any exists, it must be something very inconspicuous. So for the time being it seems more profitable to proceed on the assumption that encounter experiences can happen to *anyone*, and that it is the *state* the witness is in which is the crucial factor.

Encounter experiences are sought by some, come unsought to others. Since we have no reason to suppose that the kinds of experience these two categories have are fundamentally different, we may start with the assumption that both go through a similar process — the one deliberately, the other involuntarily — in order to have the experience.

Shamans in primitive cultures undergo training procedures in which they learn how to induce the kind of trance which seems to enable them to communicate with the divine powers. Spirit mediums attend development circles in which they heighten their ability to communicate with the dead. Religious mystics practise austerities such as fasting and penance which seem to be rewarded by visitations from divine or demonic beings.

What happens in all these processes is that the individual becomes to a greater or lesser degree 'not himself'. Unfortunately it is difficult to be more precise, for the typology of altered states is itself very imprecise. We may have a general idea of what is happening in ecstasy or trance, and so we can speak of the 'shamanistic trance' or the 'religious ecstasy' or the 'mediumistic trance' as being states which favour encounter experiences. But the parameters are not precisely drawn, and even when we can see that a person is not himself, we cannot easily say what it is that he is.

However, there seem to be grounds for believing that this doesn't very much matter, that they are all doors leading into the same room.

As to what happens in that room, there are all kinds of intriguing indications. Here are just a few, by way of reminding us what capabilities are revealed when we exchange our everyday state for another:

★ Flournoy, in his study of Hélène Smith, was puzzled by the fact that life in her imaginary world seemed to continue in her 'absence' — that is, while she was pursuing her normal earthly existence. This led him to wonder if she might have a 'second self' which existed *permanently* on the other plane of reality, but whose activities came to conscious attention only when she went into trance. [77]

★ A parallel to the foregoing is the supposition made by, amongst others, H. H. Price: 'It is plausible to suggest that we are dreaming all day long as well as at night, but only notice it when we are asleep.'[232] Should we think of our encounter experiences as only the peaks which show above the surface of a more extensive, perhaps continuous hidden parallel existence?

★ Aldous Huxley, when he took mescalin, found that he remained to all intents and purposes Aldous Huxley, with the same basic tastes and interests. Nevertheless he experienced notable sensory excitement, and reacted differently to stimuli — though perhaps hardly more than some of us do when we have a switch of mood. We remain ourselves, but in some respects our super-selves. [114]

★ Dr Linn F. Cooper, an American psychologist, performed many experiments on the experience of time in the hypnotic state. In one example, he told his hypnotized subject that he was going to give her a problem to solve in ten minutes. The problem was to advise a young couple who wished to marry but were worried by responsibilities to their families. After ten *seconds* he told her that her time was up. The subject then described how she had discussed the matter at length with the couple, asking questions and receiving answers, on the basis of which she advised them what to do. Not only had she conducted the interviews, she had dramatized the abstract problem into seemingly actual encounters with actual persons, and thought out a rational solution to their situation — and all in the space of ten seconds!

There are many other indications (dreams are of course the most familiar) that in altered states time either ceases to exist or becomes infinitely elastic. [33]

★ Elie Maron was one of the outlawed French eighteenth-century Protestants of the Cevennes known as the 'Camisards', among whom there broke out one of those epidemics of spontaneous preaching which tend to occur in revival contexts. This is how he described what happened to him:

> In my ecstasies I abandon the control of my tongue entirely to the spirit or angel of God, while my mind is occupied with thinking about God and listening to the words which my own mouth is uttering. I know that at these times a strange and superior power is making me speak. I don't think about what

I'm going to say, nor do I know ahead of time what I will say. While I'm speaking, my mind attends to what my mouth is uttering just as though it was a speech being given by somebody else. [169]

★ Hypnosis subjects are characteristically open to suggestion, and particularly to induced hallucination. A subject can readily be made to hallucinate the presence of someone who is not actually present, and he will not only describe him in great detail but relate him to the physical environment and say where he is in relation to the furniture, what he's doing in interaction with other people in the room, and so on. Since there is no question that the whole thing is anything but imaginary, it points to a remarkable capability on the part of the subject to 'dress' and 'stage' the bald suggestion which is made to him.

★ More dramatic still is the hypnosis subject's response to the suggestion that he relive a scene from an earlier existence or incarnation. Past life regression is so vivid, and subjects display such an ability to assume a role and describe scenes with verisimilitude and consistency, that many researchers — as well as the subjects themselves — have been convinced that regression is truly taking place and that they have indeed travelled back in time to rejoin a former self in a previous incarnation.

A sufficient number of such cases have been shown to contain errors, or clear indications of unconscious memory from previous reading or overhearing, for it to be very doubtful that regression actually occurs. For the purpose of our study, however, this only makes the phenomenon *more* interesting. If what we are seeing is another demonstration of latent creative powers and dramatic talent emerging in an altered state, it is an impressive indication of the way in which those resources are put to work by the subconscious mind.

Dissociation of the personality

The ability to transcend our normal selves is demonstrated most revealingly in cases where the individual personality seems to fragment — sometimes into vaguely dissociated conditions in which the individual slips in and out of 'alternate' states in which he displays alternating sets of characteristics; [123] sometimes into more dramatic conditions in which the individual seems to subdivide so completely as to give the impression that more than one person is sharing the same physical body. Almost everything that *could* be different about these secondary personalities *is* different — their attitudes, interests, values, aesthetic tastes, etc., and this is confirmed by psychological tests which reveal that the personalities are often complementary one to the other.

So vivid are some of these personalities that some researchers believe that at least some of them are instances of possession — that is, the spirit of a deceased human being, a demonic or discarnate entity, has invaded the subject and is maintaining some kind of parasitic existence at his expense.

For those who believe in demons and the possibility of demonic possession, such a hypothesis is doubtless plausible. However, one of the characteristics of dissociated personality states is the great suggestibility of the subject; it is notorious that the doctor treating such cases has often merely to hint at the existence of another personality for such a personality to manifest — a clear indication that it has been fabricated to order. If that is true of some, it is reasonable to suppose it may be true of all; in which case what appears to be possession by an external entity may be attributed to a combination of extreme suggestibility with those powers of dramatization we have already noted in other altered states.

Multiple personality states differ from hypnotic and trance states in that they are not consciously sought. The closest we come to voluntary dissociation is in the rituals of voodoo and other religious practices, in which an individual will carry out procedures supposed to induce possession by a divine or demonic entity. The cases generally classed as multiple personality cases catch the subject unawares and generally overwhelm him with their strangeness; however, a study of the factors which lead to their occurrence is immensely revealing for our inquiry.

Dissociation of the personality is, understandably, generally regarded as a malady, a psychological malfunction; just as I was writing this, researcher Lorraine Davis drew my attention to the way doctors invariably speak of MPD — multiple personality *disorder*. And so in the long run it surely is. But it is important to remember, what is so often overlooked, that dissociation confers a *short-term benefit* on the subject, enabling him to cope with a situation which he is unable to resolve in any conventional way. By allowing other facets of his total self to emerge, or by shifting the emphasis so that different characteristics become dominant, he in effect 'creates' a new personality for himself. With its aid he can either evade responsibility for what was happening to him in his primary personality, or gain access to latent abilities which his primary personality is incapable of utilizing.

Only when the emergency solution is clung to after it has served its purpose does the state start to create more problems than it solved. It is essentially an unstable state, with obvious psychological dangers for the individual who will have to cope with the social consequences of what will be seen by others as inconsistent behaviour. So it is important that as soon as his state is diagnosed, and of course when the situation which brought it about has been identified and remedied, the subject be helped towards re-integration.

Hysteria as a mode of behaviour

Diabolically inspired hallucinations are one way in which theologians account for encounter cases which are manifestly spurious; diabolically inspired hysteria is a second. Another case cited by Lhermitte concerns Madame X, a wife and mother in her 40s, who in the course of an illness began to claim encounters with Jesus, not visual but auditory and with a sense of 'presence'. She told Lhermitte:

> During this crisis, the good Lord made me understand that I would recover. I heard Christ's words well enough with my brain, but I could not explain what he said . . . when I hear Christ, it is an emotion that I feel. Quite often I have conversations with the Lord. I see him on the wood of the cross, and the divine crucified one talks to me. Once the Holy Virgin appeared to me, and once Thérèse of Lisieux.[158]

Confined to bed, she lost speech and sight, and at times would lapse into a cataleptic state in which she seemed wholly oblivious of the world outside. Then, at a time when her life was despaired of to the point where she had received the Last Rites, Jesus told her she would be cured. On this occasion her husband also reported feeling the divine presence. Suddenly all her symptoms vanished, her temperature plummeted from 42° to 36.5°, she could see and she could hear, and next morning she was back leading her normal life as wife and mother.

However, the symptoms recurred, and did so intermittently over many years, with additional features such as some rather suspect stigmata. It was, she declared, Christ's wish that she should suffer: 'all religion is suffering'. There were also encounters with the devil, in which she was tossed out of bed or thrown to the ground.

Despite the similarity of the incidents to the experiences of many of the mystics, Lhermitte diagnosed it as hysteria: her claimed encounters with Jesus were, in his view, hallucinations induced by her hysteric state. His inquiries revealed that she had been brought up by an alcoholic mother who frequently maltreated her. She had wanted to adopt the religious life, but her parents would not permit it, so she married instead. That too had not been happy at first, but things improved when the children appeared. Unfortunately, two of them died young, one of them a daughter who was especially close to her and whom she convinced herself would recover. It seems to have been the loss of this child which first brought on her sickness.

The form her hysteria took is easily accounted for by her early wish to follow a religious life. At the time of her illness she read nothing but devotional books and lives of the saints, and practised meditation, particularly on the passion of Jesus.

There is no reason why we should dispute Lhermitte's diagnosis, whether we retain the term hysteria or prefer one of those which have tended to replace it — conversion, dissociative and factitious disorders, and so on. Nevertheless we may feel that, in general, hysteria has had a rather worse press than it deserves — that, as with multiple personality, attention has been focused on hysteria as a psychological malfunction without sufficiently taking into account the positive reason for its manifestation in the first instance.

One who has taken a more positive view is the American psychologist Szasz, who has proposed that we should look on hysteria not so much as a disease but as a mode of behaviour, one which comprises both an escape *from* one mode of behaviour and a move *to* a different mode, so that — like multiple personality again — it can be seen both as positive and as negative: 'Suffering from hysteria is far from being sick, and could more accurately be thought of as playing a game, correctly or incorrectly, skilfully or clumsily, successfully or unsuccessfully, as the case might be.'[249]

The 'game' metaphor is particularly appropriate, since hysteria so frequently manifests in the form of dramatization and role-playing. But if so, it is often, and perhaps always, a very serious game with a very serious purpose. Another commentator who takes a more positive view of hysteria is Victoria Sackville West, who diagnosed Teresa d'Avila as a hysteric without any intention of denigrating the celebrated mystic. Like Szasz, she sees hysteria as a mode of behaviour selected subconsciously by the individual for a specific purpose:

> This word [hysteria] is popularly employed in a loose and misleading sense, to suggest the ranting excitability of uncontrolled emotion. In a truer sense it should be employed to denote a most variable form of neurosis, capable of producing either a complete disintegration of personality, or a schizophrenic condition of personality, or a psychological disposition inclining the subject towards involuntary auto-suggestion which may take a base and deplorable form or a form most spiritual and lofty.[221]

Once again, we see that to identify the process involved does not imply belittling the experience by behaviourist reduction: quite the contrary. For Sackville West, hysteria was the springboard which enabled Teresa to reach the heights (if also the depths) of her mysticism.

Returning to Lhermitte's Madame X, then, we can see that his negative diagnosis is inadequate. It seems probable that her experience was both an escape from her immediate situation and a seeking after some kind of justice for herself, a call for attention by one who felt that others didn't appreciate how much she had suffered — an assertion of herself as an individual.

As we shall see, this positive function of altered states is crucial to our inquiry. What all these states have in common is not simply that the individual ceases to be his normal self, but that he comes to be some other self which has, if not necessarily greater, at any rate different capabilities from those available to his normal self. In many cases, these include a capability for projection, for dramatization, for role-playing, for creative ordering of all kinds of material into coherent and meaningful scenarios which have significance for the witness.

It is clear that this spectrum of abilities is easily able to encompass the fabrication of an imaginary encounter situation.

At this stage of our study, we are still concerned only with the *process* — the means whereby the encounter situation can occur. Altered states provide that means, by giving the individual access to abilities which he is not able to command while in his everyday state, abilities which enable him to achieve his purpose.

Do we all possess these latent abilities? There is no reason to think otherwise, for we all give evidence of them every night in our dreams. What is not clear is why some people make use of them more readily than others — why there are good hypnosis subjects and others not so good, some 'natural' mediums and others who describe themselves as 'as psychic as a plank', some people who resolve their problems by resorting to hysteria or dissociation of the personality while others find less drastic solutions.

Later we shall come across some indications of what may cause that difference, though it is clear that this area of research has not been sufficiently explored. Consequently, while recognizing that the witness needs to be in a special state to have an encounter experience, we are unable to say what it is which enables some individuals to achieve that state more readily than others.

But what does emerge most clearly from this brief consideration of altered states is that the state is not entered into accidentally or arbitrarily, but with a definite purpose. What that purpose may be is something we shall be considering in a later section; first we must consider the other parameters of the process itself.

2   Appropriate circumstances

Given that the witness is in an appropriate state, what are the circumstances which will precipitate the encounter experience? We have noted cases which seem to suggest the following:

★ *External intervention*. God, an alien visitor or some other being chooses to make contact with the witness. This, as we have seen, is the ostensible cause of almost every encounter.

★ *Physiological event*. An accident, sickness, anything which upsets the body's chemical balance, seems capable of inducing the necessary state which, other conditions being fulfilled, favours an encounter experience. (We shall consider this aspect in greater detail in section 5.3.)

★ *Personal circumstances*. A sudden and intolerable crisis, such as a bereavement; or the culmination of a gradual process such as a spiritual conflict about whether or not to convert to the Christian faith. (We shall consider this aspect in greater detail in section 6.4.)

3   The process

Even if we accept that the first of the three circumstances — external intervention — is operating, and that God or an alien visitor has brought about the encounter, there is still no reason to suppose, and no evidence to suggest, that there is anything about the experience itself which is other than natural.

The mechanics of hallucination may not be fully understood, but the fact that hallucinations are known to occur, and that there is no aspect of the encounter experience which cannot be matched in the literature of hallucination, suggests that there is no need to look beyond our bodies and minds for the requisite apparatus. If an alien visitor is indeed seeking to make contact with us, he will find that we are already fully equipped physiologically for the encounter, however ill-prepared we may be psychologically.

This calls for some comment, in preparation for what we shall have to say later about *why* people have encounter experiences. We may suppose that there is no component of our bodies which was not put there for a purpose; so, to put it crudely, the fact that we have been equipped with the necessary apparatus to have encounter experiences implies that we are intended to be able to have such experiences when the need arises.

(Two objections may be made. The first, that the experience represents a malfunction of an apparatus designed for some other purpose, has I trust been fully met in our discussion of multiple personality and hysteria. The second, that if we all have this capability why do only a minority of us have encounter experiences, may be answered by saying that the fact that we have the capability does not mean we are necessarily expected to make use of it; it may be there for emergency use only.)

We have a right to conclude, therefore, that the encounter experience involves a natural process which was provided for, even foreseen, by whatever drew up the blueprint for our species. Further, since I cannot conceive of any faculty being bestowed on us which is not practical and beneficial, we may take it that though, like other human faculties, this one can doubtless be exploited, abused or misused, the encounter experience itself is fundamentally practical and beneficial.

4   Internal or external agency

The ostensible agency in virtually every encounter experience is an external entity of some kind. The alternative view is that it originates in the witness' own mind: but what in fact does this mean?

Clearly, his conscious mind is not responsible: so it must be either his subconscious mind, or his conscious mind in a state so different from its normal state that it is equivalent to a subconscious mind, or some other component of his make-up of which he and we are unaware.

In fact, the existence of such a component, however anatomists or psychologists may demur, is implicit in much of our mental activity; most notably in the fact that we dream. In a previous book[58] I predicated a component which for convenience' sake I named the *producer*, which acts autonomously to produce our dreams. Indeed, I sought to show that it is responsible for a great deal more than our dreams. I propose to retain the same working device in this study.

Briefly, the *producer* is something very like a secondary personality, but he (for since we are investing him with personality we may as well call him 'he') is not to be thought of as complementary to our conscious personality, rather as working in tandem with it. There are grounds for believing he works on a non-stop basis (as instanced by Hélène Smith's ongoing saga and H. H. Price's continuous dreaming) but that we are only intermittently aware of his activity.

Most of the time, his handiwork is displayed chiefly in dreams, and occasional waking reveries; but when a crisis develops he is liable to go more decisively into action, sometimes with quite dramatic results.

At such times he is liable to compel us to enter an altered state; conversely, if we enter such a state spontaneously, due to drugs, sickness or whatever, we find ourselves accidentally involved in the producer's activities.

As our analysis proceeds, we shall see how well the notion of a producer fits the encounter experience; for the moment it is no more than a way of showing how the encounter experience could originate within ourselves. Note, though, that in a sense the producer *is* external, in that he operates independently of our conscious selves. Moreover, the existence of a producer does not rule out a wholly external agency; we may well conceive of the producer as the man-on-the-spot organizing our end of the encounter process in co-operation with the otherworldly visitor.

5   Personal reasons
Even when the ostensible occasion for an encounter is an external visitation, personal motivations are often clearly involved. To what extent they are the decisive factor is a question we shall seek to resolve in section 7.3.

6   Interference, interpolation, substitution
Encounter experiences, for all their hallucinatory character, are frequently dramatic in form — dramatic, that is, in the sense that they are theatrical. There are *characters*, in a *setting*, who are involved in *incidents*. Sometimes it is a simple confrontation between the witness and Jesus, as in the case of Teresa d'Avila; but even then the event is fitted neatly into real space and real time.

If we find the concept of the 'producer' helpful, we may carry it further and think of him creating these psychodramas and substituting them for reality, in much the same way that we substitute a videotape on our video-player for the regular TV programme. Often this will be done so neatly that we will not notice the switch-over. Indeed, we may never know of it, but go our whole life believing we experienced it on the normal everyday plane.

To judge by accounts from witnesses, these parallel experiences can be presented in a variety of ways:

★ in the normal time-frame — for instance, if after the encounter the witness finds that some 20 minutes has elapsed, he will feel that this is consistent with the time he seemed to spend with the entity;

★ Outside real-time altogether, so that when the witness returns to reality he finds that no time has elapsed despite all that seems to have happened to him;

★ Within terrestrial time, but at a different rate, so that though time has certainly elapsed, it was by no means sufficient for him to have paid a visit to another planet, etc.

Though we might infer that these differences mean that there are three different kinds of experience, it is more reasonable to suppose that the producer or agent work within the human time-frame whenever possible, and distort it only when they have to in order to accommodate the experience. The implication is that on the level at which the encounter experience occurs, time does not exist; we shall see later that there is evidence that this is so.

7   Personal and cultural factors
What actually happens in an encounter experience is determined by such a complexity of factors, relating to the witness himself and to his interaction with the community and his cultural milieu, that the whole of section 6 is devoted to the matter.

All this may well have seemed to you to be both heavy-handedly labouring the obvious, and at the same time over-speculative. However, we had to work our way through these steps in order to establish two points which are crucial to our study:

1   The process of the encounter experience is a wholly *natural* one, whether or not supernatural or otherworldly forces are involved. So far as that process is concerned, there is no need for us to look beyond capabilities possessed by most and probably all humans.

2   The encounter experience is fundamentally a *purposeful* process, and though it may occur accidentally, is normally intended to perform a positive beneficial function.

Most behavioural scientists proceed on the assumption that the first at least of these propositions is self-evident; but those who have given these phenomena their attention — and there have been few enough of them — have not been very successful in relating the *process* to the *life-situation* of the witness. Though they recognized the hallucinatory character of the experience, and though they recognized that hallucinations are apt to occur under various circumstances, few have inquired why this particular kind of hallucination should be experienced by these particular people at these particular times.

Well, no more have we, at this stage of our inquiry. But our plodding efforts have provided the framework into which the rest can be fitted. It is not a rigid framework; there are several parts of it which permit alternative readings. In particular, as I hope you've noticed, I have been scrupulous in showing that the possibility of external intervention is by no means excluded even though the model is able to function pretty well without it.

By way of showing that others long before us have faced the range of options with which these phenomena challenge us, let us close this section with some thoughts expressed more than a century and a half ago by the German writer Görres who, while writing from within a belief system which I do not share, and without the benefit of the findings which 150 years of psychology have given us, came to conclusions reassuringly similar to ours:

> The imagination is located in the midway region of man, that is, in the soul; below it are the senses, with the common sense uniting them all, and above it are the higher powers of the spirit. Visions can therefore reach it from the external world, via the senses, or from within, from the spiritual world. However, since in either case they are related to the person who experiences them, he can in either case be responsible for them. God too can produce these visions, either by his own act or with the help of the good angels; equally, though, they can be the work of the Devil. So God and nature, angels and demons, saints and other dead persons, can alike act on the imagination, producing visions whose source it is often, for this reason, very hard to distinguish. And since error is so very easy in this field, we must observe the greatest precautions and most scrupulous attention when examining the phenomena. Indeed, this protean power which each of us possesses, which presents to our spirits in the form of dreams the memory of impressions which we have received on other occasions; which causes to float before the soul, when half-awake or when intoxicated with outward excitement, phantasms of things which have struck our senses, or even of things we have never seen, giving them such specific forms that often they are more vivid to us than reality itself; this power which, when in states of sickness the soul floats in a sort of half-state between darkness and light, evokes singular and bizarre images; this magician has set up his workshop within the imagination, and deceives not only ordinary mortals but even those who, raised by God to the mystic state, might be thought safe from illusions.[94]

5.3   TRIGGERS AND CATALYSTS

> My throat is better and I have not felt so well for some time, for I can eat almost without pain, and as the moon is full I consider this a great boon . . .
>
> The moon is full; I passed a very bad night and am suffering severely with my head today. I have been better until now; tomorrow, when the moon begins to wane, my health will improve.[250]

Those who still consider that reports of people being influenced by the phases of the moon are old wives' tales will dismiss these comments from Teresa d'Avila's autobiography as yet another example of her tendency to fantasize, and irrelevant to this study. On the other hand, those of us — and I am one — who are convinced that such claims have some kind of basis in fact, must wonder if this sensitivity on Teresa's part may be releated to her other experiences. (For opposing views on lunar influence, see [159,130])

Until recently it was not unreasonable to present, as did the learned French doctor Giscard, a study of mystical encounters under the title *Hysteria or Mysticism?*[92] with the implication that the choice between these two options is all that is on offer. Almost certainly, he would not have considered that Teresa's sensitivity to lunar phases could be significant. But there has been a growing tendency to take such physical factors into account. Towards the end of his life Jung was quoted as saying:

> Inasmuch as we have been unable to discover any psychologically understandable process to account for the schizophrenic complex, I drew the conclusion that there might be a toxic cause. That is, a physiological change has taken place because the brain cells were subjected to emotional stress beyond their capacity. I suggest that there is an almost unexplored region ready for pioneering research work.[127]

Today a substantial amount of such research work is being conducted, and findings are flooding in, showing that the mind affects the body and the body affects the mind to such an extent that we can hardly isolate a single human process which does not involve both mind and body to a greater or lesser degree.

The bearing on our study is self-evident: even if a supernaturally bestowed charisma is at the origin of the experience, as the theologians hold; or even if the witness is in some way predisposed by his body chemistry to certain hallucinatory states as the behavioural scientists suggest — even then we still cannot rule out, in determining not only *whether* a person should have an experience but also *when* and *what sort* of experience he should have, the part which may be played by such down-to-earth factors as the weather or what he ate for supper.

There is of course no question of such factors being *wholly* responsible for the experience. Whatever else the encounter experience may be, it is certainly more than the consequences of the state of the weather or the phase of the moon; or of eating mushrooms, however sacred; or getting drunk, or breathing air overcharged with positive ions, or undergoing the chemical changes which accompany puberty or the menopause. The weather is something we all have to put up with, many of us eat strange things for supper, fluctuations of body chemistry affect every one of us, yet only a few of us have encounter experiences.

What we can look for is that such elements will play a *contributory* role, interacting with the other factors involved. Sometimes they may act as *triggers*: a violent thunderstorm is notoriously apt to have this effect. Sometimes they may serve as *catalysts*, enabling factors without which the other factors would not come into play. For example, the sensory deprivation experienced by someone driving alone at night in a featureless countryside may put him into a suitable state of mind for an encounter which would be inhibited by his daytime environment, working as a shop assistant.

Micro effects

Whatever else may be involved, the encounter experience involves some components of the human machine. Even if supernatural agencies are responsible for the event, they have to make use of the mental faculties of the witness, if only that he may be aware of the event, participate in it and remember it later.

Nor are those mental faculties always the same at all times: even apart from drugs, meditation and other ways in which the witness can deliberately alter the way his mind and body operate, accidents such as sickness and the weather can have similar effects, and even the Virgin Mary would find that such factors might make a visionary sometimes more and sometimes less easy to communicate with.

The brain itself, let us remind ourselves, is an organism which functions by means of a complex of electrical and chemical processes whose sensitivity and delicacy make even the most sophisticated computer seem crude and clumsy. Anything which changes the chemical balance, and thereby the efficiency of the electrical system, will be liable to affect brain activity.

These functions do not, of course, constitute the brain itself, they are simply the means whereby it does its job; but our knowledge of brain functioning is not yet sophisticated enough for us to know whether a person's behaviour is due to a fundamental aspect of his nature, or to a momentary aberration in the way he behaves due to an interference with the channelling or data-handling functions of his brain.

Such questions puzzled Teresa d'Avila's biographer, Victoria Sackville-West:

> The question of course arises; what really ailed her? What malady or maladies produced those fearful effects of emaciation, insensibility, paralysis, cardiac agony, fever, and pains in the head which often drove her to distraction? To what extent were her disorders physical or pathological? Were they due to a combination of genuine physical infirmity aggravated by the nervous tension of her most peculiar temperament? The truth probably lies in this hypothesis. The mental and the physical are in some cases inextricably mixed up; inextricably, that is, to the incomplete attainments of our far-out knowledge. Are we perhaps putting the cart before the horse in ascribing the mental disturbance to physical causes, and would it not be truer to say that a mental composition of such excessive sensibility produced so severe a strain that the body inevitably paid? Or was it that a low physical resistance impaired the control and balance of the mind?[221]

Such questions have not often been raised by the biographers of mystics. When they have, it has generally been with the implication that if we can detect the influence of physical and physiological factors, we may dismiss the experience itself as valueless. When the sympathetic biographer of so eminent a person as Teresa takes such questions into account, it is a sign of a growing recognition that to acknowledge the part played by physical factors is not a value-judgement but a matter of fact.

Much of the misunderstanding about the value of mystical experience is due to a confusion between the means and the end-result. Zaehner, for example, has strongly criticized Aldous Huxley's endorsement of mescalin as a short-cut to the mystical experience.[114,272] Zaehner may well be right in questioning Huxley's claims, but not, I think, for this reason; for Huxley's mescalin was only one component of many, and may have played no more (and no less) a part in his experience than did, say, the phases of the moon in Teresa's case.

(If there *is* a significant difference between the experience of a Teresa and that of a Huxley, it will surely relate to subjective rather than objective factors: that is, it will derive not from such secondary circumstances as what drug or what spiritual discipline the individual employed as his *means*, but from the deeper levels of individual personality and the *ends* towards which he directs himself.)

Involuntary effects

Teresa's discomfort when the moon was at its full almost certainly has a scientific basis. But identifying that basis is complicated by the fact that it may well not be a *direct* effect. Instead, the moon may be associated with other phenomena which are actually responsible for the effect. One suggestion is that the phases of the moon may be accompanied by fluctuations in the quantity of meteoritic dust which enters Earth's atmosphere. This could lead to an increase in the count of positive ions in the atmosphere, which in turn could bring about an increase in serotonin production in the body. Serotonin being a neurotransmitter, an excess of it leads — in some but not all people — to nervousness, depression and/or irritability.

Since no two of us are perfectly alike, it follows that some people will be more affected than others: we may suppose that Teresa was one such. It is justifiable to speculate further, that the kind of person who is more affected by excessive positive ionization of the atmosphere may have other physiological and psychological correlates which may enhance the effect, or direct it in a particular way — for example, making them more suggestible.

An approach so diluted with 'possibly's and 'we may suppose's gives the sceptic ample grounds to dismiss it altogether as impossibly speculative: but the existence of the effects themselves is solidly enough established. The Israeli scientist Sulman feels justified, after fifteen years of research, in asserting that approximately one person in three displays a 'weather sensitivity' which involves some degree of personality modification as a result of meteorological conditions. However, he insists that this is not related to personality, but is 'a neurochemical reaction based on the regulatory functions of the hypothalamus, the pituitary gland, the thyroid and the adrenal gland'. [247, 233]

At the close of the nineteenth century, French hypnosis researcher Henri Durville had indicated 'sensitivity' as a crucial factor in human personality, and in 1898 another Frenchman, Dr Noriagof, proposed a specific link between 'the sensitive minority' and visionaries. Distinguishing this quality from a morbidly negative 'nervosité', he saw it positively as 'a special aptitude'. Though he dissociated it from any direct suggestion of illness such as hysteria, he recognized that it was more common among the ill, and among young people between the ages of 12 and 25. [188]

Goethe observed, 'It is a pity that just the excellent personalities suffer most from the adverse effects of the atmosphere,' characteristically not hesitating to recognize yet another indication that he was superior to the likes of you and me. It has been claimed that amongst those known to have been more than usually sensitive to weather were Dante, Darwin, Hugo, Heine, Leonardo, Luther, Michelangelo, Milton, Napoleon, Pascal, Voltaire and Wagner, but I don't suppose this is based on anything more scientific than references in their writings. I dare say quite a lot of undistinguished people, who have left us no writings which might contain such references, also suffered in the same way.

Even those who tentatively propose such ideas as these are careful not to claim too much at the present stage of our ignorance. In his foreword to Sulman's work, Charles G. Wilber, himself a Professor of Zoology, warns us:

The phenomenon of synergism [= many things acting together] must not be ignored when considering air ionization and the resulting biological responses in man. The lungs are known to be affected by modifications of the ionic composition of ambient air; but other substances also stimulate the lungs . . . these individually have a biological effect on the lungs, but they also interact among themselves and with ionized air. The resultant effects are rarely, if ever, merely additive, but are rather synergistic in nature.

So, if Eugenio Siragusa was weather-sensitive, and a storm was brewing in the Sicilian sky as he waited at the bus-stop that fateful morning, this may perhaps have triggered his experience — but so many other factors may have been involved that there can be no question of our pinpointing a precise cause-and-effect. Here are just a selection of possible factors all of which might affect the individual's body chemistry:

★ atmospheric conditions

★ lunar phase

★ fatigue

★ battle excitement, work tension and other such stresses

★ hope, fear, worry, expectation, anticipation

★ allergy

★ diet

★ drugs or medication

★ menopausal and other life-cycle changes

Many are the side-effects of actual illness. In addition, of course, there are the normal fluctuations in body chemistry which accompany the daily cycle of sleeping, waking, food intake and other activities.

It is evident that this list coincides very closely with the list we made earlier of conditions which favour the occurrence of hallucination.

A different kind of environmental factor is contributed by the earth itself. Current research into physical forces associated with geophysical activity is showing that there are some interesting correlations. Investigators claim to have detected fluctuations in electromagnetic forces related to irregularities in the underground rock structure, so that events caused by tectonic stress below the earth's surface may have effects in the atmosphere above it. The well-observed effects on animal behaviour of imminent earthquakes is a graphic example of such forces at work.[256]

Though basically physical, such phenomena could, like the meteorological effects we have noted, have psychological effects on people sensitive to such subtle modifications of the environment. Thus, some of those researching these matters claim to have demonstrated correlations between geophysical activity along fault-lines and the statistics of anomalous experiences, notably UFO sightings. [48, 193, 219]

If so, it is plausible that other kinds of unexplained behaviour — including our encounters — could be triggered by such events. Various possibilities are being proposed: one is that the geophysical events generate 'earthlights' (earthquake lights are already an observed fact) and that these lights are the basis for hallucinatory observations, which could of course lead to imaginary ET encounters.

The same stress which generates the lights would at the same time be affecting the chemical balance of a proportion of humans, who would then be ready to misinterpret anything unusual — the earthlight in particular — and suppose they had seen a UFO, the Virgin Mary or whatever.

So little scientific work has as yet been done in this field that it is too early to say how significant a part, if any, these effects may play in determining anomalous behaviour. But even if the effects are proved to be real, they are not likely to be more than one additional contributing factor, interacting with the rest, to put the individual into a suitable state, and perhaps supply him with some of his raw materials.

Sought effects

To use a thing, it is not necessary to understand how it works. Ever since man observed a cause-and-effect relationship between certain physical processes and a state in which he might have an encounter with a divine being, he has cultivated such practices.

Naturally, they have usually been associated with religion, and for this reason the priests have generally sought to control them. In many cases they have reserved the right to such privileges for themselves. Hence the shamanistic practices which are an essential part of so many religions. Elsewhere the public have been allowed to share them, but within guidelines established by the priests.

The means are many: rhythmic music and dance, ritual drug-taking and intoxication are the most frequent. Often the effect is heightened by elaborate ceremony, employing excitement, fear, sexual stimulus and so on, leading to practices ranging from 'jumping' and 'shaking' to ritual snake-handling, poison-drinking and self-mutilation.

Few, apart from those who participate in such practices, would claim that anything very worthwhile in the way of an encounter experience is likely to result. Even if genuine possession does take place in practices such as West Indian voodoo, the possessing entity is unlikely to be more than a mischievous elemental or a lost spirit. Though interesting by way of comparison for the purpose of our study, what is important about such practices is that they indicate a world-wide tradition which recognizes a connection between physical influences and encounter states.

Not all the ritual methods whereby shamans and suchlike achieve their ends employ violent battering of the senses or massive disturbance of body chemistry by means of drinks or drugs. There are many traditions in which 'quieter' means are used. Fasting, sleep deprivation, sexual deprivation and other austerities are practised, and not only within the Christian ascetic tradition.

We must therefore recognize as a simple fact that if encounter experiences happen more frequently in such places as monasteries, this is not solely because their inmates are 'better' than the rest of us, or even because they make a more determined effort, consciously or unconsciously, to obtain such experiences. There is also a strong probability that the conditions of life in such environments will be such as will *add* to the probability that hallucinatory experiences would occur.

Today, no doubt, conditions in monasteries and other enclosed communities take more account of human needs than in the past. At the same time a reduced emphasis on guilt and penance, a diminished fear of attack from the devil, will have lessened the risk of overheightened suggestibility. But negative factors can also play a part: Hebb in 1949 noted that monotonous, unchanging stimulation levels can lead to disorganization of the ability and capacity to think: he predicted that in the absence of varied stimulation brain-functioning would be impaired.[24] Seclusion, isolation, and the undifferentiating uniformity of a corporate life-style, not necessarily negative in themselves, could have negative effects on an individual who felt himself ceasing to be an individual in very much the same way as the subject in a sensory deprivation experiment.

Even in the Middle Ages, not every monk or nun saw visions: it would be interesting to establish whether encounter experiences were less frequent among those who had stimulating occupations such as playing the organ or distilling liqueurs. Similarly, it would be revealing to establish whether Teresa's visions occurred more frequently at times of the full moon; whether the number of encounters increased during Lent with its fasting and other austerities, and so on. That such factors play a part is suggested by cases such as the outbreak of convent hysteria at Hoorn in the Netherlands in 1551, when at the end of Lent, after fifty days during which they had lived on little else but turnip juice, the inmates suffered an epidemic of hallucinations and other symptons.[27a]

But even if such correlations could be traced with sufficient precision to confirm the role played by such factors in the encounter experience, that role would never be more than a secondary one. The state of the witness' health, the weather conditions, may *contribute* towards his experience, may even *enable* it to occur; but they cannot, in the absence of other factors, *cause* an individual to have an encounter experience.

5.4 PROJECTION AND PSYCHODRAMA

An encounter, by definition, takes place between the witness and another. We have seen that this 'other' may or may not be the being the witness thinks it is. A witness who has an ET encounter may be meeting:

★ an actual visitor from Outer Space;

★ a fabrication of an ET by his subconscious mind; or

★ some other being masquerading as an ET.

In either of the two alternative scenarios, the crucial point is that something is pretending to be something it isn't: role-play is occurring. As we have seen, role-playing is part of many psychological processes — most notably of dissociated personality, in which part of the individual fragments for the specific purpose of playing a role contrasting with his normal personality.

Role-playing involves *projection*, and in so far as the role is made part of a wider situation, it involves *psychodrama*. A brief look at these two processes will help us decide whether they are involved in the encounter experience.

Projection
Projection, in the general sense, occurs whenever an actor asks an audience to believe that he is Hamlet and not Laurence Olivier, or when a small child says it wasn't he that was naughty but the other naughty boy who lives inside him. More specifically, it is a psychological process in which the subject externalizes his feelings, emotions and responses by ascribing them to someone/something outside himself, or by interpreting an impersonal scene in terms of his personal attitudes.

One extreme form of projection is *identification*, which can for instance manifest as the tendency of certain mentally disturbed subjects to imagine that all kinds of things — such as newspaper headlines and posters — are directed at them personally. This process is used more positively by many schools of psychotherapy as a way to find out what is going on in the individual's subconscious. One such technique is the 'psychological tarot' employed by Canadian psychotherapist Dr Denise Roussel, who gets her subjects to lay out the cards of the Tarot, as if for a tarot-reading, and then to interpret them according to their personal situation.[216]

It is, in a sense, a confidence trick: clearly there is no inherent magic in the tarot cards. On the other hand, the symbols depicted on them were not chosen arbitrarily, but for the response they evoke, and over the centuries they have been refined and sharpened, giving them a richness and depth of potential significance. The result is that almost anyone who looks at the cards can find in them a reflection of his own preoccupations and problems, hopes and fears.

Yet for all that, the cards themselves are impersonal and objective; it is the subject himself who personalizes them and gives them subjective value. Thus one of Roussel's subjects sees a card representing a girl standing beneath an arch of flowers; he identifies with the girl, transforms the arch into a tunnel until the randomly upturned card has become a representation of himself emerging from a 'tunnel' of difficulties in which he has lately been stuck. Another subject sees a card depicting a seated couple, and spontaneously relates it to a sexual attack she recently suffered, though to the objective eye there is nothing in the card to suggest any such thing.

It is evident that what is happening is that the subject is externalizing his situation: he allows himself to be persuaded that the cards *know* that situation, and that they can help him understand it and perhaps even improve it. *Belief* that the cards possess this power is clearly a crucial factor; this will derive partly from his trust in the psychotherapist, partly from the quasi-mystical authority of the cards themselves, whose centuries-old occult reputation must impress even the most sceptical subject.

Occultists, of course, believe that some paranormal power is involved; and we should not rule out the possibility that some psi-factor is influencing the selection of the cards. However, the ability of Roussel's subjects to identify with what they want to see (or in some cases *don't* want to see) makes it clear that we have no need to look beyond projection for an explanation of the synchronicities which seem to occur, remarkable though they often are.

The 'Psychological Tarot' is an impressive demonstration, on the one hand, of the mind's *ability* to objectivize its situation by externalizing it, and on the other, of the *need* the mind has to distance itself from its preoccupations, expressing them in this way as a preliminary to understanding and then accepting or resolving them. Projection is yet another example of a process which, though it can take a negative form harmful to the individual (as in the paranoid identification with newspaper headlines) can also serve a positive and practical function: at critical times in a person's life, it can be an effective way of helping him to tackle the situation.

Psychodrama

Psychodrama is another psychotherapeutic technique, more active than simple projection, for now the subject is not merely observer and commentator, but performer. Acting out roles relevant to his situation, 'becoming' someone else, he is freed from his usual inhibitions; so he is able to express, within a sympathetic and supportive environment, needs and frustrations he would normally find it difficult if not impossible to reveal, and may not even know he possesses.

If it should turn out that the entities ostensibly involved in encounter experiences do not actually exist, then the best way of accounting for our divinities, spirits and extraterrestrials may be to see them as examples of projection and psychodrama. A God of the Thunderstorm can be seen as an expression of man's fear of the storm, a Goddess of Death as an exteriorization of man's fear of death, symbolizing the danger and justifying his powerlessness. An individual's encounter with an otherworldly entity could then be interpreted as the way he has found to personalize the otherwise impersonal forces acting upon his life, finding a place for himself in the cosmic context by presenting it as a dramatic scene in which he is a participant.

The 'theatrical' character of many encounter experiences has often received comment. French researcher Pierre Vieroudy has noted that in UFO encounters, 'everything happens as though the phenomenon was putting on an act for the witness' benefit'.[262] Here is a recent Spanish case in which the witness found himself playing a leading part in what had all the appearance of a carefully staged production:

> On 31 August 1981 Eduardo Pons Prades, an educated and intelligent Spanish writer, left his hotel in southern France, intending to spend the night at Perpignan before returning to Spain, because he disliked driving at night. Inexplicably, instead of taking the Perpignan road he took one which led directly towards Spain. About 20.15, again inexplicably, he left the main road and drove down a forest track until his motor and lights packed up. He got out, and started to walk — yet again, unaccountably — *further* down the track. This led him to a clearing, brilliantly illuminated, in which was standing a spacecraft some 50 to 75m in diameter.
>
> A voice told him not to be afraid, in perfect Spanish though he was still in France, and invited him to climb the ramp and enter the spaceship through the open door. As he did so, the voice said 'Welcome aboard the *Luz de Cosmos!*' [= Light of the Cosmos]. Inside, he was greeted by typical ET aliens in a typical ET spaceship setting, who talked to him at great length about their home planet, their mission to Earth and so on. Thanks to his journalistic training, Pons Prades was able to recall what they told him in great detail (ETs never seem to favour the use of tape recorders). It also meant that though his story contains nothing particularly new, it is better told than is usual.[199]

It is indeed the utterly stereotyped character of Pons Prades' story which is its most striking feature. It is as though he had read a dozen other ET encounter narratives, and decided to tell a similar story about himself. Yet if this were so, one would imagine that as a professional writer he could have made a better job of it. Although his account is embellished with photos and maps showing where it all happened, not a scrap of evidence is offered; nor does the 'message' which constitutes the greater part of the book contain a single verifiable fact.

Neither at the time nor later does the writer question what has happened to him, nor in the book which was published only ten months later does he express the slightest surprise at being chosen by the ETs for such an experience. This may in part be accounted for by the strong resemblance between the ETs' views and attitudes and his own — which we have seen to be true of Adamski, Angelucci and others. But for a professional journalist, Pons Prades seems to have been remarkably ready to take the incident at its face value. He does not even note the contradiction between his hosts' declared policy of non-intervention in human affairs on the one hand, and on the other the fact that within a matter of weeks after his adventure he had written an account of it and had it accepted by one of Spain's leading publishers who rushed the book into print in an edition clearly aimed at a popular market.

Not only that, but it contains an introduction by Antonio Ribera, one of Spain's leading UFO researchers. Though he does not commit himself to a total and unquestioning acceptance, there is a clear implication that Ribera accepts Pons Prades' story in principle. This could of course mean that Ribera is collaborating with Pons Prades in some kind of mystification, or that he has been hoodwinked by Pons Prades; but to me it seems more likely that Ribera, like us, is baffled by the paradox between the manifest improbability of Pons Prades' story and his naive and unquestioning narration of it, between the overall similarity to scores of other such stories and the clear belief by the witness that it was all managed for his personal benefit. What, then, are our options?

★ It really happened; in which case, so far as our inquiry is concerned, there is an end of the matter.

★ It didn't really happen; the witness thought at the time that it had happened, but doesn't think so now. If he changed his mind *before* he published his book, he is guilty of wilful deception; if he has changed his mind *since* the book was published, in all honesty he should say so.

★ It didn't really happen, but the witness thought it did, both at the time and subsequently. In which case, either he is being deceived, or he is deceiving himself.

But it may be more complicated than that. *It may be that there is one part of Pons Prades which believes the story, and another which doesn't.*

When one of Dr Roussel's subjects looks at the tarot cards laid out before him, it is as though some part of him takes off from his here-and-now commonsense self, and projects itself into the cards, involving itself in the scene depicted on the card. None of the rest of us can see the particular significance the cards have for him, because nobody else brings to them exactly the same mix of values, beliefs and preoccupations.

The process of projection, then, has much in common with a phenomenon we have already found relevant to our study, dissociated personality. In each of them there is a separation between the part of the individual's nature which stays with the here-and-now, and another part which projects itself into a kind of alternate reality.

We may speculate that in the case of Pons Prades some kind of 'second self' projected itself into the fantasized adventure of the ET encounter, and subsequently succeeded in persuading the 'real' Pons Prades to accept that it was more than fantasy, that it did actually happen.

Neither projection nor psychodrama are adequate as total explanations of the encounter experience, but they give us some idea of what the dynamics of such an experience may be. Both are purposeful procedures, performed to meet a need or resolve a problem; both do so by externalizing the subjective situation into an objective happening in which the individual is indeed involved, but only as one of the participants, and indeed an inferior participant, the leading role being played by a superior entity who thereby invests the event with authority.

Author and audience

The interaction which takes place in the psychodrama between individual experience and cultural conditioning, between what the 'author' contributes from his own resources and what he absorbs in the way of feedback from his 'audience', is tellingly depicted in an episode which occurred in December 1912. The French researcher Charles Lancelin had been carrying out a series of investigations to see if there was any substantial evidence for the existence of the devil. (For the record, he found none.)

One of his experiments was to persuade hypnotized subjects to invoke the devil — an interesting precursor of the Lawson/McCall/DeHerrera 'imaginary abductee' experiments we noted in section 4.4.

Those of our subjects who believed in the existence of the demon, or who, without positively believing in him, nourished a doubt inclining to belief, refused with every ounce of energy to receive the suggestion. We could impose our will on none of them — or rather, to insist would have meant exposing the subject to risks which we were not willing to take.

So we were obliged to fall back on a subject who was by his own admission incredulous as to the existence of the devil. But what then happened was that we obtained a phenomenon of a very remarkable kind. The suggestion that he was the devil brought to light a subliminary consciousness in the subject, where were sleeping his childhood memories. He pictured the devil as he is depicted in toy theatres or fairground sideshows, and instead of producing for us a savage and menacing devil, he presented a childish personage drawn from his former memories. He seized hold of members of the audience whom he didn't like, or who were specifically pointed out to him, and, grabbing them firmly, he dragged them into a corner of the room where he shook them, shouting, 'Off to the fiery furnace with you!'[142]

Entertaining as it is, the incident demonstrates the ability of the psychodrama to take us by surprise. Lancelin's hypnotized subject must have been aware of many other versions of the devil-entity beside the one he portrayed; what made him choose that one? Pure whim, or some deeper impulse? Did he pick up the suggestion from some member of the audience, or did it spring from within himself?

We may suppose that if that same subject were to have a serious encounter experience, a similar assortment of factors might come into play:

★ the choice of stereotype images; first, which particular entity, and then, which version of that entity?

★ the witness' personal memories and cultural acquisitions from school, family, friends, reading, TV viewing, etc.

★ suggestion from the people immediately around him at the time,

★ other effects caused by the immediate circumstances.

— let alone the weather, his state of health, his state of mind, what he had for supper . . . So many threads intertwine to make each encounter a unique event; no wonder it is so complicated to unravel!

5.5   COMMENTS ON PART FIVE

In this section we have been concerned less with the encounter experience as such, more with psychological processes which may be relevant.

Whatever the nature of the encounter experience, it involves psychological processes. Even if otherworldly entities are involved, even if the experience is all that it seems to be, psychological factors and processes are employed in the circumstances of the encounter and the way the individual responds to it.

How such an experience takes place is not its most essential or most interesting aspect, but it lays a sure foundation for our investigation of *what* is happening and *why*. We have now seen that there are other kinds of human experience which resemble the encounter experience in one way or another, which means that we can guess at what may be happening inside the individual witness when he tells us his story.

We now know that:

★ There are many processes whereby an individual may come to believe he has had a real experience, though the reality is only subjective and is generally not observed by others.

★ To have such an experience, an individual must either be of a certain disposition or be in a certain state; possibly both. Many factors may contribute: some external, such as meteorological conditions acting upon someone who is particularly sensitive to them, others internal, such as fluctuations in body chemistry. These factors, however, do not cause the experience or even determine its nature; they simply play a catalyst role, enabling the witness to have the experience.

★ Though some of these experiences occur in connection with sickness or physiological or psychological malfunction, they are for the most part initially positive and purposeful, performing a function which the individual apparently cannot accomplish in any other way. We are encouraged, therefore, to consider whether the encounter experience, too, may serve a positive and purposeful function.

★ Many of the processes involve projection, identification and dramatization — that is to say, some part of the witness seems to separate from the primary self in order to have an experience on a different level of reality. This may take the form of reading a subjective significance into objective circumstances which already exist, or it may involve creating a fantasy experience relevant to his current preoccupations.

★ Though the witness plays an essential role in these psychodramas, the leading figure is the entity he encounters, who as it were sanctions the experience by his authority. This figure seems to be someone intrinsically separate from the witness: indeed its 'otherness' is its most essential quality, giving it both credibility and authority.

However, just as we can see the actor who plays the part of the witness as a kind of dissociated self, so too the part of the entity may be played by another such self. In short, *in the psychodrama of the encounter experience, the roles of both witness and entity are played by projections from the individual's own mind.*

6.1 THE CONTEXT OF ENCOUNTER

In 1974 the American sci-fi writer Philip Dick, then aged 46, had a traumatic experience: he met God.

Being a highly intelligent person, and with the resources of modern thought and language at his disposal, Dick was able to relate himself to his experience in somewhat different terms than most witnesses of the past. None the less, he began his account in conventional terms, telling us that God 'fired a beam of pink light' directly at his head. He then experienced an 'invasion of my mind by a transcendentally rational mind, as if I had been insane all my life and had suddenly become sane'. This 'mind' he named VALIS, an acronym for Vast Active Living Intelligence System:

> This rational mind was not human. It was more like an artificial intelligence. On Thursdays and Saturdays I would think it was God, on Tuesdays and Wednesdays I would think it was extraterrestrial, sometimes I would think it was the Soviet Union Academy of Sciences trying out their psychotronic microwave telepathic transmitter.[137]

Dick sought to come to terms with his experience in a series of novels whose underlying concept is, to put it mildly, unconvincing, however stimulating or enjoyable they are as fiction. The action passes on alternate levels of reality, which the characters as well as the reader tend to find confusing. The notion that real time ceased between the fall of Jerusalem in the year 70 and the discovery of the Gnostic Scrolls in 1974 is bold but no more easily credible than the idea that President Nixon's resignation was the final event marking the culmination of the spurious reign of 'Empire' which has held the world in its sinister grip throughout the nineteen centuries of non-reality.

What is interesting to us is not so much the ideas themselves as the fact that Dick chooses to externalize his inner puzzlement in this way. We cannot easily believe it never crossed his mind that VALIS might be a part of himself, some kind of super-Dick engaged in reshaping his life: but evidently he thought he had good enough grounds for supposing it to be something 'other'.

If so, they were subjective grounds; they did not even have the support of a belief system. If VALIS exists as an independent entity, apparently it exists only for Philip Dick, whereas Delphine's Virgin is at least recognized by a consensus of belief embodied in Catholic doctrine, though that hardly constitutes proof either that the Virgin exists or, if she does, that Delphine met her.

A hundred years ago, French researcher Théodule Ribot asked:

> Certainly these voices and visions emanated from the patient. Why then does he not regard them as his own? There must exist anatomical and physiological causes, which are unfortunately hidden from us. Because we are unaware of these causes, we see only the surface symptoms which are their conscious expression. [209]

A century of research has made it seem likely that the causes lie deeper than anatomy and physiology, and that a simple behaviourist explanation will not suffice. The reason why Ribot's patient did not regard his voices and visions as his own, we may feel, is because he *needed* to believe they were external. We may go further, and think that one part of him knew perfectly well that they came from within him, but had caused them to appear to come from without for just the kind of reasons we considered in the preceding section.

Just as in that section we saw that the *form* of the encounter experience, the process by which it takes place, is affected by all kind of contributory and modifying factors, so we shall find that its *content* — who the witness encounters and in what context — is affected by his individual circumstances and those of the society within which he lives.

If people were all made alike, and lived in identical environments, we may suppose that they would all have much the same kinds of encounter experience. But of course they don't. Philip Dick, as a mature and intelligent writer living in late-twentieth-century America, has probably as great a chance to live free from hidebound belief systems and cultural constraints as any human who has ever lived. An entity which appears to him can be of many different kinds and still command his intelligent attention; and indeed if it appeared to him in a stereotyped form, Dick would probably immediately suspect he was fantasizing. His VALIS, on the other hand, carries conviction so far as he is concerned, even if his guesses as to its true identity vary with the days of the week.

An Irish or Sicilian countryperson, on the other hand, would be baffled by an entity which didn't conform to what he has been brought up to expect. As Spanish researcher Salvador Freixedo has noted, visions receive different interpretations according to the cultural setting in which they appear; seemingly identical apparitions will be identified as the Virgin in a Catholic milieu, but not in a Protestant one, and so on. [82]

But even where the social context is constant, there will be variations related to the witness himself. Two brothers from the same family, for instance, might respond quite differently to their experiences simply because one is the older, one the younger. More, the experiences themselves might be significantly different.

We must look to find, then, in every encounter experience, some elements which reflect the particular and immediate circumstances of the individual witness, along with others which reflect the more general beliefs and values of his cultural environment. In the next phase of our study, we will look at the way in which these two sets of influences interact to determine what happens, and how what happens is interpreted.

6.2 ENTITIES AND PSEUDO-ENTITIES

Even those who believe that *some* encounters are what they seem to be, are ready to admit that others are not. Catholic theologians believe that some visions of the Virgin are genuine, but dismiss others as spurious. Spiritists accept that many seeming communications from the dead are false. Those who are convinced that abductions of humans by ETs are taking place certainly don't accept every such claim. But none of these believers can provide us with foolproof tests for distinguishing the genuine article from the sham.

The matter is made more complicated because, between the definitely genuine and the definitely spurious, we have to contend with a host of ambiguous entities, such as:

★ The *devil and his minions*, who like to deceive us by masquerading as the Virgin, saints, even Jesus himself.

★ Communication between the living and the dead has to pass not only through the spirit medium, but often through his *'spirit control'* as well. Though many mediums believe that their controls are real people or real spirits, it is more generally accepted that many if not all are no more than secondary personalities of the medium himself. None the less, they claim specific identities, give themselves names (usually American Indian or Chinese), and generally act in an independent and often very convincing manner.

★ We have already considered the possibility that entities such as the Virgin Mary may be appearing to us not in their true likeness, but in the form of *stereotypes* conforming to what the witness expects to see, perhaps so as not to alarm the witness, perhaps so as to be the more readily believed.

★ It has been suggested that the ET entity, for similar reasons, reads from the witness' mind what he expects a spaceperson to be like, and matches himself to that image; so what the witness is seeing is no more than *feedback* from his own mind. A similar theory was put forward by the theosophists with regard to fairies.[89]

★ Many hypotheses have been offered which propose the existence of a species of *otherworldly beings* who occasionally interact in human affairs. For example, Salvador Freixedo suggests such a race, who in the cosmic scheme rank somewhere between God and ourselves, who thrive on human psychic energy, and manifest to us in order to obtain it. Such beings would, like the Virgin Mary and the visiting ETs, present themselves in some form we can recognize, either to deceive us or because they possess no form at all that we could perceive. This explains many ancient legends of divinities, and accounts for the majority of our puzzling encounters. [81]

If these explanations are founded in fact, it is hardly surprising that we have difficulty distinguishing genuine entities from the impostors. However, don't let's forget that these are no more than speculative hypotheses devised for the specific purpose of accounting for that difficulty; there is not a scrap of solid evidence for any of them.

The question of pseudo-entities, then, presents us with the following options:

★ If the ostensible entities actually exist, we have also to accept the existence of the pseudo-entities, and either go along with such explanations as those just cited, or think up better ones.

★ If the ostensible entities do *not* exist, the difficulty of distinguishing between genuine and spurious doesn't exist either.

Chance or chosen?

In some kinds of encounter experience — for example, abductions by ETs — it is often supposed that the event was a matter of chance. According to this view, if you or I had been driving through New Hampshire that night in 1967 instead of Barney and Betty Hill, it would have been we who would have been abducted.

This view seems to be confirmed by those instances when a witness is first selected, then rejected. This happened to 77-year-old Alfred Burtoo one August night in 1983 at Aldershot, England, when he was invited aboard an ET spacecraft which landed beside the canal where he was fishing. Soon after entering the craft he was told 'You can go; you are too old and too infirm for our purpose.' [93]

Even if it is the case that abductions are the result of mere chance, they are very much the exception. In the vast majority of encounters it is evident that the witness has been specifically selected. This is as true of ET contactees like Adamski and Siragusa as it was of religious witnesses like Teresa and Bernadette. In a great many cases, we have the word of the witnesses that they were chosen. In addition we have many cases like the current apparitions in Medjugorje, where the Virgin Mary appears nightly in a small room, seen only by the little group of visionaries without others present being able to share the experience. This suggests that the entity has a clear notion who it wants to meet and who it doesn't (though it could equally well indicate a process of self-selection on the part of the witness).

Encounters with apparitions present this problem in its most baffling form. There are many cases in which a haunting ghost is seen by someone who doesn't expect to see it. It is possible that some people are endowed with a particular ghost-seeing faculty, or possess more of it than the rest of us, which makes them more prone to such experiences than others, and that the apparition is visible only, or more readily, to those who are equipped with the appropriate receiver. This is the sort of ability which is claimed by so-called psychics, who also claim to be able to see other people's auras, have glimpses of the future, and do all kinds of paranormal things.

The evidence for the existence of a psychic faculty of some kind is very strong. What is less clear is whether it is a faculty we all possess to a greater or lesser degree, or whether humanity can be divided into those who are 'psychic' and those who are not. Confusing the issue yet further are two widely held assumptions: first, that there is something vaguely 'spiritual' about the faculty, an assumption which causes it to be associated with all kinds of weird belief systems; and second, that because the faculty has hitherto eluded scientific attempts to explain it, it is somehow outside the scope of science. There is no reason why we should accept either of these assumptions, and every reason why we should approach the psychic faculty in just the same way as any other human ability.

This matter bears on our inquiry by posing the question, is there any connection between the psychic faculty and the ability to have encounter experiences? So far as our present knowledge goes, no clear connection exists. True, many psychics are mediums and vice versa, but this may be the result of cultural conditioning and/or confusion about what the psychic faculty on the one hand and mediumship on the other really comprise. However, it may be that the same kind of psychological circumstances which encourage people to explore and develop their psychic faculties also make them liable to have encounter experiences.

The question of witness-selection, then, presents us with the following options:

★ If the ostensible entities actually exist and the encounters actually occur as reported, they occur by design rather than chance, and the witnesses have been selected for the experience; consequently we are faced with the problem of explaining why a Bernadette or an Orfeo Angelucci should be picked out from so many others seemingly just as deserving and just as gifted.

★ If the ostensible entities do not actually exist, and the encounters are some kind of psychodrama rather than physical events, the reason why Bernadette and Angelucci have the experience when others do not will be found in their personal circumstances and psychological make-up.

Purpose and need

If an encounter occurs, we must suppose there is a purpose for it; if the encounter involves an individual, we must suppose that its purpose relates to that individual.

When a leader like Moses tells us that God arranged a meeting with him, for the sake of instructing him and giving him a set of laws, this is a logical enough motive. To this day, priests in primitive communities communicate with their divinities in this way. For the most part, however, encounter experiences rarely involve public figures, and this makes it often difficult to identify and assess their purpose. A witness will often claim that the entity has a particular mission in mind, and has picked him out because he has the necessary qualities: religious visionaries possess an above-average share of spiritual gifts, spirit mediums have the right 'vibrations' to tune into the next world, contactees have developed the requisite 'philosophy'. Unfortunately, though these qualities may be just what the otherworldly entities are looking for, they are not ones which we are used to evaluating, so we have no criteria to test the witness' claims.

In the absence of any such qualification, the witness may be chosen for what he has *not* got: when the Virgin Mary appeared at Pellevoisin in 1876, she told Estelle Faguet, 'I choose the small and the feeble for my honour', and at Banneux in 1933 she told Mariette Beco 'I am the Virgin of the poor'. Again, it is not easy to see how, among so many candidates, an entity chooses a particular poor and humble individual to be the favoured recipient.[255]

When the encounter involves actitivities, not just conversation, the purpose becomes if anything even more obscure. Probably a majority of abduction experiences, for instance, describe something like a medical examination; but it is hard to believe that ETs would go to all the trouble of sending an entire crew in a spaceship to Earth for no other purpose but to spend an hour carrying out a physical inspection of a single specimen of the human species. We must not, of course, fall into the trap of judging the motives of otherworldly entities by this-worldly standards; but the abducting entities are represented as so human-like in so many other ways, it is reasonable to suppose that the logic would extend to the actual purpose of their visit.

So unconvincing are these examinations that many researchers favour the view that they are a deliberate sham, a staged performance designed to cover up some more sinister purpose (though one of the most ingenious is not sinister at all: Australian ufologist John Prytz offers the delightful suggestion that what we are seeing in many UFO visits is something of the nature of school excursions, ET children being brought to look at our planet just as our children are taken to visit the local sewage works[201]).

Other purposes attributed to the entities involve such events as mighty intergalactic struggles involving Earth, which certain privileged Earthpeople are aware of; or terrible punishments which would be inflicted on us by Jesus who, his mother tells us, is fed up with erring humanity and whose anger she is only just able to restrain. In the absence of any supporting evidence — no astronomer has reported cosmic events suggestive of space battles, and there is nothing to show that Jesus is personally responsible for the misfortunes of mankind — we have no reason to either accept or reject the statements except on grounds of probability.

But what if we look at encounters from the point of view of the *witness*? Even though we can often see that an encounter experience is beneficial to the witness, it is seldom possible to demonstrate that it occurs *on account of* that benefit. Even if it were possible to conduct a psychological investigation of the witness, our findings would fall short of scientific proof. Often, of course, the witness writes or dictates his own account of his experience, and we can give him the benefit of supposing that he has done his best to give us an honest account.

At Loudun in the seventeenth century, Soeur Jeanne des Anges convinced herself — and her spiritual counsellors — that she was possessed by the devil. Reading her account of the matter[153] we can see good grounds for believing that she was using, consciously or unconsciously, the tenets of her belief system to conceal a private motivation. What was true in the seventeenth century is just as likely to be true today, and we should be similarly hesitant about taking ET encounter reports at face value.

In a few rare cases the witness' need is so manifest that our only question is who or what was instrumental in gratifying it. Catherine Labouré was desperately anxious to meet the Virgin, and in 1830 she did so. Did Mary grant the encounter because Catherine wanted it so much, or did the force of Catherine's longing cause her to imagine the incident? Our answer will depend on which we think the more probable option.

Again, in the case of Delphine, the Virgin told the witness that her father should not drink so much. Was this a concern on the part of Mary, who may be supposed to be concerned with the welfare of every one of her flock; or a by-product of Mary's concern for Delphine, which extended to anything relating to her; or a concern on Delphine's part which (unconsciously, no doubt) she put into Mary's mouth because this would be a more effective way of persuading her father to change his ways?

In this section I have confined myself to trivial indications that the encounters meet the individual needs of the witness. Later we shall look at the deeper motivations which may be involved. This is, however, sufficient to show that the question of purpose presents us with the following options:

★ If the ostensible entities are responsible for the encounters, we have to explain why their purposes are often so obscure.

★ If the ostensible entities are *not* responsible for them, we can conjecture that the implausible purposes of the alleged entities may be a cloak for much more intelligible purposes on the part of the witness.

Social and cultural factors

The cultural environment of the witness is an important factor in determining not only what kind of encounter experience he will have, but whether he will have that kind of experience at all.

Some societies are geared to encounter situations. Without going so far as to say that the Virgin Mary is *expected* to appear to teenage Catholic children, we can say at least that nobody is unduly surprised when a teenage Catholic child makes such a claim. By contrast, similar experiences in Protestant societies are very much rarer, and in non-Christian communities rarer still. We saw, when considering encounters with Jesus, how those which occurred in England, and in the setting of a psychiatric hospital, remained as one-off events regarded as abnormal, whereas in France, similar incidents develop into rich relationships either with Jesus or with an entity purporting to be him.

There seems every reason to suppose that this difference springs from the different degree of support the witness gets from his environment. Dr Anthony Wallace of Philadelphia has commented on the need for social support felt by witnesses who have hallucinatory experiences. Primitive societies tend to accept the fact of hallucination; their concern is consequently only with its content and what they can learn from it. In Western cultures, on the other hand, it is exceptional to proceed so far as to study the content, for the fact of having the hallucination is regarded as a sign of sickness calling for treatment. Not only do the doctors and nurses have this attitude, but the patient/witness knows they have it; so he will be reluctant to report his experience, or to take it seriously himself:

> We may ask, at this point, how much anxiety, self-depreciation, and cognitive distortion are added to the miseries of mental patients by the circumstance that they have learned to fear waking hallucination in the course of living in a society in which waking hallucinatory experience is almost universally negatively valued?[263]

Dr Wallace quotes with approval A. T. Boisen's words: 'What the voices say is the important thing, not the mere fact of hearing voices'.

It is in this context that we can appreciate the value of such events as the annual Rocky Mountain Conferences held by Dr Leo Sprinkle at the University of Wyoming, Laramie, where UFO contactees are able to come together in an encouraging and supportive environment to discuss their experiences with Sprinkle and his colleagues on the one hand, and also with one another. Here, at least, they can be sure their experiences will be valued positively rather than negatively. Though Sprinkle himself holds certain working hypotheses about what is happening to his delegates, he maintains a scrupulous impartiality when counselling individual witnesses:

> From an investigator's standpoint I'm puzzled. But from a psychologist's point of view I know it's helping people for them to sit down and talk to somebody; they feel better. We don't know what's going to come of this conference, scientifically speaking; but from a social standpoint we *know* that it's helpful.
>
> Anthropologists know that you can have one kind of anthropology where you stand outside the society and look at it, and another kind where you are *inside* the society; and I think I have decided that I might as well be a contactee, be inside; because I *feel* like I'm one! Now, someone may come along and judge that as bad science, and I'll accept that verdict. But I made a choice. I guess in a few years we'll find out whether it was wasted effort or not![236]

It could be argued that Sprinkle is providing an artificially supportive environment for his contactees, and thereby encouraging them in what may well be delusions.

To this, we must answer, first, that even if we knew for certain that a witness was deluded, it is questionable whether the best course would be to tell him so, without first finding out *why* he is having the delusion and dealing with that cause.

As it is, we do *not* know for sure that these witnesses are deluded, and so we certainly have no right to impose our own views, however sure of them we may be. In the present state of our ignorance, Sprinkle's supportive neutrality is the only morally defensible position.

Though attempts to establish a common psychological make-up for encounter witnesses have not yet been very helpful, it is clear enough even from the handful of cases presented in these pages that most witnesses are 'loners' by temperament, isolated to some degree from the rest of society. French contactee Monnet, American contactee Menger, English psychic Eileen Garrett, Spanish mystic Teresa — each runs true to type in telling us of a childhood during which they preferred not to join in the other children's games, but pursued their own private interests.

Did this voluntary isolation make them into the kind of people who would be more likely than the rest of us to have encounter experiences, or was it the premonition of later experiences which set them apart in the first instance? Once again we come up against the difficulty of identifying cause and effect. If we think their experiences were 'real', we may well favour the latter view, and see the witnesses as in some way predestined: if we think they were fantasy or delusion, we shall see them as part of a larger psychological process.

Either way, we may doubt if there is a single witness who does not welcome the approval of others as a *validation* of his experience (though he may pretend and even believe he doesn't give a damn). All four of the witnesses named above, and probably a majority of the others quoted in this book, published accounts of their experiences. ET contactees are eager to lecture about their experiences or make radio and TV appearances, while on a less popular level the enthusiasm of contactees to attend Leo Sprinkle's conferences is an indication of their wish to have their stories taken seriously.

We must further consider the possibility that the encounter experience may not occur at all unless the witness is sure in advance of a reasonably sympathetic hearing. This sounds as though to have an encounter is something the witness decides for himself; but that is not quite the implication. In the first place, the witness' feelings are likely to be unconscious; and secondly, the expectation of an unsympathetic reception would be simply an inhibiting factor, *preventing* the process just as we have seen other factors play an *enabling* role.

The question of social acceptance, then, presents us with the following options:

★ If the ostensible entities are responsible for the encounters, we have to explain why they permit them to be so ambiguous that the witness is affected by his social environment, both in the way he interprets his experience and even as to whether he has it at all.

★ If the ostensible entities are *not* responsible for them, we may conjecture that what happens to the witness is shaped and even instigated by the beliefs of those around him.

In this chapter we have considered a variety of features of the encounter experience bearing on whether or not the ostensible entities are in fact responsible for them. In each case we see that taking the experiences at face value presents difficulties which do not arise when we hypothesize that the ostensible event is a facade concealing something more obscure. But any such hypothesis must also explain why a facade is required at all, and why it should take one form rather than another.

6.3   MODELS AND MYTHS

If a short, tubby, clean-shaven, crop-headed individual with a laughing face were to present himself to us as Jesus, we would at once reject his claim; for we know, don't we, that Jesus is tall, lean, bearded, long-haired and unremittingly serious?

But of course we don't know any such thing. No authentic portrait of Jesus exists, not even a verbal description. All we have is a general consensus as to his appearance, a stereotype to which we all give assent.

In the same way, if you ask any child of the 1980s to describe a spaceman, he will cheerfully do so. Yet neither he nor we have ever seen a spaceman, nor is it even certain that spacemen exist. We are watching the creation of a new mythology.

Mythology is what you have when you don't have the real thing. It may be that the real thing doesn't exist — like the Age of Gold or Valhalla or Hell — or it may be that it exists too intangibly, and we feel a need to give the airy nothing a local habitation and a name — like The Evil One or Guardian Angels. We have seen that many of our encounters are with entities who seem little more than stereotypes: we must now ask, are they that and nothing more?

Need and consensus

The entities in encounter experiences seem to be of two kinds: stock figures like 'The Evil One' or 'A Space Alien,' or individual beings such as Delphine's Virgin Mary or Canon Phillips' C. S. Lewis. But we may be mistaken in thinking of them as two separate kinds; suppose we think, instead, of what they share in common.

When we were considering the *process* of encounter, we found it helpful to think of the witness as two persons in one: at the time of the encounter, one part of him as it were distances itself from the other, and engages itself in the action. There is another sense in which he is two persons in one: he is at the same time an individual, with unique personal needs, and a member of his social group, with needs that he shares with his fellows.

The entity has to satisfy both sets of needs: it must meet his personal hopes, fears, preconceptions and expectations, and it must also meet those he shares with others.

At the same time, it must also satisfy two subsidiary requirements:

it must possess the *authority* to perform its role in the encounter drama, and it must possess sufficient *credibility* to win the acceptance not only of the witness himself but also of his fellows — which is quite a lot to ask an entity to do. If it really is the Virgin Mary, or Ashtar from Alpha Centauri, who is responsible for the encounter, we may sympathize with the dilemma of how they should manifest.

What happens, in practice, is that they manifest as stereotypes — but stereotypes with variations: as standard models, but customized for the individual.

Here, I suggest, is the way to resolve the paradox presented by the same-but-different characteristics of our entities. Ufologists have been baffled by the fact that no two contactees seem to encounter the same spaceship crews. Parapsychologists have been stumped by the inconsistencies and contradictions displayed by the spirits of the dead. Even the most ingenious theologians have found it hard to explain why the Mary met by Bernadette at Lourdes in 1858 wasn't at all like the Mary encountered by Mélanie and Maximin at La Salette in 1846, while the Mary that appeared to Lucia, Francisco and Jacinta at Fatima in 1917 was different from either of the others.

Not only does the Mary-entity look different every time it appears, but it doesn't look like the consensus-Mary as depicted in holy pictures or church statuary, which we might think would provide a source of inspiration for the visionaries. Still less, needless to say, does it resemble any plausible notion of how a middle-aged first-century Palestinian carpenter's wife might be supposed to look.

And yet there was no serious problem in identifying each of these entities as the Virgin. Bernadette, like many visionaries, had moments of doubt; but the entity, though differing from the consensus-Mary, was not *too* different to be accepted.

A revealing incident occured when Bernadette was confronted with the statue Fabisch made, supposedly in accordance with her description:

> Bernadette joins her hands and contemplates the image 'with a look full of tenderness and appeal'. She tries to acquiesce in the representation, accustomed as she is to be obedient, and says, feebly, Yes, that is it.
> But at once her temperament, her natural frankness, assert themselves— No, that *isn't* it, she protests. And ever afterwards she would maintain this definitive verdict: No, that isn't her . . . but in any case, one couldn't represent her as she was.[145]

We can see that little episode as the outward expression of a conflict within Bernadette herself. Had she been asked, before her encounters, to give a description of the Virgin, she would surely have done so along conventional lines: only now, after her meetings with *'une fille blanche, pas plus grande que moi'* (a girl in white, no bigger than myself), did she have ideas of her own which departed from the consensus-image.

So it must have been with the others; but of course the consensus prevailed. The Mary you see today portrayed in the statues erected on the visionary sites, or reproduced millionfold on postcards, is not the visionary's Mary but the stereotype Mary; not what the witness saw, but what people thought she *ought* to have seen.

An interesting experiment is said to have been carried out by the French Cathar heretics, presumably with the intention of ridiculing Catholic piety:

> The Cathari of Monceval made a portrait of the Virgin, representing her as one-eyed and toothless, saying that, in his humility, Christ had chosen a very ugly woman for mother. They had no difficulty in healing several cases of disease by its means; the image became famous, was venerated almost everywhere, and accomplished many miracles, until the day when the heretics divulged the deception.[264]

If this story is true, it shows that people *can* be made to discard their stereotypes, provided they are given a plausible reason for doing so. In general, though, stereotypes are not lightly abandoned, for the reason that they are not lightly held. If a stereotype is to carry conviction, it must be strongly believed in — which means it must be believed to be *real*. If the Cathars were able to convince the good folk of Monceval to change their pretty young Virgin for a toothless old one, it must have been because theirs was more convincing.

Evidently none of the Marys described by the visionaries has been sufficiently imposing to replace the conventional image, except, of course so far as the witnesses themselves are concerned. With extraterrestrials, on the other hand, the situation is quite different, because though there are general notions current as to the way ET-entities may be supposed to look and act, there exists nowhere near so clear-cut a stereotype. Rather, it is the reports of the witnesses which are helping to shape and define such a stereotype.

In the early days of ET-encounters, the notion of 'little green men' prevailed. This seems to have been borrowed from science fiction, with a secondary debt to the 'Little People' of folklore; but there were some UFO-related reports to confirm the description, notably the notorious shoot-out at Kelly, Kentucky, in 1955, when the Sutton family were besieged by a number of gnome-like creatures who, though they displayed no hostility, were fired upon in the classic Western tradition. (You'll be glad to learn the bullets just bounced off them.)[245]

Adamski and his fellow-contactees soon changed the paradigm for something more adult. His Venusian was depicted as very similar to the Jesus stereotype, and set a pattern for extremely handsome ETs with shoulder-length blonde hair and warm, caring expressions. No ET-entity wears spectacles or suffers from acne; they would doubtless attribute their good health to their vegetarian principles, their abstention from drink and drugs, the pollution-free environments in which they live except when visiting our disgusting planet, and the inner health which comes from not being greedy and aggressive like you and me.

Abducting ETs are less sympathetically portrayed; they tend to be hairless, unsmiling, leanly built characters, more or less human in appearance (except for the hairy ones) apart from their big wrap-round eyes. Just as we saw abduction stories as reflecting an increasing maturity and sophistication compared with the contactees, so the progression from caring Jesus-figures to dispassionate abductors seems to parallel our passage from the age of hippies and flower power to that of the computer.

The extent to which entities reflect our expectations is well exemplified by the clothes they wear — or indeed, by the fact that they wear clothes at all. Man is the only species on this planet which has developed the habit of wearing clothes; yet it is taken for granted that any ET visitor will have developed the same habit. This is strangely at variance with other folk beliefs, for the Bible makes it clear that the adoption of clothing is a consequence of the loss of innocence. Evidently, the ETs too had their Fall. Only one of our contactees reports that people on other planets go naked, and even in their case it was a question of leaving off clothes, not of not having them in the first instance.[46]

It may be no more than coincidence that most contactee reports come from the United States, one of the most puritanical nations on earth. But there is no escaping the match between the appearance of the female ET crewpersons, as reported by Bethurum, Menger, Angelucci and others, and the then-current American notions of female attractiveness. Not only are the female ETs invariably described as facially extremely beautiful, but their shapes receive enthusiastic comment. The hypothesis that the ETs adapt their appearance to match the expectations of the witnesses is inadequate to explan why entities who wish to impress us with their superior wisdom, and who frequently declare themselves to be hundreds of years old, should manifest in the form of a sex-magazine pin-up.

Spirits of the dead

Apparitions of the dead also run to stereotypes, but these tend to be less elaborate. Typically, a recently bereaved lady will see her dead husband gazing at her wordlessly from the foot of the bed, or a child will speak of an old lady who comes into his bedroom, who is later identified as a former occupant of the house.

Clearly, when named individuals are concerned, there can be no question of stereotypes; they are themselves. But they may, none the less, be performing stock roles: it is by no means uncommon for an individual, in the throes of a personal problem, to receive a visit from a dead grandparent, aunt or uncle, to whom he was accustomed to turn for comfort or advice during their lifetime.

Among unnamed apparitions, there is a notable tendency for veiled nuns and cowled monks to appear. A typical case occurred in 1976, when

Lou Eden of Bromley, Kent, five months pregnant with her first child, had a succession of encounters with monk-like figures around the house, which her husband was unable to see:

> I was so sure I'd seen someone. He had been so real, so vivid. He had been wearing a medieval cowled hood and ankle-length light-brown habit of rough woolen cloth, hairy and coarse, tied round the waist by a rope with tasseled ends. His face was concealed in the darkness of the hood . . . How could I have seen all that in the pitch darkness? Was I mad? [69]

Subsequently she saw not only single monks or pairs but whole processions of them. She speculated that the house might have been built near the site of an old monastery; but that doesn't explain why she should join the great number of witnesses who have seen this particular type of ghost.

There may be fact-based reasons for such sightings; but it is also possible that monks have attained some kind of symbolic status for many of us. Their piety; their celibacy; their voluntary self-exile from worldly affairs; their lack of individual identity in their all-concealing robes — all these make them sinister, menacing figures whom, I suggest, we sense to be already half-way out of this world and into the next . . .

From belief to reality

A particularly rich category of encounter experiences is that which involves the 'phantom hitchhiker'. Reported world-wide over many years in many forms, the myth is a stereotype with infinite variations. Here is a recurrent favourite:

> A motorist is driving (usually alone, and often at night) when he sees a person (usually female) by the side of the road, thumbing a lift. He stops and she gets in. If she speaks it is to warn him not to drive too fast at the next bend. To humour her, he takes it slowly, then turns his head for her approval — only to find that she has vanished. He looks for her without success. Subsequently he learns that some time before, a young lady had been killed in an accident on that very bend.

Michael Goss, a leading investigator of the legend, has not only unearthed a great many different versions, but has shown that there is substantial evidence to show that, *subsequent* to the story attaining world-wide circulation, genuine cases of phantom hitchhikers are occurring. [95]

If this is so, then it seems that belief in a myth has led to its becoming reality; and if that is the case, the implications are awesome. It could mean, for example, that the widespread stereotype of encounters with the Virgin, whether or not they are founded in fact, could lead to *real* encounters. The current encounters, with Mary at Medjugorje, let's say, may be real encounters which came into being only because the visionaries were aware of other such incidents and believed that the same thing could happen to them also.

It is a possibility we should bear in mind, but we can do no more with it as things stand; we don't know whether this is really occurring, or if it is simply another instance of the mythmaking process at work.

Conclusion

The encounter entity, as the witness meets and reports it, is a composite creature. It is what the witness *expects* to meet, and it is what the witness *wants or needs* to meet.

It remains possible that this is done by the express intention of the entity itself, who chooses to appear in this form so as to fulfil its function with the greatest effectiveness. But even if that is so, it is evidently the *need of the witness* which is the dominant factor; for otherwise the entity could appear in its consensus form, there would be no argument or doubt, and everyone would be satisfied.

If, on the other hand, it is the witness who brings about the encounter, he too may seem to be making a concession in giving the star part in his little drama to an off-the-shelf stereotype. But the advantages are many:

★ He doesn't have to invent the character; it's ready made, and all he needs to do is a little remodelling to fit the present circumstances.

★ By using an authorized stereotype, he gains increased credibility so far as others are concerned.

★ The entity comes with built-in qualities, such as authority, warmth, concern, all of which are attributes which have been fed into the stereotype by popular assent, in much the same way as we saw that the tarot pack has acquired 'authority' as the result of repeated use.

If entities have a general tendency to resemble one another, it is because the witnesses who encounter them are members of a community whose ideas and beliefs they in general share.

If, despite the foregoing, no two entities are precisely alike, it is because no two witnesses are precisely alike.

If encounter experiences have a general tendency to resemble one another, it is because the witnesses who have them need the reassurance of a shared experience and authorized precedent.

If, despite the foregoing, no two encounter experiences are precisely alike, it is because no two witnesses have precisely the same needs nor can resolve them in precisely the same way.

6.4 THE NEED-BASED ENCOUNTER

No matter whether the entities encountered are genuine or spurious, no matter how much the circumstances of the encounter are determined by the cultural context, the crucial factor in virtually every case is the *need* of the witness to have the encounter.

In some cases the need is clear and unambiguous: for example, the reappearance of a dead husband to his recently bereaved widow. This can be interpreted as either:

★ the dead actually 'returning' to comfort the living;

★ the living fantasizing a psychodrama in which the dead returns;

★ some kind of mutual arrangement between the subconscious mind of the witness and the spirit of the dead.

But whichever explanation we prefer, the need of the witness is evidently the reason why the encounter occurs.

It will not always be so apparent. To some, indeed, it will seem monstrous to suggest that little Bernadette may have brought about her encounter to serve her personal ends. Nevertheless this is a possibility that must be considered.

It is unlikely that we shall be able to indicate more than a possibility, in most instances, for the need — and the meeting of that need — will seldom be anything measurable. No doubt some encounters have been fakes staged for financial gain or to achieve status in the community, and perhaps some of our contactee cases were instances of jumping on a fashionable bandwagon. But the overwhelming majority of witnesses give an impression of sincerity; few have benefited financially or socially as a result of their experience; so that both the benefit and the need which that benefit answers must be looked for on a deeper, psychological level.

Unfortunately, since few witnesses have been examined with this sort of intensity, we can rarely prove the occurrence of the need-benefit process. The most we are likely to be able to do is to show:

★ that it is likely that the witness had a need, to which his encounter may have supplied an answer;

★ that parallels exist in more explicit situations, such as clinically observed mentally disturbed patients whose behaviour may clearly indicate need-benefit processes;

★ that the need-benefit explanation provides a plausible explanation when we have no other.

Encounter experiences are rarely enjoyed by the well-off, secure and contented: virtually every one of our encounter witnesses was in some way underprivileged, or — what is for our purposes equally significant — felt himself to be so. Bernadette, for instance, had a miserable life even in a society where life for all was a continual struggle for mere existence; an out-of-work and ne'er-do-well father, herself sent away from home to work, the loss of their home and makeshift accommodation in the town gaol, these were specific circumstances which added to a way of life which was in any case appallingly poor and devoid of excitement or hope for the future.

The lives of the mystic visionaries nearly always start with an unhappy childhood. Saint Marguerite-Marie Alacoque (1647–1690) is typical. Daughter of a notary, in a respectable family, her father died when she was young and, in accordance with the laws of heritage of the time, an uncle moved in and took over the family home. The new family treated the widow and her five children harshly, so that Marguerite-Marie's childhood was very much a Cinderella one. Her mother was often ill, and not able to take proper care of her children. Marguerite-Marie found comfort in solitude, and from the age of 8 felt destined for the religious life. This was exacerbated by ill health: for four years from age 8 to 12 she was unable to walk. When she eventually recovered, she credited the Virgin Mary to whom she had prayed. Her mother sought to get her married, but after six years of struggle Marguerite-Marie succeeded in becoming a nun.

We read so many such stories in the pious biographies that it requires an effort to imagine what such an upbringing would mean to *any* child, let alone one more than averagely sensitive as Marguerite-Marie evidently was. Some excerpts from her autobiography will help us to share her feelings:

> I was sent to a church school, where I made my First Communion when I was 9. This Communion gave me such a distaste for my petty pleasures and amusements that I could never again derive any joy from them. When I sought to join in the games of my schoolfellows, I always felt something drawing me away to find solitude. I was happy only when I was praying, on my bare knees, provided there was no one to see me, for I felt strangely uncomfortable if I met anyone at these times . . .
>
> I was so ill that for four years I could not walk; my bones came through my skin in every direction. The only remedy was to dedicate myself to the holy Virgin, promising her that if I recovered, I would one day be one of her daughters. No sooner did I make this vow than I was cured. From this

time on she made herself mistress of my heart, treating me as her own child, controlling my conduct and correcting my misbehaviour.

One day while I was sitting saying my rosary, she presented herself in front of me and reproached me: 'My daughter, I'm astonished that you serve me so negligently!' These words made such an impression on my soul, that they have guided me all my life . . .

[Her family often prevented her from going to church, accusing her of using it as an excuse for meeting some boy.] Not knowing where to go, I hid myself in some corner of the garden, or a stable, or some other secret place where I could go on my knees to relieve my feelings in tears . . . I would stay there for the entire day, without food or drink. Sometimes the good people of the village would give me a little milk or some fruit. When I returned home, I was in fear and trembling, as if I were some criminal.[5]

The interacting physical and psychological circumstances of Marguerite-Marie's life are just as we have seen to be conducive to altered states, and all that they make possible. Not every child would have responded to those circumstances in the same way; her disposition must also have played a crucial part. But underlying it all was her need to resolve her situation, her need for comfort and understanding, her need to be recognized as an individual, her need to live her own life in her own way. Only the Virgin Mary, it must have seemed to her, could meet those needs.

In Marguerite-Marie's case, the physical circumstances of her life are such that we can understand how she might have felt even without her own account; in others, the outward circumstances are less obviously desperate. We saw that Hélène Smith's life was comfortable enough, nevertheless Flournoy revealed her dissatisfaction, her sense of not belonging which even made her feel her father and mother were not her true parents. Jung, speaking of his patient 'Sophie', who like Hélène enjoyed comfortable enough material circumstances, wrote: 'She longs to get out of this world, she returns unwillingly to reality, she bemoans her hard lot, her odious family circumstances.'[124]

The phrase 'identity crisis' is over-used, but it does seem to be precisely what many of our witnesses are experiencing. There is of course a very real sense in which every adolescent has an identity problem; the achievement and assertion of individual identity is the single most important stage in the development of every one of us, and often the most traumatic. Some of us achieve it easily and relatively painlessly; some have to weather the usual storms of adolescence; yet others fail to find a way along conventional lines, and have to resort to more extreme measures.

The finding and establishing of his own identity is a complex process for any individual, whether he achieves it easily or with difficulty and pain. It involves, first and foremost, an act of separation from those who have hitherto controlled his life: chiefly his parents, but to some extent also others who have had a hand in shaping his ideas, setting his values, directing his activities. All these he will start to question, some he will

reject. Often it will be a question of initial rejection, followed by
re-acceptance.

Much will depend on the sympathy and understanding he gets from
others; much too on whether his present environment is sufficiently flexible
to allow him to reshape his life without breaking out of it. A restrictive
family context will not necessarily be *over*-restrictive; a dominant parent
will not necessarily have to be rebelled against; the values and beliefs in
which he has been brought up will not necessarily have to be rejected,
if the adolescent is temperamentally suited to them. But where conflict
occurs, and where no other way of resolving the matter presents itself,
the individual may have recourse to an extreme solution.

It is not only at adolescence that identity crises occur; moments may
come at any time of our lives when circumstances call for reappraisal or
readjustment. If a correlation indeed exists between identity crises and
encounter experiences, it will not be mere coincidence that so many of
our witnesses are teenage children, that a high proportion of ET encounter
witnesses were at the time suffering from marital stress, or that 'displaced
persons' such as immigrants and members of ethnic minorities seem
particularly prone to encounter experiences.

The entity as authority figure

The Virgin Mary, Mrs Coombe-Tennant, Ashtar from the Intergalactic
Parliament — at first sight, the beings encountered have so little in common
that it is not surprising they have hitherto been thought of as separate
categories. But they *do* share certain characteristics, and these become
apparent when we look at the encounter experience in the light of a
psychodrama designed to resolve a need on the witness' part. We then
see that the entities are of a sort to play an appropriate role in that drama.

First and foremost, they represent *authority*. Divinity-entities, of course,
derive their authority from their place in the belief system. Spirits of the
dead are supposed to have passed beyond this life to a higher level of
existence where they have been invested with greater knowledge and
understanding. As for the ETs, they are invariably beings of superior
wisdom, superior morality, superior everything: a recurrent phrase in
their messages is 'Our civilization is x-thousand years ahead of yours'
The notion that the superiority of a civilization can be measured in time-
units is of course totally meaningless: if it is put into the mouths of the
entities, this can only be to indicate how much more advanced they are
and therefore how much right they have to tell us humans what to do.

This sense of 'authority' gives force to the experience. It makes the
witness himself, and the community to whom he reports his experience,
more willing to accept the message. At the same time it enables the witness,
in all sincerity because it is what he truly believes, to dissociate himself
from aspects of the experience which others may not easily accept, for
example when Jeanne d'Arc proposes herself as the potential saviour of
France, a suggestion which would hardly have been taken seriously

had she not had Saint Michel and Saint Catherine as her sponsors.

This process is of course wholly *subconscious*. If Jeanne needed the authority of her 'voices' to impress others, she needed them first and even more importantly for herself. No one in her position could have felt herself capable of such a venture had she not been utterly convinced that it was required of her by an authority in which she had absolute belief, for which she had total respect, and of whose support she was totally confident.

There are many instances in which it seems as though the witness is exploiting for his personal ends the authority of his entity. We frequently find Teresa d'Avila, for instance, announcing that her entity has ordered something which, while it suits her book, might not be favourably received by her superiors did they not accept her visionary encounters as genuine. It is easy to see this as opportunism, and indeed so it is: but that does not mean that Teresa was not herself convinced that the orders came from above.

A more complex example of this kind of projection occurs in the case of Lydwine of Schiedam (1380–1433), whose entire life is a chronicle of appalling physical afflictions, supported with pious fortitude because she is in almost daily communication with Jesus and Mary. Her parents hope she will marry, but she is committed to becoming the bride of Christ, and begs him to help her. She is at once struck with ill health, and becomes fat and ugly. This serves the double function of destroying the beauty which might have made her marriageable, and at the same time providing her with the opportunity of suffering for Jesus' sake. (We have to remember that what most of us would regard as affliction is positively welcomed by religious mystics as a sign of grace) It may seem crudely unsympathetic to suggest that the entire life-history of this tormented saint derived from her reluctance to marry; but if Huysmans, her devoted biographer, can see her ill health as Jesus' way of permanently ruling out the possibility of her marriage, we are justified in offering an alternative scenario in which Lydwine casts Jesus in the role of an authority-figure onto whom she can project her own subconscious wish. [115]

Not only does the encounter experience come about as the result of a need, its purpose is to *resolve* that need. And just as the need may not be consciously felt by the individual, so the way in which it is resolved may well be something that has not consciously occurred to him; indeed it may be something that he would consciously reject unless it was presented to him in a form which he is constrained to accept. Hence, of course, the necessity for the encountered entity to be a figure of authority. It is important that we recognize that a very important part of the function of the encounter experience is *to get the individual to do something which he might not otherwise have done*. To take a trivial instance: if Delphine is really meeting the Virgin, we must suppose it is the Virgin who wants her to give up eating so many bonbons; if it is really Delphine herself who is responsible, it is because she subconsciously knows she eats too many bonbons, but cannot make herself give them up without this subterfuge of putting the prohibition into the mouth of an external authority.

Secrets and missions

Not only must the entity possess authority, but the witness himself must feel that he is *authorised*. We have already noted the sense of being 'chosen' which is common to a very great number of encounters. Thus when Marion Keech and her colleagues were told by the 'Guardians' that mankind was about to be overtaken by catastrophe, they were also told that because they had taken the warnings seriously they would be evacuated to safety. [74]

Many encounter witnesses are entrusted with secrets: Agnes of Bohemia was just one of the religious mystics who claimed that 'she had contemplated the secrets of God, which it is not permitted to anyone to reveal', [208] and the visionaries of La Salette, Fatima, Garabandal and elsewhere have made similar claims.

When the German stigmatic Emilie Schneider of Dusseldorf talked with Jesus in 1856, he showed her his wounds, telling her:

> There are few who recognise these things, and fewer still who approach them closely; but you, you share my sufferings with me . . . Come close to the wellsprings of my love; they are open for everyone, but few find the way which leads to them. You have discovered it, so drink at this spring, for yourself and others.

The phrase 'for yourself and for others' is significant, for a feature of encounter cases is that while the witness inevitably plays the leading role, he generally expresses his surprise at being chosen — 'Why me?' — and, in contexts where to have an encounter is considered a privilege, his humility.

Perhaps because they do indeed feel unworthy of being singled out in this way, and that their story may not be believed for this reason, witnesses tend to emphasize that they are no more than chosen representatives. George King was just one of many contactees who, though selected for his individual merits, was expected to share his experience with others. Those who have received messages are asked to pass them on; many believe they have a duty to fulfil, a mission to carry out:

> Madame Guyon had a burning piety and performed notable acts of virtue. But all in her was spoiled by her exalted imagination, her obstinacy, and above all her mad belief in a mission in the Church. She never doubted that she was led infallibly by her alleged revelations and her interior impulses. She was encouraged in this by Père Lacombe, who told her, 'I have consulted many pious ladies, and all unite in affirming that you are destined for an extraordinary mission.' [34]

But the sense of having a mission not only justifies the experience, it gives it a *purpose*. And if it forces the witness to change his life-style, well, perhaps that is what the whole episode was designed to do.

The encounter experience as rite of passage

A parallel with anthropology may be revealing at this stage. Most cultures have 'rites of passage' — ceremonials which mark a crucial stage in the individual's life, when he reaches puberty, makes a marriage relationship, when he dies, and so on.

In primitive societies these rites are open and explicit. They take a myriad different forms, often including dramatic spectacles which are unforgettable — frequently terrifyingly so — for the individual, and leave an indelible mark. But while they may be alarming, they are also reassuring; while painful, also a privilege; for they are an acknowledgement of the fact that he has reached a certain stage in his development, and that his community recognizes this. So not only do they register the fact but they help the individual to come to terms with it.

In sophisticated societies, much less is made of these critical phases. Weddings and funerals grow less and less formal, their deeper meanings hidden in ceremonies whose point is forgotten by all but the folklorist. In consequence, the impact on the individual is proportionately less.

Most evident of all is the decline of ritual associated with attaining puberty, when the individual exchanges the world of children for the world of grown-ups. Yet in many ways this is the most traumatic of all, for it is also the moment when the individual *becomes* an individual in his own right, not a mere appendage of his parents.

Most of us accomplish this without too much difficulty, beyond the usual storm of adolescence. But where the adolescent finds no guidelines to follow he may undergo an identity crisis of the kind we were considering a few pages earlier: and if this takes the form of trafficking with the forces of evil, ostensible encounters with those forces may be the consequence.

When considering encounters with the devil, we saw that they may be for some people not so much a pursuit of evil for its own sake, as a means of rejecting parental and other authority. Satan is seen not as an evil power but as a symbol of liberty, as Milton depicted him. For rejection can also be *assertion*: the negative step of cutting himself loose from parental apron-strings is also the *positive* step of starting out on his own feet.

Such a phase is not likely to be more than a short-lived flirtation, lasting no longer than is needed for the individual to accomplish the process of emergence into adulthood. But for a few the effects will be longer-lasting, the flirtation will become infatuation, and what began as a positive step turns to a self-destructive one.

This is particularly likely to occur in a culture with a strong but naive belief system — for instance, where there is a belief in the devil as a real and personal being. Such a case occurred in Switzerland in the 1960s, when a 17-year-old country girl, Bernadette Hasler, became enslaved by a small fanatical German religious sect who called themselves 'The Holy Family'. The sect leaders persuaded Bernadette's parents that the girl was possessed by the devil. The pressure of their accusations created in the girl's mind what German investigator Hans Bender labelled a 'sin mania'. She was forced to write hundreds of pages of confessions, admitting to sexual liaisons with the devil and all manner of other religious and sexual sins; for these she was physically and psychologically punished by all the members of the sect, who were persuaded they were doing God's will in helping to drive the devil away. In the end she died in 1966 as a result of their tortures: she was found to be still a virgin. [143]

The Hasler case may seem to be exceptional; but fundamentalist religion derives much of its impetus from its sustained battle with an alleged devil, and its literature is full of cases only marginally less alarming than Bernadette Hasler's. Even where the 'exorcism' is 'successful', the individual will suffer psychological damage from which he may never recover. Yet all that is happening is that the individual has been given a pseudo-cure for a pseudo-ailment. Had his trouble been recognized for what it was, and the causes sought, some quiet counselling would have achieved far more, and achieved it both less painfully and more effectively.

We have already noted the correlation between adolescence and the occurrence of visionary and encounter phenomena, to which could be added poltergeist outbreaks and other 'psychic' manifestations. It may seem naive to attribute all these to a lack of a 'rite of passage' to mark these individuals' transition to adulthood: yet it is not only the personal and social circumstances of the witness which favour the notion that a crisis of identity may underlie them. There are also features of the experiences themselves which suggest that they may be attempts to resolve such a crisis.

Rebirth

An element of 'rebirth' is evident in many encounter experiences. In almost every instance, the event marks a new start in life for the witness. Most religious visionaries, if they have not already adopted the religious life, do so as a result of their visions. ET contactees change their life-styles, become vegetarians, campaign for ecology.

In his *Birth and Rebirth* Mircea Eliade indicates seven stages in the ritual process, one of which is the *regressus ad uterum* in which the initiate 'clears' himself for his new life by returning symbolically to the womb. It can hardly be coincidence that American researcher Alvin Lawson has proposed a 'birth trauma' explanation for many of the details of ET abductions. He has persuasively demonstrated the parallels between witness accounts of their abduction experiences and the birth process, and goes so far as to propose that the experience is no less than the individual's recollection of his own birth-occasion. [149]

The evidence Lawson produces is impressive, but his ideas have not only failed to win general acceptance, but met considerable resistance.

While this may in part be attributed to a cultural reluctance to ascribe so ostensibly objective an event as a UFO abduction to so subjective a cause as memories of birth, there is the additional stumbling block that there is no obvious reason *why* this fantasy should occur, and on so widespread a scale. To put it bluntly, why, all of a sudden, should so many people start remembering their births and turning those memories into stories about being abducted by UFOs?

Our analysis of the encounter experience suggests an answer. If we are right to see the encounter experience as something like a self-administered rite of passage, and if Eliade is right in asserting that such a rite is likely to include a return-to-the-womb element, then it is by no means ridiculous to suggest that the encounter experience will incorporate elements of the *regressus ad uterum*. The psychodrama of the UFO abduction is simply the outer shell of the experience, chosen because of the currently available myths it happens to be the one most likely to win social acceptability; inside the public shell is the private experience, which may well take the symbolic form of a birth trauma.

John Rimmer, in his authoritative study of abductions, has demonstrated how the abduction scenario, nonsensical in itself, makes sense as some kind of subjective rebirth process. He cites the Aveley abductees, John and Elaine Avis, whose 1974 experience led to radical changes in their life-style. Apart from details like giving up smoking and becoming vegetarian, Rimmer notes more profound developments:

> John's inability to settle to a regular routine seems to have been channelled into bringing out a suppressed artistic facility . . . he has taken up sculpture, apparently with a certain amount of critical success — at least one of his works has been bought for display in a public building. Elaine also has changed. Besides becoming more self-confident and extrovert she began attending college and continuing the studies which were interrupted by her marriage . . .
>
> Consideration of this must prompt the question of the fundamental nature of their shared abduction experience. Were all these changes triggered off by the experience, or is the event itself a result of some emotional crisis or turning point that the couple — consciously or unconsciously — were going through? There is a strong suggestion that the abduction, in this case at least, was a *symptom* of a more personal emotional experience.[211]

If we add Lawson's suggestions to Rimmer's, and stir in our own conclusions drawn from a comparison with other types of encounter experience, we get an intriguingly plausible model of the abduction encounter experience as an archetypal initiation process:

★ It is nearly always a *solitary* experience. In the rare cases where it is shared, as in the Hill and Avis cases, the partner is someone very close — wife, lover, close friend — which makes it likely that something like a *folie à deux* is involved.

★ Characteristically it occurs in an *isolated location* — in a desert or mountain, such as those where Adamski, Vorilhon, Siragusa, Menger, Bethurum, Monnet and so many others met their contacts.

★ The witness is guided by wise *superior beings* who perform the priestlike task of initiation.

★ An emphasis on *light* — shafts and beams of light, tunnels of light, rooms with no obvious source of light — seems so pervasive as to have some symbolic significance, almost as though the witnesses were literally 'seeing the light' as well as remembering the emerging-into-light = emerging-into-life which birth represents.

★ The preoccupation with *genitals* in the 'medical examination' of abduction experiences is perhaps only to be expected — for after all, our reproductive system is likely to interest otherworldly visitors. But where everything else about the inspection is so *un*realistic, we may be excused for looking for a deeper significance. If so, then it conforms neatly with the idea of a rite of passage which marks puberty and the ability to procreate. Nor should we forget in how many religious encounters there is reference to the 'mystical marriage' in which the witness dedicates herself to earthly virginity in order to save herself as the 'bride of Christ'.

★ A curious detail of traditional initiation rituals is the crossing of the *enchanted forest* in which, amongst other details, no birds sing. A curious detail which is nevertheless specifically remarked by many encounter witnesses is the absence of birdsong and other animal noises.

Researcher Jenny Randles has frequently referred to what she names the 'Oz factor'[204] in which a sense of unreality overtakes the witness at the onset of the experience. Many ET encounters are supposed to have taken place in public places, yet there is never an uninvolved witness to observe the event. Is the event somehow cloaked from others' sight? Does it happen outside the normal time frame, in some other dimension? If so, have the witness' car, family and so on accompanied him into the enchanted realm, or is the enchantment, like the experience itself, occurring within his own mind?

Whether or not we should see the encounter experience *as* an initiatory rite of passage is not important; what *is* important, because it suggests a meaning and a purpose for events that otherwise seem arbitrary and pointless, is that we recognize how much encounters have *in common* with rites of passage. In each case, the individual is discovering a new identity, changing the direction of his life; in each case he has found an identity for himself and at the same time a place in the community. In primitive societies this is achieved by a dramatic ritual in which a shaman leads him from childhood into adulthood: in the encounter experience he is involved (whether by himself or by guiding entities, we leave for the moment undecided) in a psychodrama in which he learns, in the course of playing the role of witness, what his future course of life must be.

6.5 COMMENTS ON PART SIX

In seeking to understand what is happening in encounter experiences, we have had to dissect them in a way which must have seemed to you, as it certainly did to me, inappropriate to the intensely emotional nature of those experiences. It is easy to forget that these encounters were, to their witnesses, of profound and life-transforming importance.

This subjective importance is there, whatever the objective nature of the experience. In a sense, therefore, it is immaterial whether the entities are genuine or spurious, or on what level of reality the encounter takes place. For perhaps the majority of witnesses, the fact that the encounter occurs, and does its job, may be enough. They can proceed in whatever direction their experiences point them, confident in the power that has changed their lives.

Unfortunately, for some it is not so rosy. There is the witness who is puzzled or frightened by his experience, on whom it has a negative rather than a positive effect. There is the witness who is encouraged by his experience to nourish false hopes and expectations; when they do not materialize, he may be psychologically shattered. There is the witness who takes his experience as a sign that he has been chosen by God or the Extraterrestrials for some mighty mission, and leads not only himself but his followers along dangerous paths. For the sake of these people, it is essential we learn what is really happening.

We have seen that there is good reason to doubt that any encounter experience can be taken at its face value. The ambiguities and contradictions are too many. Only if we are so committed to a belief system or so anxious to accept the surface 'story' that we are willing to suspend normal critical standards can we override the objections of common sense and accept the ostensible entities, and the incidents in which they are encountered, for what they claim to be.

On the other hand, we have seen that we cannot dismiss the experience simply because it is not what it seems to be. Clearly, it happens, and if it happens it must serve some purpose. Clearly, moreover, that purpose was envisaged by whoever/whatever built into us the capability of having such experiences. So, though we may allow that some of them are accidental (the cat setting off the burglar alarm), we must suppose that the majority are meant to happen, by whatever agency is responsible.

Faced with an event which is not what it seems to be, but which none the less seems to be intended and purposeful, the obvious inference is that it is some kind of mask for an event of a different kind. We have seen that certain situations may arise where an individual, unable to cope on the conscious everyday level, has subconscious recourse to some psychological device: multiple personality was the most striking example. We may ask whether some such process may be taking place in encounters.

Could the encounter experience be no more than a display (which would account for its unrealistic character) mounted either by or with the complicity of the witness' subconscious mind (which would account for his unawareness on the conscious level of what is happening) whereby a personal crisis (most likely a spiritual dilemma or an identity crisis of some kind) is expressed, and maybe resolved, by being projected externally (thus distancing the individual from his problem and giving him a degree of perspective) in the form of a symbolic drama (in which the role of guide/guardian/guru is played by an entity with the appropriate authority and cultural acceptability.)?

In the final part of our study we shall see if this model helps us to understand the encounter experience.

7.1 UNDERSTANDING THE ENCOUNTER EXPERIENCE

We have considered what may be happening to the encounter witness in psycho-physiological terms, and we have considered how the process might be modified by social, cultural and personal factors, so that what might have happened to anyone at any time becomes something that could have happened only to *this* person at *this* time. But we have still not resolved the question, does this process originate with the individual, or with some agency external to him?

Virtually every case we have looked at is ambiguous in this respect. Though it is well-nigh certain that the encounter does not occur on our everyday level of reality, it is equally certain that it *does* occur in some sense of the word. But this is by no means tantamount to saying it possesses objective reality. Similarly, it is well-nigh certain that the experience takes place in or through the mind of the witness; but this is by no means tantamount to saying that it *originates* in the mind.

Our options remain:

★ *All encounters are the externally originating events they seem to be* (omitting obvious hoaxes and self-deceptions). Teresa really did talk with Jesus, Siragusa really did meet extraterrestrials.

★ *All are of internal origin.* Each witness creates his own experience in his own subconscious mind, without his conscious mind being aware of the process.

★ *Some are what they seem to be, others are pseudo-events of some kind.* Some visions of the Virgin are genuine, others originate with Satan, say, or are an accidental symptom of fever or drug-taking.

★ *The events are 'real', but are not what they appear to be.* For example, some unknown agency may stage an encounter with extraterrestrials in a form it knows will be meaningful to the witness, though this may not be the true nature of the event.

If incontrovertible proof existed for any of these options, we may suppose it would have been found by now. The most we can expect to achieve, in these concluding chapters, is to show that the evidence favours one probability rather than another.

First, though, we must comment on some objections which if valid would mean we cannot with our present knowledge hope to resolve these questions. It has been variously asserted that encounter experiences are beyond our comprehension (1) because they are caused by super-beings who are essentially unknowable; (2) because they are inherently pathological; (3) because they occur on the undefinable boundaries of the self; or (4) because they are essentially miraculous. We will now deal with these points in turn.

The encounter experience and belief in super-beings

No matter which of our options is valid, implicit in the encounter experience is the belief that there exist 'super-beings' of some kind, with the corollary that it is reasonable to expect them to intervene — or to turn to them ourselves — when human resources prove inadequate.

This is often supposed to be a fundamental human trait universally possessed. Swedenborg in his *Dream Diary* speaks of 'that which belongs to man alone, the spiritual and religious need inborn in the psyche'. I have no intention of embroiling us in the question of the origins of religious belief; but I suggest that the assertion that we all need religious belief of some kind is of the same order as that made by married folk that everyone should get married.

Much of the confusion stems from a failure to distinguish the idea that there is probably some kind of purposeful agency behind the universe, which is hardly a religious belief so much as a logical inference, from projections of that idea which embody the agency in specific superhuman powers.

It is far from certain that a need to believe in such superhuman powers is inborn in us all. It is equally plausible to see such beliefs as relics of primitive attempts to explain the cosmos; though mankind in general has outgrown them, many of us cannot bring ourselves to part with them, with the result that we all grow up in awareness of them even if we do not share them. Consequently they continue to influence our subconscious minds as symbols and archetypes even when our conscious minds reject them as literal truths.

Suppose, however, we had incontrovertible and independent evidence that the superhuman entity really exists. It might then seem at first sight as though our problem would be over: the reality of the entity would prove the reality of the encounter. Unfortunately, it isn't as simple as that. When Victor Hugo practised spiritism during his exile on Jersey, he believed he was in communication with, among others, Shakespeare. On the basis of the messages Hugo received, which revealed that Shakespeare wrote French in a style very like Hugo's, we can be pretty sure that Hugo was *not* communicating with his fellow dramatist. Nevertheless Shakespeare existed . . .[184]

In short, neither the fact that the witness believes in the existence of the entity, nor even the knowledge that the entity exists, are here or there when it comes to assessing the validity of the claim.

The encounter experience as pathological symptom

A proportion of encounters occur in a mob situation, by which I mean one in which a more or less stable and structured group has been replaced by a more or less unstable and unstructured aggregate whose cohesion is due to the leadership of a charismatic individual or to a shared impulse towards some compelling goal. Mob dynamics is an insufficiently understood subject, but it is at least clear that in a mob context individual behaviour can be modified to a degree that is almost equivalent to an altered state. In his classic study, Le Bon speaks of the crowd as

> perpetually hovering on the borderland of unconsciousness, readily yielding to all suggestions, deprived of all critical faculty, excessively credulous . . . The improbable does not exist for a crowd . . . a crowd scarcely distinguishes between the subjective and the objective. It accepts as real the images evoked in its mind, though they most often have only a very distant relation with the observed fact.[150]

Another French researcher, Philippe de Félice, has suggested we see mob behaviour not as a return to the primitive *un*organization characteristic of man before he became civilized, but as a *dis*organization of what civilized man has achieved: a breakdown. What happens to the crowd as a whole is paralleled by what happens to the individual: his everyday safeguards and inhibitions lose their force, his repressed desires are able to emerge. Simultaneously, increased suggestibility and the suspension of his usual reality-testing mean, first, that hallucinatory and near-hallucinatory phenomena may occur, and second, that when they do he will accept them as real.[70]

The *dancing mania* of the Middle Ages, the Paris *convulsionnaires* of the eighteenth century, the Jonestown mass suicide of 1978, are three examples of the extremes to which mob dynamics linked to specific beliefs may lead: characteristic of such movements are visionary and encounter claims, whereby the leaders claim to be guided and sanctioned by otherworldly authority. On a smaller scale such claims are made every day by 'ordinary' people who have got into extraordinary situations in which they believe they are being attacked by the devil, directed by some occult force to kill, or menaced by former occupants of the house. Even as I write this, news comes in of a 57-year-old London grandmother who has stabbed to death her two little granddaughters because she thought aliens were trying to beam them up into space. She 'believed space ships visited her regularly and beamed her aboard' and 'kept plastic bags full of clothing and personal belongings ready for the day they took her away for good'. Three top psychiatrists told the Old Bailey court that she was mentally ill.[37]

Ill she no doubt is; and because her case differs from so many others only in the extreme lengths her delusion led her to, there is a natural temptation to conclude that *all* encounter witnesses are mentally ill.

This is a possibility we have to face; for though attempts to correlate encounter witnesses with specific psychological types have failed to produce significant results, it does seem as though encounters may correlate with certain mental *states*. If so, it could be argued that to be in such a state is tantamount to being mentally ill. Thus the French researcher Dr E. Dupouy proposed that *all* encounter experiences are pathological.[54] and Thulié, generally so perceptive, committed himself to this blunt assertion: 'Hallucination is always the symptom of a mental illness, the certain sign of a serious affection of the nervous system.'[251]

Fortunately, other early writers on the subject took a broader view. Thus, writing of the Hélène Smith case, Flournoy wrote:

> Even if it should be shown that mediumship is a pathological fact, a sick disposition, a form of hysteria, a near kin to madness, it would not follow that mediums were any less deserving of esteem, consideration and regard, or that they are any the less fitted to play their role in society, than the great army of so-called normal people . . .
>
> But in any case, it is far from proven that mediumship is a pathological phenomenon. Abnormal in the sense of rare, exceptional, out of the ordinary, granted; but that is something other than morbidity. It is far too early in the study of mediumship to pronounce on its true nature. There are as many opinions as there are observers. However it is interesting to note that in those countries where research has been carried farthest — England and America — the general tendency among scholars is far from being unfavourable towards mediumship. Far from regarding it as a special form of hysteria, they see it as a superior faculty, beneficial and healthy, of which hysteria is a degenerate form, a pathological counterfeit, a morbid caricature.[77]

What has happened since the days of both Thulié and Flournoy is that we are learning that many states which might be labelled 'sick' are nevertheless beneficial from the patient's point of view: multiple personality we have already seen to be one such. Even psychosomatic illnesses are an attempt at resolving a problem, though we might say that to seek to resolve a problem by evading it by taking to one's bed is the sign of a sick mind.

These are deep waters, and I want to wade into them only far enough for it to become obvious that to say that an encounter witness is mentally ill will get us nowhere. Much that is classified as mental illness is simply the individual signalling his need of help; the same is liable to be true of encounter experiences, though encounters, far more than mental illnesses as such, don't just signal a problem, they point the way to a solution, and sometimes even embody one.

The boundaries of the self

Because unexplained phenomena — of which encounters are just one example — have for so long resisted our questioning, some researchers suggest this is because we are asking the wrong sort of questions. American investigator J. T. Richards is one:

> PK (psychokinesis) phenomena often take place without conscious intent on the part of anyone. This raises an old question: Is it more appropriate to explain the events in terms of the unconscious minds of the participants or in terms of autonomous agencies (call them spirits or what you will)? This question may in the end have no satisfactory solution since the boundaries of the self elude precise definition. [210]

I am no more about to get involved in the nature of the self than in the origins of religion; nevertheless we must take this suggestion into account because it implies that we are asking ourselves a question which is intrinsically unanswerable.

Those Eastern mystics may indeed turn out to be right who assert that we are all one with the universe, or their Western fellows whose aim is to lose the Each in the All. The fact remains that whoever/whatever is responsible for the universe evidently thought fit to make it a solid physical universe, containing solid physical planets like Earth, peopled by solid physical individuals like you and me, capable of independent and autonomous thought, including the thought that there may be other kinds of reality than the one we know. All this may be a cunningly contrived illusion; nevertheless it is clearly within this framework that you and I are intended to function, and it is within this framework that this study of ours is being conducted even if in the end it should turn out to have as much validity as a recipe-book in a dolls' house.

For you and me, here and now, the question 'Do these encounters have a basis in reality?' has a real meaning. So does the question, 'Do they originate from within the witness or without?' We accept the possibility that they may occur within the witness yet originate outside him, or originate within him yet occur outside him; but the very fact that I can use such terms as 'inside' and 'outside', and that you understand more or less what I mean, supports the view that these terms have meaning. And so long as that is so, we have no right to seize on metaphysical speculation as an excuse for not facing up to one of the supreme problems of existence: are otherworldly beings intervening in human life?

There is nothing new about these difficulties. More than a century ago the German writer Görres wrote:

> It is often difficult in the early stages of mystical development to distinguish what should be attributed to earthly influences, what to celestial, and what to divine, and to determine whether the phenomena which occur should be assigned to church or science. [94]

Fortunately, most of us have learned that the interests of Church and science are not as incompatible as they seemed in Görres' day. Nevertheless a school of thought persists which holds that there are matters of the spirit which are beyond the reach of science. Implicit in this book is my belief that this is nonsense. If I am wrong, and they are right to hold that there are some areas of experience where the scientific method is no longer valid, well, we shall have done no harm by our ineffectual probing. If, on the other hand, those areas of experience formerly declared off-limits to science should turn out after all to be accessible to human explorers, then religion should welcome the directing of light into corners where formerly was only darkness. We may even help save a child from the fantasies of its space-deluded grandparent.

A brief note on miracles

Many of our encounters are classified as 'miracles' by the Catholic Church. Many writers have tried to define what constitutes a miracle — and tried in vain. The consensus agreement, however, is that when an event involves suspension of the 'laws of nature', that suspension could only have been brought about by some literally supernatural agency, so it qualifies for classification as a miracle.

Miracles can only occur, then, where we have hard-and-fast distinctions between what nature can do and what it can't. None of us today would claim that such distinctions can be drawn. The most we can do is to say that such-and-such is likely or unlikely. But the moment we substitute 'laws of probability' for 'laws of nature', the concept of miracle becomes meaningless.

So many things which were formerly believed to be miraculous, such as stigmata and spontaneous remission, have now been brought within the scope of the just-possible, even if they have not been fully explained, that we should be wary of labelling our encounters as miraculous until we are sure that nature does not offer a possible explanation, however improbable.

7.2   THE ENCOUNTER EXPERIENCE AS OBJECTIVE EVENT

Jung's patient whom we have earlier called Sophie told him, 'I do not know if what the spirits say and teach me is true, nor do I know if they really are the people they call themselves; but that my spirits exist is beyond question.'

Despite Sophie's certainty, we *do* have to question — because thanks to her spirits, she takes a fellow rail traveller, whom her doctor by fortunate chance is able to identify as an innocent citizen of Zurich, for a Martian. And while in this instance that isn't too serious a delusion, we have seen how a less balanced person killed her two grandchildren because she, too, believed herself to be in communication with otherworldly agencies. If there are indeed spirits who are inciting us to kill our grandchildren, then we should do something to discourage them.

Do the entities exist? Proving a negative is difficult enough at any time; when it comes to otherworldly beings who do not present themselves for testing by any of the usual means of human senses or scientific instruments, it becomes almost impossible. Certainly I do not know of any way to prove that Sophie's spirits, or any other of our entities, do not exist.

What we *can* do is show that the evidence for their existence is frail and ambiguous. Many of them seem to want us to believe in their existence — they traverse light-years of space for the express purpose of bringing us messages and warnings — yet they avoid, almost it seems deliberately, giving us grounds for believing them. Couldn't they at least have given George King a framed certificate, printed on some convincingly non-Earthly material, to authenticate his status as Earth's representative in Interplanetary Parliament?

This lack of evidence has not of course discouraged people from accepting their existence as a matter of faith. Theologians have done better still, they have devised *a priori* arguments which show that some of the entities at least *must* exist because logic demands it. Unfortunately, one theologian's notion of logical necessity differs so much from his colleagues' that their arguments carry conviction only to those who have already convinced themselves on less intellectual, more intuitive grounds.

Which brings us to consensus belief. Irrespective of *a priori* arguments and logical necessities, millions of people do believe in these entities. While so broad a consensus doesn't mean they're right, it is certainly no light thing to assert that they are wrong.

If the entities exist, do they cause the encounter experiences?

Some witnesses seek their encounters: notably the spiritists at their seance tables, and magicians in their charmed circles. Many visionaries wish explicitly for their visions. But, ostensibly at least, the vast majority of encounters seem to have been brought about by the entity rather than the witness.

Almost as vast a majority of witnesses, too, would claim to have been taken by surprise by their encounters; but of course it may only be their conscious minds that are taken by surprise. In his study of religious conversion, De Sanctis notes the emphasis placed by witnesses (and their biographers) on the 'lightning' conversion: 'It is certainly strange how almost all converts like to believe in the suddenness of their mutation.' He narrates the case of Alphonse Ratisbonne, a French Jew who at the age of 28 went with a friend to attend a funeral at the church of Sant' Andrea delle Fratte in Rome. Afterwards, left alone in the church by chance, he 'saw something like a veil before me, and in the centre of the dimness the image of the Virgin . . . at this vision I fell upon my knees . . . I knew the horror of my state . . . and the beauty of the Catholic religion, I understood all'.[47]

However, as De Sanctis demonstrates, Ratisbonne had been hesitating for quite a while whether to desert Judaism for Christianity. On the day of his conversion he was actually wearing a pious Catholic medal; he had visited many other churches during his stay in Rome; his mind and spirit were already prepared, and indeed only the previous night he had awakened and seen a vision of a great dark cross, which had so impressed him that he had been unable to sleep afterwards.

Clearly, Ratisbonne's conversion was not the bolt from the blue that he pretended. This in itself does not make it any the less genuine, of course, but it does set us thinking about the psychological factors involved. Why do converts like to think of their conversion as being like that of Saul on the road to Damascus?

It strikes me that there may be a sound psychological explanation. A sudden conversion carries the implication that it was effected by a *force majeure*, something *external to* and *stronger than* the witness. Consequently he can attribute the event not to his own weakness but to the greater strength of the divinity. Not only that, but he can claim to have been *chosen*: so urgent a summons is a sign that the divinity is really concerned about him, and as an *individual*.

This sense the witness has of being chosen is a factor we have noted in all kinds of encounter cases; and if we are right in thinking that one of the purposes of the encounter experience is to help the witness through an identity crisis, clearly to be picked out in this way by the divinity is, to say the least, a splendid affirmation of identity!

This still leaves open the question, did the Virgin arrange the encounter because she was so keen to number M. Ratisbonne among her faithful, or did he himself bring it about in order to resolve his personal dilemma?

Do the entities participate in the encounter?

The only substantial evidence that encounters occur is the testimony of the witnesses involved. If we accept their testimony that an objective event took place, then we must accept that an actual entity was involved. That entity can be only (1) the ostensible entity or (2) a pseudo-entity.

While occasionally the circumstances are such that it is impossible to believe that the ostensible entity is involved, we must remember that the existence of pseudo-entities is even less well established than that of the entities themselves, and is in any case contingent on the existence of the 'real' entities. (That is, there would be no point in Satan impersonating the Virgin Mary if there was no genuine Virgin Mary for him to impersonate.)

In short, if we accept that objective encounters occur, we should accept that *it is the ostensible entities who are involved* except where we have strong grounds to suspect that pseudo-entities are impersonating them.

If the entities participate, do they do so in their true form?

In virtually every case, the witness describes the entities as more or less human in appearance, and able to communicate and interact with humans. We have seen that this is in many cases improbable; so we must consider the alternative possibility that though the ostensible entities are indeed involved, they have adapted their 'real' nature in order to effect the encounter.

Eduardo Pons Prades, speaking of the ET entities he encountered, said:

> For four generations my family have been totally uninvolved in religious matters. None of us was ever involved in a 'crisis of faith' — we left such traumas to others. So the crew of the *Luz del Cosmos* didn't present themselves to me in the form of virgins or saints, as others have reported; nor as demons or genies, as followers of esoteric traditions describe them; still less in the form of mysterious adepts, as are said to have been glimpsed by students or pseudo-students of the occult.[199]

Pons Prades implies that he was seeing his entities in their 'true' form, but of course he may have been just as much deceived as the others he refers to so contemptuously. Many researchers have hypothesized categories of entities who assumed the appearance of divinities, ETs and so on for convenience' sake. In the course of five books Salvador Freixedo has developed the thesis that there exists a class of beings intermediate between humanity and God, who masquerade as 'gods', spirits of the dead, cosmic visitors, or whatever seems appropriate to the individual occasion. These beings are no more malevolent but also no more benevolent than, say, a farmer in regard to his livestock; and indeed, Freixedo suggests that they exploit us in much the same way.[81]

Such ideas are ingenious, and often make sense of an otherwise nonsensical state of affairs; but they remain no more than speculation. The question, 'Are we seeing the entities as they 'really are'?' takes us into areas where our knowledge and our reasoning can do no more than suggest possibilities.

In summary, we see that the best reason for accepting the encounter experience as objective event is because that is what the witness says it is.

He cannot prove that his entities exist; he cannot prove that they are responsible for the encounter; he cannot prove that they participate in the encounter; he cannot prove that he is seeing them in their true likeness. But we cannot prove the contrary.

7.3   THE ENCOUNTER EXPERIENCE AS SUBJECTIVE EVENT

It is certain that some encounter experiences are *not* what they seem to be; it is by no means certain that any *is* what it seems to be. We must therefore take seriously the possibility that *none* of them is what it seems to be.

Though we are by no means committed to finding a common explanation for all encounter experiences, throughout this study we have seen so many parallels, both in the outward aspects of the event and in its social and psychological aspects, that it is at least reasonable to proceed as though they are all manifestations of the same fundamental process.

If the encounter is not what it seems to be, the main reason must be because the entity is not what it seems to be. What else can it be? We have these options:

★ An undifferentiated being with the ability to take any form it chooses, like the theosophists' fairies.

★ A being which sheds its own appearance and takes any form it chooses, like the Catholics' Devil.

★ A pseudo-entity specifically created by some external agency in an appropriate form, like Freixedo's 'intermediate beings'.

★ A pseudo-entity created by the witness' own mental powers and projected in such a way as to give an illusion of external existence.

Various schools of esoteric thought have promoted each of the first three of these options, but none has been able to produce convincing evidence that such beings exist or that such processes occur. On the other hand, we *do* have evidence that our minds possess considerable powers to create fantasy figures, to devise dramatic situations in which those figures appear, and to project those situations in such a way as to give to the conscious mind the illusion of reality. In short, the means exist.

What encourages us to think that those means are in fact being employed?

First, it is evident that whatever sets it in motion, there are generally clear indications that *the encounter process is related to the individual witness*. Furthermore, it is generally no less clear that *it is related to a* particular problem, crisis or need in the witness' affairs.

Second, there is no need to suppose that exceptional faculties are involved in the encounter experience, or that the witness must be an exceptional being. As Catholic psychologist Jean Lhermitte has written in his *Mystiques et faux mystiques*:

> However great the mystics may be, they are made of the same stuff as the rest of us, subject to the same affects; their mental mechanisms are in no way different from ours. If they are superior to us, it is because they have ideas and feelings that are superior to ours, and because their conduct earns them higher graces; but they remain human beings for all that. Are we to suppose that God miraculously creates new mechanisms in certain people, when there already exist in them the necessary dispositions? The psychophysiologist can abandon the search for specific indications in these cases, for in each of them the same mechanism is involved; what differs, and leads to different consequences, is the principle which sets that mechanism in movement.[158]

The implication is clear: the same process is involved *whether or not the witness' interpretation of his experience is the correct one*. No wonder Lhermitte finds it so hard to distinguish between his mystics and his false mystics! When a Teresa d'Avila has an encounter with Jesus, and when a Mary Smith makes the same claim, there is no difference in the mental process involved, whatever difference there may or may not be in the other circumstances.

Third, many bothersome discrepancies and contradictions in the witness reports become comprehensible within the framework of a mental event. Anomalous details of description (for example the incidents in the Andreasson ET encounter) can often be traced to the witness' personal experience; the interest shown by entities in matters which are also the witness' personal or cultural preoccupations (for example the Fatima Virgin's hostility to Communism) is explained; the disconcerting similarity between cases (for example the patterns displayed in visions of the Virgin, seance-room communications with spirits of the dead, and ET contactee encounters) is more easily attributed to unconscious mimicry on the part of the witness than to any formal necessity that these experiences should occur along set lines.

All these *can* be explained otherwise; but the subjective-process hypothesis enables us to account for them *all*, rather than having to find a separate explanation for each difficulty, and to account for them plausibly rather than with far-fetched speculation.

Finally, the subjective hypothesis is in no way a denial that such events occur: it simply offers an explanation for them in human rather than otherworldly terms. It is, therefore, the *simplest* form of explanation, in that it requires no support from belief systems or *a priori* doctrines, it makes no assumptions but proceeds from experience.

Moreover, if the thesis presented in this study is valid, we do not have to look on the encounter process as negative simply because the witness seems to have been deluded. On the contrary, it proposes a positive and purposeful interpretation.

Two awkward categories

There are two categories of encounter which it hardly seems possible can be explained on the subjective hypothesis.

The first is the *multiple experience*, in which more than one witness is involved in what appears to be the same encounter experience. A case like the Kentucky abduction, in which three people had first a UFO sighting, then a missing-time experience, and eventually a shared remembrance under hypnosis, seems unquestionably to point to an objective event. To account for it subjectively we would have to establish, first, that all three witnesses were in a state where such an experience could occur; second, that all three were sufficiently alike psychologically that the same trigger could set them fantasizing; and third, that all three had sufficient in common individually and socially for their fantasies to be substantially so similar.

No more than any other researcher do I pretend to be able to offer a definitive explanation of this case. Accounts of it are tantalizingly incomplete; a great many questions seem never to have been asked, in part no doubt because of witness reluctance, but also because no one knew what questions *should* be asked. Apart from witness testimony there is, as usual, no other evidence; and it must be said that all abduction testimony is ambiguous in itself and, because it is generally retrieved (as in this case) via hypnosis, requires that we be on the lookout for fiction mixed in with the fact.

There are some known psychological processes which may be relevant: *folie à deux* (in this case trois) and *multiple hallucination*. But 'known' is hardly the word for these processes. 'Folie à deux' is no more than a label to describe any kind of shared fantasy, without any pretension to explaining how the sharing is effected: 'multiple hallucination' is a process easily conceived in principle but by no means established in practice. We certainly don't know enough about either to say that it may have been involved in the Kentucky case.

But that same ignorance also permits us to think that a subjective explanation for the case may be forthcoming, even though we have none in our armoury at present. A case reported in 1942 involved two identical twins whose behaviour when they enlisted in the army in 1941 led to admission to the neuropsychiatric ward:

From the moment they entered the ward every movement and, apparently, every impulse were identical. When one removed his clothes, so did the other. When one stood rigidly to attention the second did likewise, and for the same length of time. A question addressed to one twin was answered by both. Usually J.C. spoke a fraction of a second later than J.D., but the time interval was so short that to casual observation they seemed to speak the same words simultaneously. They combed their hair at the same time, leaned on the table in exactly the same posture, became agitated in the same manner at the same moment; this mirroring of activity had so much the appearance of a carefully-timed and well-rehearsed act that more than one medical officer felt that the brothers were malingering.[189]

It was noted that one of the twins was generally the leader — but not invariably the same one. Whoever was leader would be followed unfalteringly and unquestioningly by the other.

Such cases indicate the existence of abilities which perhaps some humans may possess more than others, or which we all may possess intermittently when the need arises. They may be 'psychic' faculties, they may be senses akin to those displayed by birds when flocking, they may be the effects of some such subliminal information transfer as is implicit in Sheldrake's morphic resonance.[228] The very fact that I can throw you a handful of such untried and unproven possibilities is an indication of how little we know about these matters, but it also indicates our awareness of our ignorance, and therefore suggests that research may reduce that ignorance before too long. When it does, it may help us to understand what happened to the three abducted ladies of Kentucky.

The second category of case for which the subjective hypothesis seems inadequate is the *crisis apparition*: here it seems both apparent and witness must be involved, because only the apparent knows that a crisis has happened and only the witness knows his own whereabouts.

Since science recognizes no way the witness could have access to the necessary information, we seem to be obliged to accept external intervention; which means something like an actual manifestation of the apparent in some more or less physical form.

For those of us, however, who are prepared to admit the possibility, some form of ESP could provide the explanation, though it would have to be in a complex form involving some kind of co-operation between apparent and witness.

So, while the subjective hypothesis is not able to provide a watertight explanation for these awkward cases, it can at least suggest the sort of explanation which may eventually be forthcoming; and in any case, the difficulties which arise when we try to explain them by the objective hypothesis are hardly less formidable.

This setting-out of the case for the objective and subjective hypotheses has revealed their respective strengths and weaknesses in accounting for our encounters.

Of the objective hypothesis it may be said, echoing Samuel Butler, that 'all reason is against it, and all healthy instinct is for it', though theologians might argue the first half of the proposition and psychologists the second. However improbable, these encounters are what tens of thousands of seemingly sincere and honest people have believed happened to them: common sense says there must be some meaning and purpose behind such a wealth of experience.

Of the subjective hypothesis it may be said that while it frees us from having to account for the contradictions and inconsistencies, there is something distastefully negative about an explanation which asserts that those tens of thousands of witnesses are one and all deluded, and something distastefully reductionist about an explanation which drags a revered mystic down to the same level as a mid-western housewife who claims she's been visited by a cosmic brother on her back porch.

Any conclusion, to be convincing, must show that there is more to the encounter experience than a lot of foolish people mistaking fantasy for reality; that though it may involve illusion the process may none the less be purposeful and positive; and that such a process can be meaningful on any level from that of a Teresa or a Jeanne d'Arc to that of a Betty Andreasson or a Eugenio Siragusa.

7.4 INDIVIDUAL EXPERIENCE AND COSMIC PROCESS

Throughout this study we have been aware that some of those who have had encounter experiences, and some of those who have sought to understand them, have felt that they had significance for more than the individual, were intended for mankind at large.

We see this at its most explicit in the cases of those who are entrusted with messages which they are instructed to pass on to others. The visionaries tell us that the Virgin Mary tells us to pray more and sin less or she won't be able to hold back her son's wrath: the contactees tell us that the extraterrestrials tell us to abandon nuclear power and learn to love one another or we shall destroy our planet.

Ostensibly, one of two things is happening:

1   If the encounter is occurring *objectively*, real entities are giving us real warnings (or impersonating entities are giving us false warnings) via the witness who is no more than a chosen mouthpiece.

2   If the encounter is occurring *subjectively*, the witness is projecting his 'social' fears along with his private preoccupations.

But is it as simple as that? A number of researchers are exploring the concept that certain strange experiences — in particular, those involving interaction with ET entities — are part of a wider process. One of the most thoughtful exponents of these views is Dr Leo Sprinkle of the University of Wyoming, whom I have already quoted in connection with contactees. Sprinkle proposes a theoretical model which would account for the sudden spate of contactee activity:

> The model suggests that UFO experiences are educational events, which are presented to UFO observers, who become witnesses, who become contactees, who are impelled to learn more about the 'outer' world and 'inner' world, to share knowledge, and to become advocates for transformation in human awareness. [235]

Sprinkle's work with contactees — and there is probably no one living who has had more to do with them — has led him to the working hypothesis that *UFO experiences are one segment of a plan to transform evolved earthlings from planetary persons to cosmic citizens*. This he infers from individual accounts, which when added together seem to compose the following picture:

1   UFO contactees have been chosen; no UFO contact is accidental.

2   Contactees are ordinary people, who exhibit a caring or a loving concern for all humankind.

3   Contactees have an experience which can be viewed as a manifestation of their ideas of reality.

4   UFO experiences include paraphysical, parabiological, parapsychological and paraspiritual manifestations which are designed to influence the 'world view' of contactees.

5   Contactees receive information during and after their UFO experience which is related to their life interests, e.g. natural sciences, social sciences, music and art, ancient civilizations, psychic phenomena, reincarnation, metaphysical and spiritual knowledge, etc.

6   Contactees are gently coerced into studies and activities which blend with the ultimate purpose of UFO entities; they are not forced to be obedient to 'Ufolks'.

7   Contacts are initiated and maintained within the general framework of contactees' views of reality. (Thus, UFO contacts can be viewed as physical, face-to-face encounters with flesh and blood beings, or out-of-body experiences, or mental programming by Ufolks; or as dreams, fantasies, and/or subconscious ideas which are manifested consciously, without external stimulus.)

8   Contactees are programmed for a variety of 'future' activities, including awareness of their own contacts and desire to share their messages and knowledge with other contactees.

9   The lives of contactees move in the direction of greater self-awareness, greater concern for the welfare of the Planet Earth, and a greater sense of Cosmic Citizenship with other beings in the Universe.

10   The personal metamorphosis of UFO contactees is the forerunner of a social transformation in human consciousness, which now is leading to changes in the economic, educational, military, political and religious institutions of nations of the Earth.

Sprinkle's model is both plausible and attractive. It is consistent with the current *Zeitgeist* to which Jung and Sheldrake have in their different ways given expression, which invites us to think of the individual as part of a larger community on a deeper level than merely a member of a biological species or social group. At the same time it relieves us of having to account for those encounters which simply don't make sense in terms of individual experience, by inviting us to think that Siragusa's traumatic encounter on the slopes of Mount Etna was a symbolic educational lesson meant for you and me as much as for Siragusa himself.

This would account, among other things, for the ready acceptance which the ET-encounter has had among so many, from the hundreds of ET-related cults and New Age groups to the thousands of individuals who buy the books and attend the lectures where such ideas are propagated. It would also account for the hostility with which such ideas have been greeted by others. The former can be seen as the willing pupils who are ready to learn, the latter as those less willing, stuck in the old ways.

But a model which so sweepingly explains any and every experience does not really explain anything at all; for could it not be said that *all* human experiences are part of the great process of human development? To show that ET-encounters are specifically part of a cosmically timetabled educational programme, it would be necessary to demonstrate that they are indeed contributing to speed up the process of adaptation from 'planetary person' to 'cosmic citizen'. Some contactees, at least, should emerge from their educational crash-course as manifestly superior beings; there should, in short, be some self-evident *results*.

Champions of such ideas would say that we are indeed seeing such results in the way encounters benefit individuals; if each individual is part of the whole, then each man's improvement benefits the community; you and I are the better off because Siragusa has got himself sorted out.

But even if this be granted, we have yet to see evidence that what happened to Siragusa was the result of external programming rather than a self-improvement plan activated by his own subconscious mind.

If a team of Cosmic Guardians were to beam themselves down onto the surface of our planet for all to see, and set about an explicit educational programme, there would be none of this ambiguity; but as it is, working undercover as they seem to be, through dubious individuals with no credentials but their personal say-so, providing no evidence of any sort and no information that is not either ambiguous, contradictory or downright false, their track record is, to put it mildly, unimpressive.

Here, for example, is a sample communication from an alleged ET entity, taken almost at random from the vast quantity of such stuff that is being channelled to humanity via the contactees:

> The planet Earth, or Terra, is a fallen planet, fallen in the sense that it has fallen from its correct frequency band level and is vibrating at a slower vibratory rate than the life waves existing on other planets in this system. As you become less densified, you move into the correct frequency band. And it is then, our brothers, our sisters, as we slightly reduce our own vibratory rate and as you raise yours, Spaceman meets Earthman and the reunion of that which was lost within the system takes place, and the fallen planet is restored in Light . . . I again draw your attention to the tremendous upliftment of attunement with the highest frequencies of Universal Light as they now flow in. Attunement at these levels may bring about spiritual

experiences, spiritual rebirth, and what could be called, a type of spiritual ecstasy. Yours, oh people of Earth is the choice! We know which choice we would make but we cannot choose for you. [80]

I do not wish to seem negative or dogmatic, so I will not assert that the foregoing is nonsense. What I *will* say, though, is that it is not very helpful. Leaving aside the poor grammar, which may be forgiven a visitor from another world, the sloppy terminology is surprising from a culture whose technology is so far advanced compared with ours that they can cross space to visit us.

The *least* unsatisfactory encounter with Cosmic Guardians is the extraordinary affair of Ummo. If we are to believe the story they tell us, some inhabitants of the planet Ummo, some 14 light years from Earth came to our planet in 1950, and spent the next 15 years establishing their bases and acclimatizing themselves to our physical conditions and our way of life. Then in 1965 they started to make contact, by letter or telephone, with selected individuals; most of them were Spanish, and included several well-known personalities. For example, engineer Enrique Villagrassa Novoa received a phone call late at night on 28 November 1966. The speaker identified himself as an ET, and spoke fluently and intelligently, though in a voice that was faintly foreign and mechanical, for some two hours. He discussed engineering and obviously knew his subject; a few days later he followed up the call with a batch of documents.

Those documents certainly exist, and number some 7000 to date. They indicate considerable but not extraordinary learning — certainly nothing beyond the capability of well-informed Earthpersons. A certain amount of back-up evidence has been offered, but invariably this has been found — as with all ET evidence — to be ambiguous, contradictory or downright false. On one occasion a UFO sighting was promised: and photographs were duly published, allegedly taken by witnesses who obeyed instructions and went to the assigned place. Unfortunately, the photographs were found to be faked.

The views of researchers are divided. Veteran ufologist Antonio Ribera, himself one of the recipients of Ummo contact, is impressed to the point of belief: others remain sceptical, in the light of the inconsistencies. We have been given examples of the Ummite language, for instance: but though Ribera described it as 'a structured language, with its own characteristic manner of forming adverbs and derivatives, its laws of grammar and so on', it is in fact pathetically crude even when compared with Hélène Smith's pseudo-Martian language.

The most impressive features of the Ummo contact are the sheer weight of material generated, and the time-period over which it has spread — for Ummo is still active as I write. If it is a hoax, it is the most elaborate hoax ever perpetrated in this field; if it is what it claims to be, on the other hand, it has failed to convince. If there really are Ummites trying to function as Cosmic Guardians of humanity, they have failed in their mission. [207, 59]

Yet Ummo represents ET contact at its *most* explicit, *most* practical, *most* plausible. Most other contact messages offer nothing but vague 'philosophy' and pleas for humanity to give up its aggressiveness: Ummo offers something approaching hard fact, with its specifications for spacecraft and detailed accounts of life on their planet. Most other contacts are directed at solitary and nameless individuals: Ummo addresses itself to people with some standing in the community. If Ummo fails to convince, how much less will the rest of our encounter claims persuade us that Sprinkle's cosmic educational programme is more than a sci-fi fantasy?

The idea that encounters are part of a wider process is by no means confined to ET encounters. A substantial school of thought proposes that the entities encountered by mystics and spiritists are simply Cosmic Guardians suitably disguised. This magnificent proposal would resolve virtually all our difficulties in one sweep, and for that reason has inspired substantial literature over recent decades; in books entitled *God Drives a Flying Saucer*[49] or *Jesus Christus, Erbe der Astronauten*[241] or *Nos ancêtres venus du Cosmos*[31] or *Nosostros los Extra-terrestres*,[161] writers the world over have purveyed infinite variations on the theme of 'ancient astronauts'. In some scenarios we are ourselves the lineal descendants of these beings; in others we are farmed like cattle; a large category see today's UFOs as signalling the return of the astronauts, who had left us to sink or swim much as did the Christian God, but feel the need to intervene today because our combination of sophisticated technology with primitive morality makes us a menace to the rest of the cosmos.

Hence, of course, the need for an educational programme à la Sprinkle . . .

The cynic will recognize that much of this has happened before in previous millenarist scenarios; the philosopher will acknowledge yet another instance of man's ability to transcend his earthly reality with cosmic dreams. The proponents of competing belief systems — whether religious or scientific — don't find such speculations in the least amusing, and a number of well-meaning but rather drab books have been written to debunk them. [29,243-4,265,267-8]

There is no need, for the purposes of this study, for us to take sides in this matter; personally, I enjoy both the orgy of wild speculation and the salutary purging which follows. Both the capacity to fantasize, and the ability to distinguish truth from fantasy, are valuable gifts.

Does it help us to understand our encounters to see them as part of an ongoing cosmic educational process? The short answer is no, I don't think it does. The Virgin's messages at La Salette give no indication that she was concerned to show these simple peasant children how they could raise their existence onto a higher cosmic plane; rather they tended to confirm a narrow sectarianism and traditional values which are anything but consciousness-raising. Even her more productive encounters with Teresa d'Avila, though they may have helped that good lady find her feet as an energetic religious reformer, hardly made her a more valuable citizen

of the world at large, less still a cosmic citizen who would help herald
a New Age.

Communication with spirits of the dead is, if anything, even less
uplifting. The petty concern with trivia displayed by the average
communicating spirit is poor publicity for a wider, richer life to come.
The dead show every sign of being less concerned with cosmic
development than we who are living.

Everything we know about the encounter experience points to it as being
from first to last an *individual* experience. There is nothing to support
the view that it is part of a deliberate and specifically programmed cosmic
process.

But individuals are themselves changing. Each encounter witness is a
child of his time. So it is not surprising that for an unlettered countryperson
of the mid-nineteenth century, whose imagination could not easily travel
beyond the confines of his immediate earthly existence, his encounter
would take place within the belief system of his cultural milieu. For the
seance-goer of a later period, the stage would have expanded to
accommodate the wider possibilities of life beyond earth.

For today's space-age citizen, particularly in the more highly developed
cultures where most ET encounters are reported, the stage has enlarged
to cosmic dimensions. So, where the peasants of La Salette had their
encounter in terms of the Virgin Mary, the seance-visitor communicated
with the dead, and today's witness contacts the Cosmic Guardians.

Seen in this light, the individual experience does indeed become part
of a wider pattern. Seen in this light, the untruths become meaningful.
Seen in this light, what may have seemed for some readers a negative
and reductionist debunking has, on the contrary, revealed that though
we account for the ecstasies of a Teresa or the sci-fi fantasies of an ET
contactee in terms of a psychological process, this is in no way to detract
from the value and significance of their experiences.

In fact, for those of us who never thought much of gods and spirits
anyway, it is to enhance the stature of the encounter experience to see
it as an expression of man's ability to achieve self-enhancement without
the help of divinities, spirits or cosmic guardians.

8   THE REALITY OF ENCOUNTER

Lies, mademoiselle, tell a listener just as much as truth can. Sometimes they tell more.

Hercule Poirot in Agatha Christie's *Sad Cypress*

I suppose that you and I both started out on this inquiry with a suspicion that some, perhaps many, perhaps most, perhaps all encounter experiences are lies. And we have found our worst suspicions confirmed. Lies, indeed, they are. Lies, by definition, because what the witness sees is not 'true' by the yardstick of conventional reality.

But we have also found that to see in the encounter experiences nothing more than lies and illusion is to miss their deeper function. They serve a purpose, and more often a beneficent than a harmful one. So, while as a rule it is better to confront the truth than to take refuge in illusion, there can be exceptions to that rule. Ideally, no doubt, every encounter witness should be sufficiently balanced to see his encounter for the illusion it is; but we must not expect him to be ready for it at the time, or even soon after; and we must be prepared to find that he is never ready to accept the truth. Some lies have to be lived with.

It is with this overall proviso that we now set about gathering together what we have learned, in hope that from it we can construct a plausible model for what is happening in the encounter experience.

To prevent the discussion from getting too abstract, let us start with a specific case. In 1952 Rosalind Heywood, an educated lady with a lifelong interest in the paranormal, voluntarily took mescalin to help a doctor with his experimental research. Here is part of what she experienced:

In a flash that filled me with awe there appeared a supreme figure, motionless, Buddha-like, eternally at peace . . . out of the gold there appeared a figure clothed in soft blues and greens and purples, infinitely benign and compassionate. I knew it to be the Divine Mother. It appeared that I asked the magic question which enabled the Divine Mother to come to answer it. And her answer was to swing me round so that I could look with a fraction of her eyes outward on all created things. In this way she gave me a glimpse of what love was: infinitely far from possessive doting, quite unsentimental, yet warm and comforting — and above all personal. That was the Divine Mother's attitude to all and everything. She was literally in love with the whole universe. [107]

She received many explanations from the proponents of different schools of thought. A Freudian told her, 'Your Divine Mother was a construct of your own. You were doubtless brought up in an Edwardian nursery and saw too little of your own mother.' A Jungian saw it as an archetype, a Catholic said 'Our Lady', a psychiatrist said she was seeing her own self.

> That enraged me at first. Then I saw that it was very funny. What label the experts choose to give this product of my model psychosis seems of no importance at all. They can say she was due to artificial over-stimulation of the parasympathetic nervous system if they like. I know that, whatever she was, she represented all that I could possibly grasp of perfection.

Our immediate reaction will be that something good, beneficent, illuminating, helpful, happened to Rosalind Heywood. On the other hand, it was part of an experiment. It didn't happen spontaneously — it was drug-induced. Without the mescalin, presumably it wouldn't have happened. It was a side-effect of a chemical imbalance in her biological system. It was accidental, not purposeful. It wasn't meant to happen.

So, unless we suppose that the Divine Mother worked on Heywood's subconscious mind to encourage her to take the mescalin in order to be in a suitable state for whatever the Divine Mother had lined up for her, we must conclude that no planned supernatural intervention occurred.

Heywood's immediate and unquestioning recognition of the being is significant, considering that we have no independent evidence that any such being as her 'Divine Mother' actually exists. The words are simply a useful label to define a concept. No doubt any of us, challenged by the term, would come up with some kind of mental image, and possibly there's a sufficiently general consensus so that everyone who uses the concept comes up with a roughly similar mental picture, as with angels or spacemen. But to exist as a convenient label is a long way short of existing as an autonomous entity.

What we would really like to know is whether Heywood herself had a private belief in a Divine Mother? Was the image she saw the reflection of something which already existed in her subconscious mind? Did it symbolize for her some preoccupying concept, the essential nature of love, say? To answer that, we would have to know much more about her mental, emotional and spiritual state at that time. But even without that knowledge, we may reasonably suppose that the entire experience originated within her own mind, and proceeded along the lines we have earlier elaborated. That is to say, in the favourable state induced by the mescalin, the 'producer' component of her subconscious mind was able to substitute, for everyday reality, a psychodrama embodying images and concepts expressing her beliefs and interests. We may suppose that the experience reflected either a current preoccupation or a subject of chronic concern. This we can infer from the way she welcomed and accepted an experience which many might have found surprising and alarming.

Does this imply that her producer had the encounter already scripted and ready for showing, like a videotape? There is no need to suppose so; our dreams give ample evidence that the producer possesses an infinite talent for improvization.

This account of what happened in Heywood's case is, I suggest, more or less what happens in most other encounter experiences.

I say 'more or less' because though the underlying process may be much the same, there are as many different kinds of encounter as there are witnesses; each is a unique experience.

I say 'most' because we may have to recognize some exceptions; crisis apparitions (whose exceptional character we have already considered) are one, and there may be others. For instance, pseudo-encounters, such as may occur during the delirious hallucinations induced by fever, while they employ the same physiological machinery, do not appear to do so in a purposeful and meaningful manner; yet even in these cases it is possible that an opportunistic producer might seize the occasion to stage one of his little shows.

Supermind

An interesting model for the abduction experience, which could be no less applicable to other kinds of encounter, has been proposed by American researcher Scott Rogo, who of all writers on the subject has shown the greatest insight into what the abduction event involves. In the course of his evaluation of his investigation of the Tujunga Canyon abductions which occurred over a period of years from 1953 to 1975, he surmised:

> UFO abductions occur when the witness is in a state of psychological need, and when the unconscious mind needs to impart an important message to the conscious mind. Once contacted by a human mind in such a state, the supermind creates an abduction experience for the witness by drawing upon information and preoccupations buried deep within his mind. It structures this information as part of the abduction scenario and presents it to the witness in objectified form. The supermind does all this by relying upon a prototypical experience, which it then individually models to best communicate a vital message in symbolic form to the witness. [53]

Clearly this is very close to the psychological model which we are considering. Where ours differs from Rogo's, of course, is in dispensing with his hypothesis of a 'supermind' which he evidently sees as something *external* to, or at any rate independent of, the witness, and with which the witness' subconscious mind makes contact in time of need. The supermind then lays on a psychodrama which is also, I take it, to be thought of as occurring externally.

My own view is that there is no need to hypothesize either an external supermind nor an externally occurring encounter experience: I suggest that we contain the necessary resources within us. Our 'producer' does the work of his 'supermind', and our producer's projected psychodrama performs the function of his objectified scenario.

However, though the differences between the two hypotheses are of evident importance, to choose one rather than the other in the present state of our knowledge would be hardly more than to voice a personal inclination. Much more important, as I think Rogo would agree, is what both approaches have in common. Both envisage the same kind of process: the resolution of the individual's need by means of a fantasy in which the subconscious mind conveys a message to the conscious mind in the most impactful way it knows, a psychodrama in which the individual himself plays a starring role.

There is a nice confirmation of this in a case which Rogo includes in another of his books. The primary witness in the remarkable 'Dapple Gray Lane' abduction case remarked in retrospect to Californian investigator Ann Druffel: 'I think the entire thing was a fantastic, beautifully executed theatre . . . a display solely for my benefit to convey something that right now is unbeknown to me.'[215]

The need-based experience
In broad outline, it seems that what may be happening in an encounter experience is this:

The individual has a need (not necessarily one that he is aware of) which can be either:

★ an *immediate* crisis, usually of a personal nature, or

★ a *temporary* awkward phase in his development which he finds it difficult to surmount, such as adolescence or menopause, which may well be accompanied by an identity crisis; or

★ a *long-term* uncertainty, such as a religious doubt; or

★ a *chronic* frustration, such as a boring or humiliating existence.

Unable to resolve this need by normal means, *his subconscious mind devises and projects to his conscious mind as simulated reality a dramatic episode in which he seems to encounter an otherworldly being* which, to him, represents authority together with whatever other attributes are required.

To make the incident effective, it must be believable; to be believable, it must be lifelike. So *it is presented in such a way that the conscious mind accepts it as reality*. Even if liberties are taken with time and place, these are smoothed over so that they are not at the time, if ever, apparent.

Again, to make the experience both credible and effective, *the figure chosen for the otherworldly entity is one which will command the necessary authority*, together with whatever other attributes — sympathy in the case of the Virgin Mary, fear in the case of the devil, advanced knowledge in the case of a Space Brother — are appropriate for the circumstances. Thus Delphine meets the Virgin, Canon Phillips meets C. S. Lewis, Siragusa meets Cosmic Guardians, and so on.

So, either by the simple reassurance of its presence, or by explicit action, *the entity helps the witness to resolve, satisfy or redirect his need*. Often the mere affirmation of identity — the suggestion that the witness has been 'chosen' — is enough; in other cases a specific change of direction is encouraged.

Some encounters are manifestly on a 'higher' level than others, which is why some of us have difficulty in taking a visit from a spaceman as seriously as a mystic's communion with the Almighty. The simple answer is that some people live on a higher level than others, their problems are commensurate with that level and so are the encounters which resolve them.

But the experiences are no less important to those involved, no matter at what level they occur. Because we honour and respect Teresa d'Avila, we value her experiences: because Delphine is a nobody, we consider hers trivial. But not to Delphine they weren't. They were all the world to her; they altered the course of her life; they made her whatever she is.

So we must avoid falling into the trap of thinking that because we can see that some encounters are 'higher' than others, they have a different origin and serve a different purpose. There are no class distinctions in psychology; we have no better grounds for thinking the highest encounters are too good to have been created by humans and must be credited to supernatural agencies, than we have for thinking the lower kind serve no better purpose than to fill the case-books of morbid psychology.

In the end it comes down, predictably, to our adherence or non-adherence to belief systems, and to our greater or lesser estimate of human capabilities.

Those of us who subscribe to a specific belief system, be it a religious creed or a faith in cosmic benevolence, may prefer to believe that encounter experiences are brought about by the beings associated with those systems, as gifts of grace, comfort or concern; and that those which are manifestly of a malevolent kind either are engineered by Dark Forces or are the morbid symptoms of sick minds.

Those, however, who believe that man has an infinitely greater potential than is normally displayed in his daily life, may find it easier to believe that he has within himself the resources to fabricate, at times of need, an encounter experience, even though to ensure its effectiveness he has to play tricks on himself by drawing on his cultural background for its characters and script.

If this view is the correct one, then when Delphine is visited by the Virgin Mary in her garden, when Teresa meets the infant Jesus on the convent stairs at Avila, when Canon Phillips is reassured by C. S. Lewis or Eugenio Siragusa meets The Brothers on Mount Etna, their encounters are not with gods, not with spirits, not with cosmic guardians, but with the higher aspects of their own selves.

BIBLIOGRAPHY AND REFERENCES

1 Adamski, George, *Pioneers of space* (Private, California, 1949).

2 ——, *Inside the space ships* (Arco/Spearman, London, 1956).

3 ——, *Flying saucers farewell* (Abelard-Schuman London/NY, 1961).

4 Adamski, George, with Desmond Leslie, *Flying saucers have landed* (British Book Centre, New York, 1953).

5 Alacoque, Marguerite-Marie, *Entretiens mystiques* (Written in 17th century, reprinted Editions Spes, Paris, 1947).

6 Alberione, Very Revd J., *The glories and virtues of Mary* (Daughters of St Paul Editions, Boston, 1958).

7 Allison, Ralph, *Minds in many pieces* (Rawson, Wade, New York, 1980).

8 Angelucci, Orfeo, *The twentieth century times* (Private, February 1953).

9 ——, *The secret of the saucers* ed. Ray Palmer (Amherst Press, Wisconsin, 1955).

10 ——, *Million year prophecy* (Golden Dawn Press, 1959).

11 Anon *Letters from the planets* (in *Cassells Magazine*, London 1887).

12 Auclair, Raoul, *Kerizinen, apparitions en Bretagne* (Nouvelles Editions Latines, Paris, 1968).

13 Barker, Gray, (ed.) *The book of Adamski* (Saucerian, Clarksburg VA, 1966).

14 ——, *Gray Barker at Giant Rock* (Saucerian, 1976).

15 Bassette, Louis, *Le fait de La Salette*, (Editions du Cerf, Paris, 1965).

16 Bayle, Pierre, *Les apparitions de Vallensanges* (Pensée Universelle, Paris, 1978).

17 Bethurum, Truman, *Aboard a flying saucer* (De Vorss, Los Angeles, 1954).

18 ——, *People of Planet Clarion* (Saucerian Press, Clarksburg VA, 1970).

19 ——, *Personal scrapbook* (facsimile; Arcturus, Scotia NY, 1982).

20 Bible, the, Exodus 31, for Moses and 10 Commandments. 1 Samuel 28 for Witch of Endor.

21 Bodin, Jean, *De la demonomanie des sorciers* (Paris, 1587).

22 Britten, Emma Hardinge, *Modern American spiritualism* (The author, New York, 1870).

23 Brotteaux, Pascal, *Hallucinations ou miracles? Les apparitions d'Exquioga et de Beauraing* (Vega, Paris, 1934).

24 Brownfield, Charles A., *The brain-benders* (Exposition-University, New York, 1972).

25 Bruno de Jésus-Marie, *Les faits mystérieux de Beauraing* (in *Etudes Carmélitaines*, 18e Année vol 1, Desclée de Brouwer, Paris, 1933).

26 Burge, Weldon, *The UFO cults* (Pamphlet Publications, Cincinatti OH, 1979).

27 Bushman, Richard L., *Joseph Smith and the beginnings of Mormonism* (University of Illinois Press, Urbana, 1984).

27aCalmeil, L. F., *De la folie* (Baillière, Paris, 1845).

28 Campbell, Stuart, *The strong delusion* (Private, London, 1961).

29 Castle, E. W., and Thiering, B. B., *Some trust in chariots!* (Bailey Bros. & Swinfen, Folkestone, 1973).

30 Chastenet, Patrick et Philippe, *Prophéties pour la fin des temps* (Denoël, Paris, 1983).

31 Châtelain, Maurice, *Nos ancêtres venus du cosmos* (trans. *Our ancestors came from outer space*; Doubleday, New York, 1978).

32 'Churchwoman, A', *The chariots of God* (Stockwell, London, 1915).

33 Cooper, L. F., 'Time distortion in hypnosis', *Journal of Psychology* vol. XXXIV, 1952, cited in Estabrooks & Gross, *The future of the human mind* (Dutton, NY, 1961).

34 Coynart, Ch., de *Une sorcière au XVIIIe siécle; Marie Anne de la Ville* (Hachette, Paris, 1902).

35 Cristiani, Mgr. L., *Présence de Satan dans le monde moderne* (France-Empire, Paris, 1902).

36 Cummins, Geraldine, *Swan on a black sea* (Routledge, London, 1965).

37 *Daily Mirror* (London, 6 June 1986).

38 Davidson, Leon, 'Why I believe Adamski', (*Flying Saucer Review* vol. 6 no. 1 1960).

39 Davies, Charles Maurice, *Mystic London* (Tinsley, London, 1875).

40 Davis, Isabel, with Bloecher, Ted, *Close encounter at Kelly* (Center for UFO Studies, Evanston IL, 1978).

41 Davy, Humphry, *Consolations of travel*, in Collected Works, various editions.

42 DeHerrera, John, *The Etherean invasion* (Hwong, Los Alamitos, CA, 1978).

43 Deikman, Arthur J., in Ornstein, R., *The Nature of Human Consciousness* (Viking, NY, 1973).

44 Denaerde, Stefan, *UFO contact from Iarga* (UFO photo Archives, Tucson, 1982; trans. from *Buitenarrdse Beschaving*, Ankh-Hermes, Deventer, 1969).

45 Deonna, W., *De la planète Mars en Terre Sainte* (De Boccard, Paris, 1932).

46 Derenberger, Woodrow, as told to H. W. Hubbard, *Visitors from Lanulos* (Vantage, NY, 1971).

47 De Sanctis, Sante, *Religious conversion* (Kegan Paul, London, 1927).

48 Devereux, Paul, *Earthlights* (Turnstone, Wellingborough, 1982).

49 Dione, R. L., *God drives a flying saucer* (Exposition, NY, 1969).

50 Dixon, Norman E., *On the psychology of military incompetence* (Cape, London, 1976).

51 Dong, Paul, and Stevens, Wendelle, *UFOs over modern China* (UFO photo Archives, Tucson, 1983).

52 Drake, W. Raymond, *Gods and spacemen throughout history* (Spearman, London, 1975; and several other books in the series).

53 Druffel, Ann, and Rogo, Scott, *The Tujunga Canyon contacts* (Prentice Hall, NJ, 1980).

54 Dupouy, E., *Psychologie morbide* (Leymarie, Paris, 1907).

55 Eliade, Mircea, *Shamanism* (Princeton University Press, NJ, 1964).

56 Ennemoser, Joseph, *The history of magic* (trans. from the German by William Howitt) Orig. German 1843 (Bohn, London, 1854).

57 Evans, Hilary, *The evidence for UFOs* (Aquarian, Wellingborough, 1983).

58 ——, *Visions, apparitions, alien visitors* (Thorsons, 1983).

59 ——, 'UMMO, a perfect case?', in *The unexplained* (Orbis, London, 1983).

60 ——, 'A night to remember', in *The unexplained* (1983).

61 ——, *Intrusions* (Routledge, London, 1982).

62 Evans, Hilary, with Evans, Dik, *Beyond the gaslight* (Muller, London, 1976).

63 Evans-Wentz, W. Y., *The fairy faith in celtic countries* (Frowde, London, 1911).

64 *Fate* magazine, Highland Park, Illinois, Arnold, 'I did see the flying saucers', in vol. 1, no. 1, Spring 1948.

65 ——, Adamski, 'I photographed space ships', in vol.4, no. 5, July 1951.

66 ——, Stupple, 'The man who talked to Venusians', in vol. 32, no. 1, Jan 1979.

67 ——, Pflock, 'Anatomy of a UFO hoax', in vol. 33, no. 11, November 1980.

68 ——, Story of boy with puppy in Curtis Fuller's 'I see by the papers', in vol. 39, no. 11, November 1986.

69 ——, Lou Eden, 'A ghostly order of monks', ibid.

70 Félice, Philippe de, *Foules en délire, extases collectives* (Albin Michel, Paris, 1947).

71 Ferguson, William, *My trip to Mars* (Galaxy Press, Ontario, 1973).

72 Fernandes, Joaquim, 'Extraterrestrial interference at Fatima', paper presented at 2nd London International UFO Congress, May 1981.

73 Fernandes, Joaquim, with Fina d'Amanda, *Intervencao extraterestre em Fatima* (Livraria Bertrand, Amadora, 1982).

74 Festinger, L., Riecken, H. W., and Schachter, S., *When prophecy fails* (University of Minnesota, 1956).

75 Ffoulkes, Maude, Letter in *Occult Review* (London, December 1918).

76 Field, M. J., *Angels and ministers of grace* (Longman, Harlow, 1971).

77 Flournoy, Théodore, *Des Indes à la Planète Mars* (Atar, Geneva, 1899).

78 Fort, Charles, *The books of Charles Fort* (Holt, NY, 1941).

79 Fowler, Raymond, *The Andreasson affair* and *The Andreasson affair phase two* (Prentice Hall, NJ, 1979 and 1982).

80 Francesca, Aleuti, *Starcraft* (leaflet of Solar Light Retreat, Oregon, no date).

81 Freixedo, Salvador, *El diabolico inconsciente* (Orion, Mexico, 1977).

*82 ——, *Las apariciones de El Escorial* (Quintá, Madrid, 1985).

83 Fry, Daniel W., *The White Sands incident* and *To men of Earth* (New Age, Los Angeles, 1954, revised 1966).

84 ——, *Steps to the stars* (Understanding, El Monte CA, 1956).

85 Fuller, John G., *The interrupted journey* (Dial, NY, 1966).

86 Fund for UFO Research, *Final report on the psychological testing of UFO 'abductees'* (Mt Rainier, MD, 1985).

87 Gansberg, Judith M. and Alan L., *Direct encounters* (Walker, NY, 1980).

88 Garçon, Maurice, *Rosette Tamisier ou la miraculeuse aventure* (L'Artisan du livre, Paris, 1929).

89 Gardner, E. L., *The theosophic view of fairies* in Doyle, A. C., *The coming of the fairies* (Hodder & Stoughton, London, 1922).

90 Garrett, Eileen J., *Many voices* (Allen & Unwin, London, 1969).

91 Giraud, Jean (ed.), *Les soucoupes volantes — le grand refus* (Moutet, Régusse, 1978).

92 Giscard, Pierre, *Mystique ou hystérie* (La Colombe, Paris, 1953).

93 Good, Timothy, News item in *Aldershot News* (25 November 1983).

94 Görres, Johann Joseph von, *La mystique divine, naturelle et diabolique* (trans. from German by Sainte Foi, Paris, 1854). Orig. 1842.

95 Goss, Michael, *The evidence for phantom hitch-hikers* (Aquarian, Wellingborough, 1984).

96 G.R. *Les apparitions de Bayside* (Nouvelles éditions Latines, Paris, 1975).

97 Graham, Billy, *Angels, God's secret agents* (Guideposts Associates, NY, 1975).

98 Green, Michael, *I believe in Satan's downfall* (Hodder & Stoughton, London, 1981).

99 Gregory, William, *Letters to a candid inquirer on animal magnetism* (Taylor, Walton & Maberly, London, 1851).

100 Haines, Richard (ed.), *UFO phenomena and the behavioral scientist* (Scarecrow, Metuchen NJ, 1979).

101 Harper, Clive, 'The witches' flying ointment', *Folklore* 88 (London, 1977).

102 Hartland, Edwin Sidney, *The science of fairy tales* (Walter Scott, London, 1891).

103 Hastings, James (ed.), *Encyclopedia of religion and ethics* (T. & T. Clark, Edinburgh, 1912).

104 Hawker, R. S., 'The Botathen Ghost', in *Prose Works* (Blackwood, Edinburgh, 1893).

105 Hawthorne, Nathaniel, *Passages from the French and Italian notebooks* (Complete Works vol. 10; Kegan Paul, London, 1893).

106 Hendry, Allen, *The UFO handbook* (Doubleday, NY, 1979).

107 Heywood, Rosalind, *The infinite hive* (Chatto, London, 1964).

108 Hickson, C., and Mendez, W., *UFO contact at Pascagoula* (UFO Photo Archives, Tucson, 1983).

109 Hill, J. Arthur, *Psychical investigations* (Cassell, London, 1917).

110 Hind, Cynthia, *UFOs — African encounters* (Gemini, Zimbabwe, 1982).

111 Hookham, Paul, *'Raymond', a rejoinder* (Blackwell, Oxford, 1917).

112 Hopkins, Budd, *Missing time* (Marek, NY, 1981).

113 Hufford, David J., *The terror that comes in the night* (University of Pennsylvania Press, Philadelphia, 1982).

114 Huxley, Aldous, *The doors of perception* (Chatto & Windus, London, 1954).

115 Huysmans, Joris Karl, *Sainte Lydwine de Schiedam* (Plon, Paris, 1917).

116 Hyslop, James H., *Psychical research and the resurrection*(Fisher Unwin, London, 1908).

117 Inge, Dean, 'Ecstasy', in Hastings, op.cit.

118 Innes, Michael, *The daffodil affair* (Gollancz, London, 1942).

119 *International UFO reporter* vol. 2 no. 11, La Rubia case.

120 Jacobs, David Michael, *The UFO controversy in America* (Indiana University Press, Bloomington, 1975).

121 Jaffe, Aniela, *Apparitions and precognition* (University Books, NY, 1963).

122 Janet, Pierre, *L'automatisme psychologique* (Alcan, Paris, 1889).

123 ——, *L'état mental des hystériques* (Alcan, 1911).

124 Jung, Carl Gustav, *Zur Psychologie und Pathologie sogennanter occulter Phänomene* Leipzig, 1902 (trans. as *On the psychology and pathology of so-called occult phenomena* in Collected Works vol. 1, Routledge & Kegan Paul).

125 ——, *Uber die Archtypen des Kollektiven Unbewussten* 1954 (trans. as *Archetypes and the collective unconscious* in Collected Works vol. 9 part 1).

126 ——,*Ein moderner Mythus: Von Dingen, die am Himmel gesehen werden* Zurich, 1958 (trans. as *Flying saucers: a modern myth of things seen in the skies* in Collected Works vol. 10).

127 ——, Interview in *Time* magazine, date unknown.

128 Keel, John A., *UFOs: Operation Trojan Horse* (Souvenir, London, 1970).

129 Kelly, Henry Ansgar, *Towards the death of Satan* (Chapman, London, 1968).

130 Kelly, I. W., Rotton, J., and Culver, R., 'The moon was full and nothing happened', *The Skeptical Inquirer* vol. x, no. 2, Winter 1985–6.

131 Keul, A., and Phillips, K., 'The unidentified witness', *ASSAP News* (London, 1985).

132 King, George, *You are responsible* (Aetherius Society, London, 1961).

133 ——, *The nine freedoms* (Aetherius Society, Los Angeles, 1963).

134 ——, *The flying saucers* (Aetherius Society, London, 1964).

135 ——, *The day the gods came* (Aetherius Society, Los Angeles, 1965).

136 King, George, with Mary King, *Cosmic voice: Mars and Venus speak to Earth* (Aetherius Society, London/Los Angeles, 1958).

137 Kinney, Jay, 'The mysterious gnosis of Philip K. Dick', *Critique* 11–12 (Santa Rosa, CA, 1983).

138 Klarer, Elizabeth, *Jenseits der Lichtmauer* Ventla, Wiesbaden, 1977 (trans. as *Beyond the light barrier* Timmins, Cape Town, 1980).

139 Klass, Philip J., *UFOs explained* (Random House, NY, 1974).

140 Kraspedon, Dino, *My contact with Flying Saucers* (trans. from Portuguese, Spearman, London, 1959).

141 Kroll, J., and Bachrach, B., 'Visions and psychopathology in the Middle Ages', *Journal of nervous and mental disease* vol. 170.1, 1982.

142 Lancelin, Charles, *Mes rapports avec le diable* (Durville, Paris, 1913).

143 Langdon, Paul, 'Twentieth century victim', in Ebon, *Witchcraft today* (Lombard, NY, 1971).

144 Laski, Marghanita, *Ecstasy* (Cresset, London, 1961).

145 Laurentin, René, *Lourdes; documents authentiques* vol. 7, (Lethielleux, Paris, 1965).

146 Laurentin, René, with Rupcic, Ljuderit, *La Vierge apparaît-Elle à Medjugorje?* (Oeil, Paris, 1984).

147 Lawren, Bill, Dreamless sleep', *OMNI* vol. 8, no. 6, 1986.

148 Lawson, Alvin H., 'The hypnosis of imaginary UFO "abductees"', *Journal of UFO Studies* 1.1, Evanston, no date (c 1983).

149 ——, 'The Birth Trauma Hypothesis in *Magonia* no. 10 (London, 1982).

150 Le Bon, Gustave, *The crowd* (Fisher Unwin, 1896; trans. from French *La psychologie des foules*).

151 Lee, F. G., *Glimpses of the supernatural* (H. S. King, London, 1875).

152 Lefebure, Francis, *Lourdes et le phosphenisme* (Bersez, Paris, 1980).

153 Legue, G., and Tourette, G. de la, *Soeur Jeanne des Anges* (Bureau de Progrès Médical, Paris, 1886).

154 Leuba, James H., *The psychology of religious mysticism* (Kegan Paul, London, 1929).

155 ——, *God or man?* (Kegan Paul, London, 1934).

156 Lévi, Eliphas, *Dogme et rituel de la haute magie* (Baillière, Paris, 1861; trans. as *Transcendental magic*).

157 Lhermitte, Jean, *Origine et mécanismes des hallucinations* in *Etudes Carmelitaines* (Desclée & Brouwer, Paris, 1933).

158 ——, *Mystiques et faux mystiques* (Blond & Gay, Paris 1952).

159 Lieber, Arnold L., *The lunar effect* (Anchor/Doubleday, NY, 1978).

160 Ligeron, Jean Michel, *OVNI en Ardennes* (private, Charleville, 1981).

161 Lleget, Marius, *Nosotros los extraterrestres* (Karma-7, Barcelona, 1974).

162 Lodge, Sir Oliver, *Raymond, or life and death* (Methuen, London, 1916).

163 Lukianowicz, N., 'Hallucinations à trois', *Archives of general psychiatry* (1959.1).

164 Mackay, Charles, *The mormons* (no publisher named, London, 1852; cites Orson Pratt, *Remarkable visions*).

165 Maindron, Gabriel, *Les apparitions à Kibeho; annonce de Marie au coeur de l'Afrique* (Oeil, Paris, 1984).

166 Manning, Matthew, *The strangers* (Allen, London, 1978).

167 Marie, A., *Mysticisme et folie* (Giard & Brière, Paris, 1907).

168 Marie de Sainte Thérèse, *L'union mystique à Marie* (trans. from Flemish, Les Cahiers de la Vierge, Du Cerf, Juvisy, 1936; orig. written end of 17th century).

169 Mathieu, P. F., *Histoire des miraculés et des convulsionnaires de St Médard* (Didier, Paris, 1864).

170 Maudsley, Henry, *Natural causes and supernatural seemings* (abridged edn.; Watts, London, 1939; orig. London 1886).

171 Méheust, Bertrand, 'Le Projet Nabokok', *Inforespace* no. 55 (Bruxelles, 1981).

172 ——, *Science fiction et Soucoupes Volantes* (Mercure de France, Paris, 1978).

173 ——, *Soucoupes Volantes et Folklore* (Mercure de France, 1985).

174 Menger, Connie, *Song of Saturn* (Saucerian, Clarksburg, 1968).

175 Menger, Howard, *From outer space to you* (Saucerian, 1959).

176 Mirville, J. E. DE, *Des esprits* (Vrayet de Surcy, Paris, 1863).

177 Mitchell, Helen, and Mitchell, Betty, *We met the space people* (Saucerian, Clarksburg, 1959).

178 Monnerie, Michel, *Et si les OVNIs n'existaient pas?* (Les Humanoïdes Associés, Paris, 1977).

179 ——, *Le naufrage des extra-terrestres* (Nouvelles éditions rationnalistes, Paris, 1979).

180 Monnet, Pierre, *Les extra-terrestres m'ont dit* (Lefebvre, Paris, 1978).

181 Monroe, Robert, *Journeys out of the body* (Doubleday, NY, 1972).

182 Montmorand, Maxime de, *Psychologie des mystiques catholiques orthodoxes* (Alcan, Paris, 1920).

183 Moses, Stainton, Notebooks in possession of College of Psychic Studies, London.

184 Mutigny, Jean de, *Victor Hugo et le spiritisme* (Nathan, Paris, 1981).

185 Nebel, Long John, *Way out world* (Prentice Hall, New Jersey, 1961).

186 Nevius, John L., *Demon possession and allied themes* (Revell, Chicago, 1893).

187 *Nexus* vol. 2, no. 6 (June–July 1955).

188 Noriagof, Dr., *Notre Dame de Lourdes et la science de l'occulte* (Charmuel, Paris, 1898).

189 Oatman, Jack G., 'Folie à deux: report of a case in identical twins', *American Journal of Psychiatry* 93, 1942, cited in Corliss, W. G., *The unfathomed mind* (Sourcebook Project, Glen Arm, 1982).

190 Pannet, Robert, *Marie au buisson ardent* (S.O.S., Paris, 1982).

191 ——, *Epiphanie Mariale en 5 actes* (S.O.S., 1983).

192 Pelton, Robert W., *Confrontations with the devil* (Barnes, S. Brunswick, 1979).

193 Persinger, Michael, 'Possible infrequent geophysical sources of close UFO encounters', in Haines (op.cit.) and many papers in *Perceptual and motor skills* and elsewhere.

194 Petitalot, Jean-Baptiste, *The Virgin Mother according to theology* (trans. from French; St Anselm's Society, London, 1896).

195 Peze, Emmanuel, *Les nouveaux lieux miraculeux* (Balland, Paris, 1984).

196 Pinotti, Roberto, *UFO: missione uomo* (Armenia, Milano, 1976).

197 Plato, *Phaedo* (trans. Jowett).

198 Podmore, Frank, *The newer spiritualism* (Fisher & Unwin, London, 1910).

199 Pons Prades, Eduardo, *El mensaje de otros mundos* (Planeta, Barcelona, 1982).

200 Pozo, Victorino del, *Siragusa, mensajero de los extraterrestres* (EDAF, Madrid, 1977); *Siragusa, el anunciador* (Barath, Madrid, 1979); *Y III, verdad y persecucion de Siragusa* (Barath, Madrid, 1984).

201 Prytz, John, 'The school excursion hypothesis', *Journal of the Australian Centre for UFO studies* vol. 6, no. 4, (Prospect, 1985).

202 Quinones, Pedro A., *Los OVNIs y el fin del mundo* (Ramon Plana, Barcelona, 1979).

203 Randles, Jenny, *The Pennine UFO mystery* (Granada, London, 1983).

204 ——, *UFO reality* (Hale, London, 1983).

205 Raupert, J. Godfrey, *The dangers of spiritualism* (Kegan Paul, London, 1906).

206 Reyt, Daniel, *Les apparitions religieuses à la lumière des faits de Dozulé* (Corlet, Condé-sur-Noireau, 1983).

207 Ribera, Antonio, *El misterio de Ummo* (Plaza y Janes, Barcelona, 1979).

208 Ribet, M. J., *La mystique divine* (Poussielgue, Paris, 1879).

209 Ribot, Théodule, *Maladies de la personnalité* (Paris, c 1880).

210 Richards, John Thomas, *Sorrat, a history of the Neihardt PK experiments* (Scarecrow, Metuchen, NJ, 1982).

211 Rimmer, John, *The evidence for alien abductions* (Aquarian, Wellingborough, 1984).

212 Ring, Kenneth, *Life at death* (Coward, McCann & Geoghegan, NY, 1980).

213 Robertson, John M., *Christianity and mythology* (Watts, London, 1910; orig. 1899).

214 Rochas, Albert de, *Les vies successives* (Leymarie, Paris, 1924).

215 Rogo, Scott, *UFO abductions* (Signet, NY, 1980; see also under Druffel).

216 Roussel, Denise, *Le tarot psychologique, miroir de soi* (ed. de Mortagne, Québec, 1983).

217 Rowe, Kelvin, *A call at dawn* (Understanding, El Monte, CA, 1958).

218 Rufinus, *On Origen's De Principiis* cited in Kelly *Toward the death of Satan* (q.v.).

219 Rutkowski, Chris, 'Geophysical variables and human behavior: some criticisms', (*Perceptual and motor skills* 1984, 58).

220 Sachs, Margaret, *The UFO encyclopedia* (Putnam, NY, 1980).

221 Sackville-West, Victoria, *The eagle and the dove* (Michael Joseph, London, 1943).

222 Saint Denys, Hervey de, *Les rêves et les moyens de les diriger* (Amyot, Paris, 1867; new ed. Tchou, 1964).

223 Saintyves, P., *En marge de la Légende Dorée* (Nourry, Paris, 1931).

224 Sanchez-Ventura y Pascual, F., *La Vierge est-elle apparue à Garabandal?* (trans. from Spanish *Los apariciones no son un mito*; Nouvelles éditions Latines, Paris, 1966).

225 Saudreau, Auguste, *L'état mystique, sa nature et ses phases* (Grassin & Richou, Angers, 1903).

226 Schwarz, Berthold, *UFO dynamics: psychiatric and psychic aspects of the UFO syndrome* (Rainbow, Moore Haven FL, 1983).

227 Sedman, G., 'A phenomenonological study of pseudohallucinations and related experiences', in *Acta Psychiatrica Scandinavia* vol. 42 fasc. 1, 1966.

228 Sheldrake, Rupert, *A new science of life* (Blond & Briggs, London, 1981).

229 Sleigh, Bernard, *The gates of horn* (Aldine House, London, 1926).

230 Smith, Hester Travers, *The return of Oscar Wilde* in *Occult Review* August 1923.

231 Society for Psychical Research, *Journal*, vol. 20, no. 373, March 1921 (Alleyne fairy); vol. 45, no. 746, Dec. 1970 (Phillips-Lewis case).

232 ——, *Proceedings*, vol. 3, 1895: Mrs Sidgwick, 'Phantasms of the dead', case of Mrs W; vol. 5, 1889: Edmund Gurney, 'On apparitions occurring soon after death'; vol. 23, 1909: William James, 'Report on Mrs Piper's Hodgson-Control'; and Sir Oliver Lodge, 'Trance communications received chiefly through Mrs Piper'; vol. 29, 1918: Mrs Sidgwick, reviewing *Raymond*; vol. 35, 1926: S. G. Soal, 'Some communications received through Mrs Blanche Cooper', vol. 44, 1939: H. H. Price, 'Haunting and the psychic ether hypothesis'.

233 Soyka, Fred, with Edmonds, Alan, *The ion effect* (Dutton, NY, 1977).

234 Sprinkle, Leo, (Director) *Proceedings of the Rocky Mountain Conferences*, annually from 1980, Laramie WY.

235 ——, 'UFO activity and human consciousness', paper given at APRO UFO Ohio, Cleveland, June 1981.

236 ——, Personal interview, Laramie, 1984.

237 Stanford, Ray, quoted in Jerome Clark, 'The Pascagoula and Adamski abductions' in *Saga UFO Report* vol. 6, no. 2, August 1978.

238 Steiger, Brad, *Encounters of the angelic kind* (Esoteric Publications, Cottonwood AZ, 1979).

239 ——, *The Seed* (Berkley, NY, 1983).

240 Steiger, Brad, with Steiger, Francie, *The Star People* (Berkley, NY, 1981).

241 Steinhauser, Gerhard R., *Jesus Christus, Erbe der Astronauten* (trans. as *Jesus*

Christ, heir to the astronauts; Abelard Schuman, London/NY, 1974).

242 Stevens, Wendelle C., *UFO contact from the Pleiades: a preliminary investigation report* (UFO Photo Archives, Tucson, 1982).

243 Story, Ronald, *The spacegods revealed* (Harper & Row, NY, 1976).

244 ——, *Guardians of the universe* (New English Library, London, 1980).

245 ——, *The encyclopedia of UFOs* (Doubleday, NY, New English Library, London, 1980).

246 Strentz, Herbert J., *A survey of press coverage of UFOs 1947–1966* (degree dissertation, repr. Arcturus, Scotia NY, 1982).

247 Sulman, Felix Gad, *The effect of air ionization, electric fields, atmospherics and other electric phenomena on man and animal* (Thomas, Springfield, NY, 1980).

248 Swedenborg, Imanuel, *Arcana Coelesta, The earths in the universe, Heaven and hell* in Collected Works (various editions).

249 Szasz, Thomas S., *The myth of mental illness* (Secker & Warburg, London, 1961).

250 Teresa d'Avila, *The life of the Holy Mother Teresa of Jesus* (trans. from Spanish by E. Allison Peers; in Complete Works, Sheed & Ward, London, 1946).

251 Thulié, Dr A., *La mystique divine, diabolique et naturelle des théologiens* (Vigot, Paris, 1912).

252 Thurston, Herbert, 'Some knotty points for spiritualists', *The Month*, 1938.

252a ——, *The Church and spiritualism* (Bruce, Milwaukee, 1933).

253 ——, *The physical phenomena of mysticism* (Burns Oates, London, 1952).

254 ——, *Surprising mystics* (Burns Oates, London, 1955).

255 Tizané, Emile, *Les apparitions de la Vierge* (Tchou, Paris, 1977).

256 Tributsch, Helmut, *When the snakes awake* (trans. from German *Wenn die Schlangen erwachen*; MIT Press, Cambridge, MA, 1982).

257 Trochu, Abbé Francis, *Le curé d'Ars* (Vitte, Lyon, 1925).

258 Tylor, Edward B., *Primitive culture* (Murray, London, 1871).

259 *UFO Investigator*, vol. 1, no. 8, 'Adamski's latest claim', (NICAP, Washington, June 1959).

260 Vallée, Jacques, *Passport to Magonia* (Regnery, Chicago, 1969).

261 Van Tassel, George, *I rode a Flying Saucer* (New Age, Los Angeles, 1952).

262 Vieroudy, Pierre, *Ces OVNI qui annoncent le surhomme* (Tchou, Paris, 1977).

263 Wallace, Anthony F. C., 'Cultural determinants of response to hallucinatory experience', *Archives of General Psychiatry*, vol. 1, no. 1, 1959.

264 Warfield, B. B., *Counterfeit miracles* (Banner of Truth Editions, Edinburgh, 1972; orig. 1918).

265 White, Peter, *The past is human* (Angus & Robertson, Sydney, 1974).

266 Williamson, G. H., and McCoy, J., *UFOs confidential* (Essene Press, Corpus Christi TX, 1958).

267 Wilson, Clifford, *Crash go the chariots* (Lancer, NY, 1972).

268 ——, *The chariots still crash* (Signet, NY, 1975).

269 Winkler, Louis, *Catalog of UFO-like data before 1947* (Fund for UFO Research, Mt Rainier, MD, 1984).

270 Wooden, Kenneth, *The children of Jonestown* (McGraw Hill, NY, 1981).

271 Woolcott, Judie, Interviews in *Northwestern*, Oshkosh WI, 4.8.1985, and *Post-Crescent*, Appleton WI, 21.8.1985 and 21.9.1986, both reprinted in Farish newsclipping service, nos. 194 and 207.

272 Zaehner, R. C., *Mysticism sacred and profane* (Oxford University Press, 1957).

273 Zinsstag, L., and Good, T., *George Adamski, the untold story* (CETI, Beckenham, 1983).

INDEX

Of further interest

VISIONS ★ APPARITIONS ★ ALIEN VISITORS

A Comparative Study Of The Entity Enigma

The first comparative study of ghosts, apparitions, astral doubles, alien visitors and the many other non-human entities with which ordinary people throughout history and to the present day have claimed to have come into contact. Through a careful analysis and assessment of the available evidence and the latest theoretical approaches, **Hilary Evans** offers an original and convincing explanation of the Entity Enigma. Covers such topics as: entities in folklore, thought forms, religious visions, spirits of the dead, UFO occupants and much more. One of the most ambitious works on the paranormal to be published in recent years.